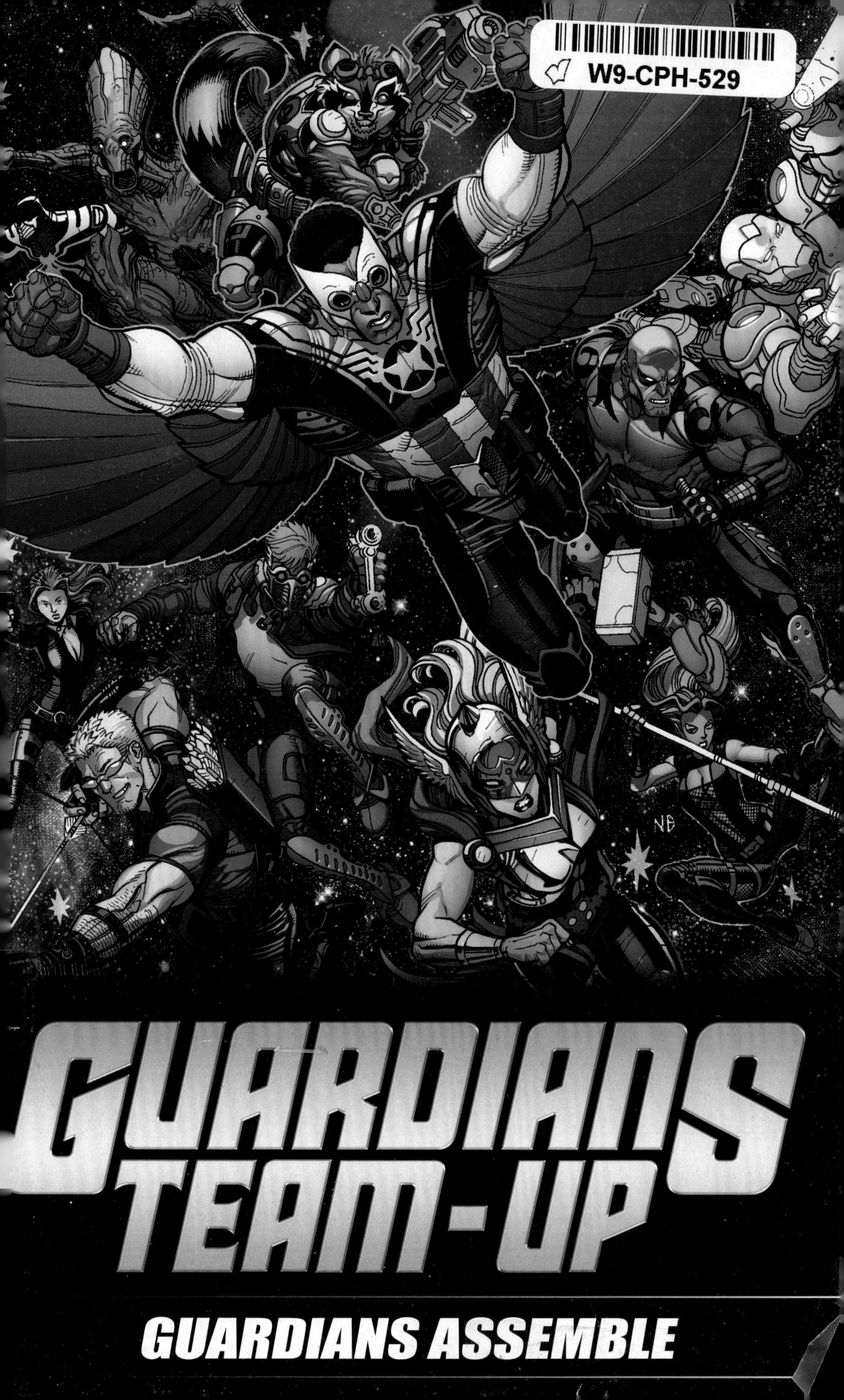

GUARDIANS TEAM-UP

GUARDIANS ASSEMBLE

GUARDIANS TEAM-UP
GUARDIANS ASSEMBLE

GUARDIANS TEAM-UP VOL. 1: GUARDIANS ASSEMBLE. Contains material originally published in magazine form as GUARDIANS TEAM-UP #1-5 and TAILS OF THE PET AVENGERS #1. First printing 2015. ISBN# 97 0-7851-9714-0. Published by MARVEL WORLDWIDE, INC., a subsidiary of MARVEL ENTERTAINMENT, LLC. OFFICE OF PUBLICATION: 135 West 50th Street, New York, NY 10020. Copyright © 2015 MARVEL No similar between any of the names, characters, persons, and/or institutions in this magazine with those of any living or dead person or institution is intended, and any such similarity which may exist is purely coincidental. **Print in Canada.** ALAN FINE, President, Marvel Entertainment; DAN BUCKLEY, President, TV, Publishing and Brand Management; JOE QUESADA, Chief Creative Officer; TOM BREVOORT, SVP of Publishing; DAVID BOGART, S of Operations & Procurement, Publishing; C.B. CEBULSKI, VP of International Development & Brand Management; DAVID GABRIEL, SVP Print, Sales & Marketing; JIM O'KEEFE, VP of Operations & Logistics; DAN CAI Executive Director of Publishing Technology; SUSAN CRESPI, Editorial Operations Manager; ALEX MORALES, Publishing Operations Manager; STAN LEE, Chairman Emeritus. For information regarding advertising in Mar Comics or on Marvel.com, please contact Jonathan Rheingold, VP of Custom Solutions & Ad Sales, at jrheingold@marvel.com. For Marvel subscription inquiries, please call 800-217-9158. **Manufactured betwe** 9/4/2015 and 10/12/2015 by SOLISCO PRINTERS, SCOTT, QC, CANADA.

10 9 8 7 6 5 4 3 2 1

GUARDIANS TEAM-UP #1-5

WRITERS: **BRIAN MICHAEL BENDIS** (#1-2),
SAM HUMPHRIES (#3), **JOHN LAYMAN** (#4) AND
ANDY LANNING & **ANDY SCHMIDT** (#5)

ARTISTS: **ART ADAMS** (#1), **STEPHANE ROUX** &
JAY LEISTEN (#2), **MIKE MAYHEW** (#3),
OTTO SCHMIDT (#4) AND **GUSTAVO DUARTE** (#5)

COLORISTS: **PAUL MOUNTS** (#1), **BRETT SMITH** (#2),
RAIN BEREDO (#3) AND **MARCELO MAIOLO** (#5)

LETTERER: **VC's CORY PETIT**

COVER ART: **ART ADAMS** & **IAN HERRING** (#1),
STEPHANE ROUX (#2), **MIKE MAYHEW** &
RAIN BEREDO (#3), **OTTO SCHMIDT** (#4) AND
HUMBERTO RAMOS & **EDGAR DELGADO** (#5)

ASSISTANT EDITOR: **XANDER JAROWEY**
EDITOR: **KATIE KUBERT**
GROUP EDITOR: **MIKE MARTS**

TAILS OF THE PET AVENGERS #1

"BEGINNINGS AND ENDINGS"
WRITER & LETTERER: **CHRIS ELIOPOULOS**
ARTIST: **IG GUARA**
COLORIST: **CHRIS SOTOMAYOR**

"MY ENEMY, MY FRIEND"
WRITER & LETTERER: **CHRIS ELIOPOULOS**
ARTIST: **GURIHURU**

"TERRIER ON THE HIGH SEAS"
WRITER, ARTIST & LETTERER: **COLLEEN COOVER**

"TOP DOG"
WRITER: **SCOTT GRAY**
ARTIST: **GURIHURU**
LETTERER: **DAVE SHARPE**

"PROM QUEEN"
WRITERS: **BUDDY SCALERA** WITH
CHRIS ELIOPOULOS
ARTIST: **CHRIS ELIOPOULOS**
COLORIST: **SOTOCOLOR'S C. GARCIA**
LETTERER: **CHRIS ELIOPOULOS**

"BIRDS OF A DIFFERENT FEATHER"
WRITER: **JOE CARAMAGNA**
ARTIST & LETTERER: **COLLEEN COOVER**

COVER ART: **HUMBERTO RAMOS** & **CHRIS SOTOMAYOR**
ASSISTANT EDITOR: **MIKE HORWITZ**
EDITOR: **NATHAN COSBY**

COLLECTION EDITOR: SARAH BRUNSTAD
ASSOCIATE MANAGING EDITOR: ALEX STARBUCK
EDITORS, SPECIAL PROJECTS: JENNIFER GRÜNWALD & MARK D. BEAZLEY
SENIOR EDITOR, SPECIAL PROJECTS: JEFF YOUNGQUIST
SVP PRINT, SALES & MARKETING: DAVID GABRIEL
BOOK DESIGNER: ADAM DEL RE

EDITOR IN CHIEF: AXEL ALONSO
CHIEF CREATIVE OFFICER: JOE QUESADA
PUBLISHER: DAN BUCKLEY
EXECUTIVE PRODUCER: ALAN FINE

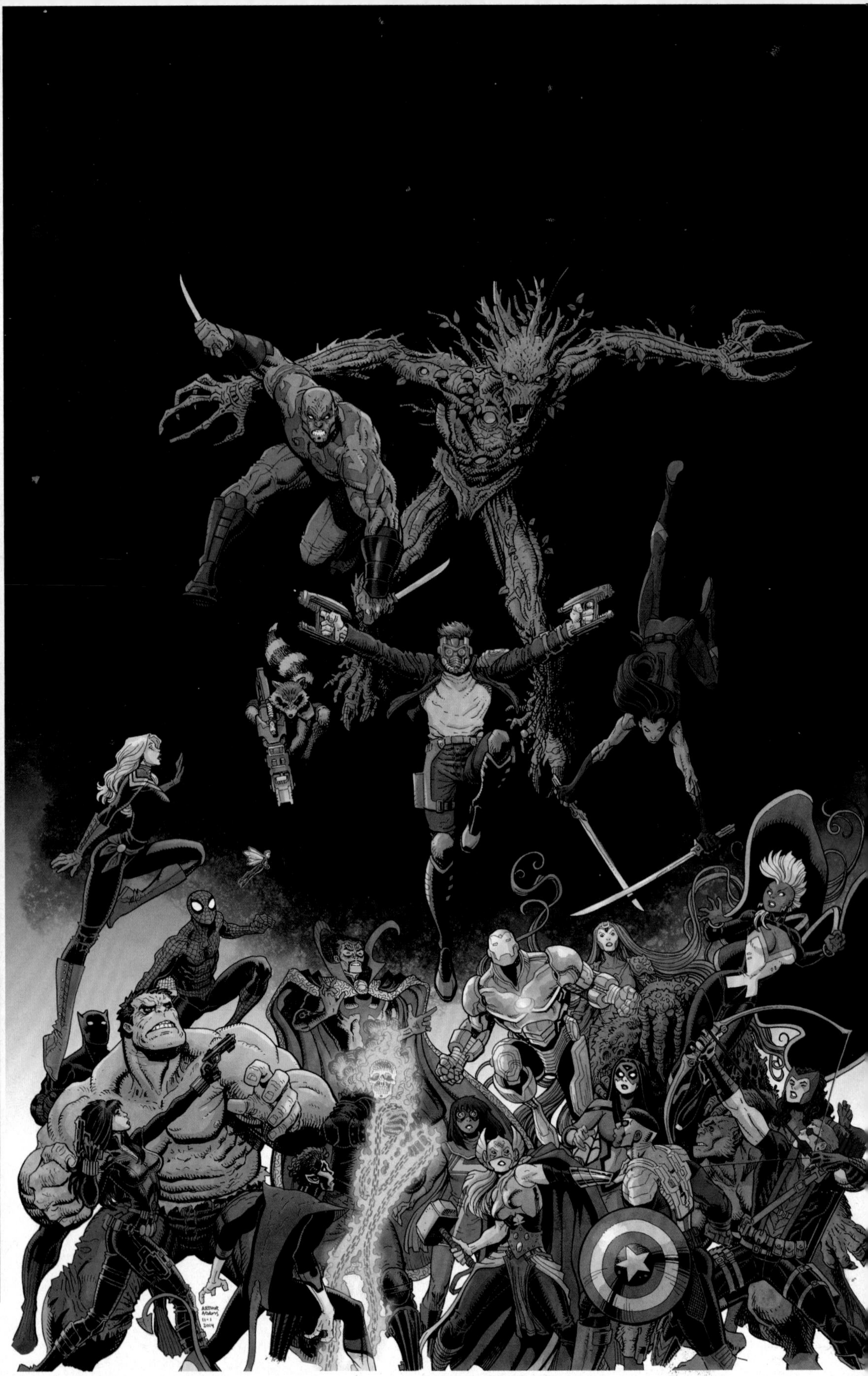

THE ENTIRE GALAXY IS A MESS. WARRING EMPIRES AND COSMIC TERRORISTS PLAGUE EVERY CORNER. SOMEONE HAS TO RISE ABOVE IT ALL AND FIGHT FOR THOSE WHO HAVE NO ONE TO FIGHT FOR THEM.

THE GUARDIANS OF THE GALAXY ARE PETER QUILL A.K.A. STAR-LORD, GAMORA, THE MOST DANGEROUS WOMAN IN THE UNIVERSE, DRAX THE DESTROYER, THE MYSTERIOUS WARRIOR ANGELA, VENOM, CAPTAIN MARVEL, ROCKET RACCOON AND GROOT.

PREVIOUSLY IN...

GUARDIANS OF THE GALAXY

THE GUARDIANS THEMSELVES HAVE BEEN STRAINED OVER RECENT CONFESSIONS OF PAST SINS. PETER OUSTED HIS CRIMINAL FATHER AS THE PRESIDENT OF THE SPARTAX EMPIRE.

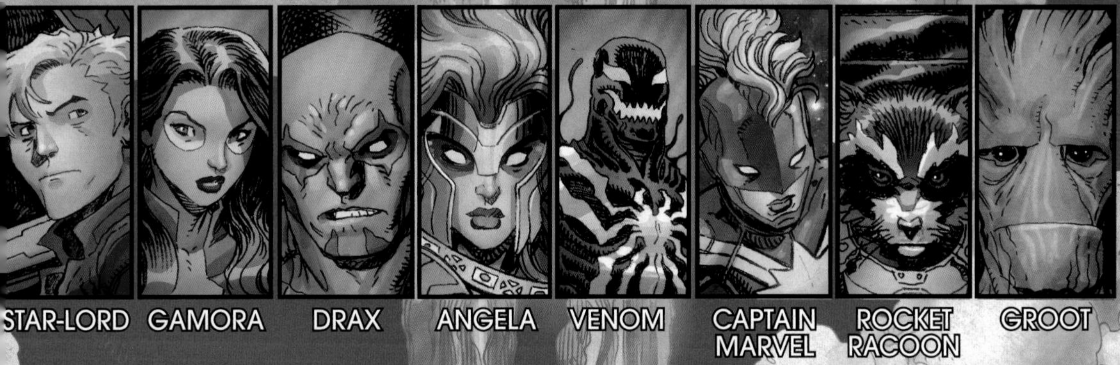

STAR-LORD
GAMORA
DRAX
ANGELA
VENOM
CAPTAIN MARVEL
ROCKET RACOON
GROOT

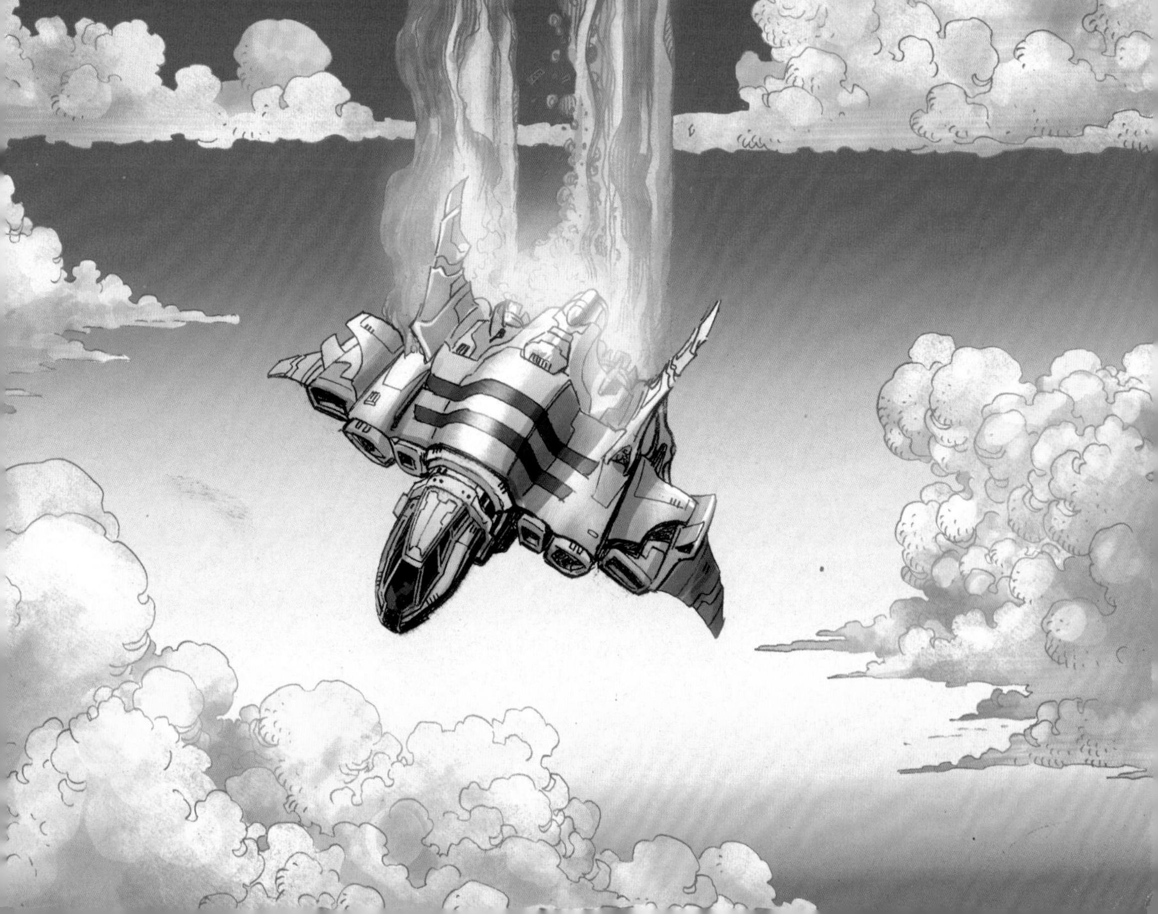

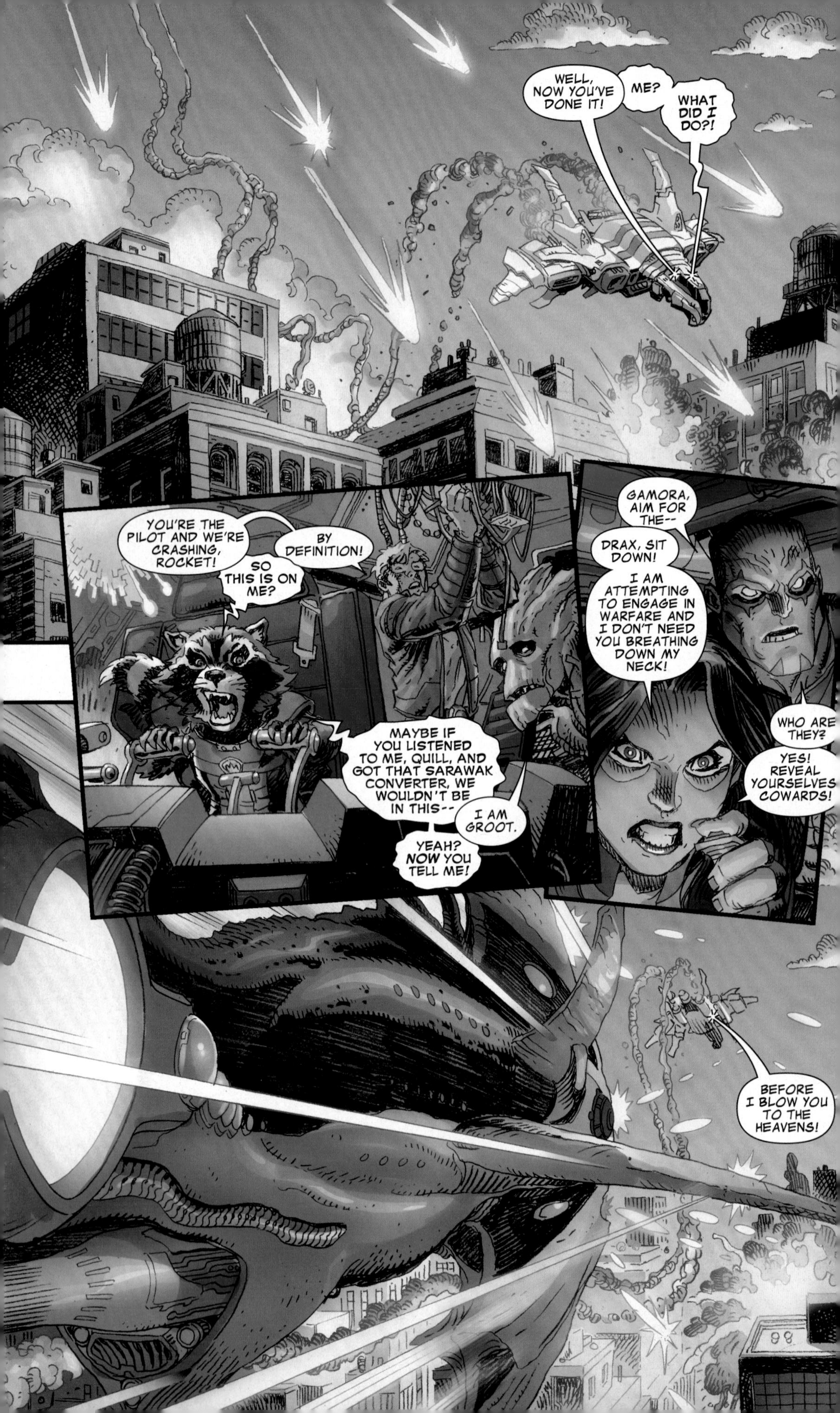
WELL, NOW YOU'VE DONE IT!
ME?
WHAT DID I DO?!
YOU'RE THE PILOT AND WE'RE CRASHING, ROCKET!
BY DEFINITION!
SO THIS IS ON ME?
MAYBE IF YOU LISTENED TO ME, QUILL, AND GOT THAT SARAWAK CONVERTER, WE WOULDN'T BE IN THIS--
I AM GROOT.
YEAH? NOW YOU TELL ME!
GAMORA, AIM FOR THE--
DRAX, SIT DOWN!
I AM ATTEMPTING TO ENGAGE IN WARFARE AND I DON'T NEED YOU BREATHING DOWN MY NECK!
WHO ARE THEY?
YES! REVEAL YOURSELVES COWARDS!
BEFORE I BLOW YOU TO THE HEAVENS!

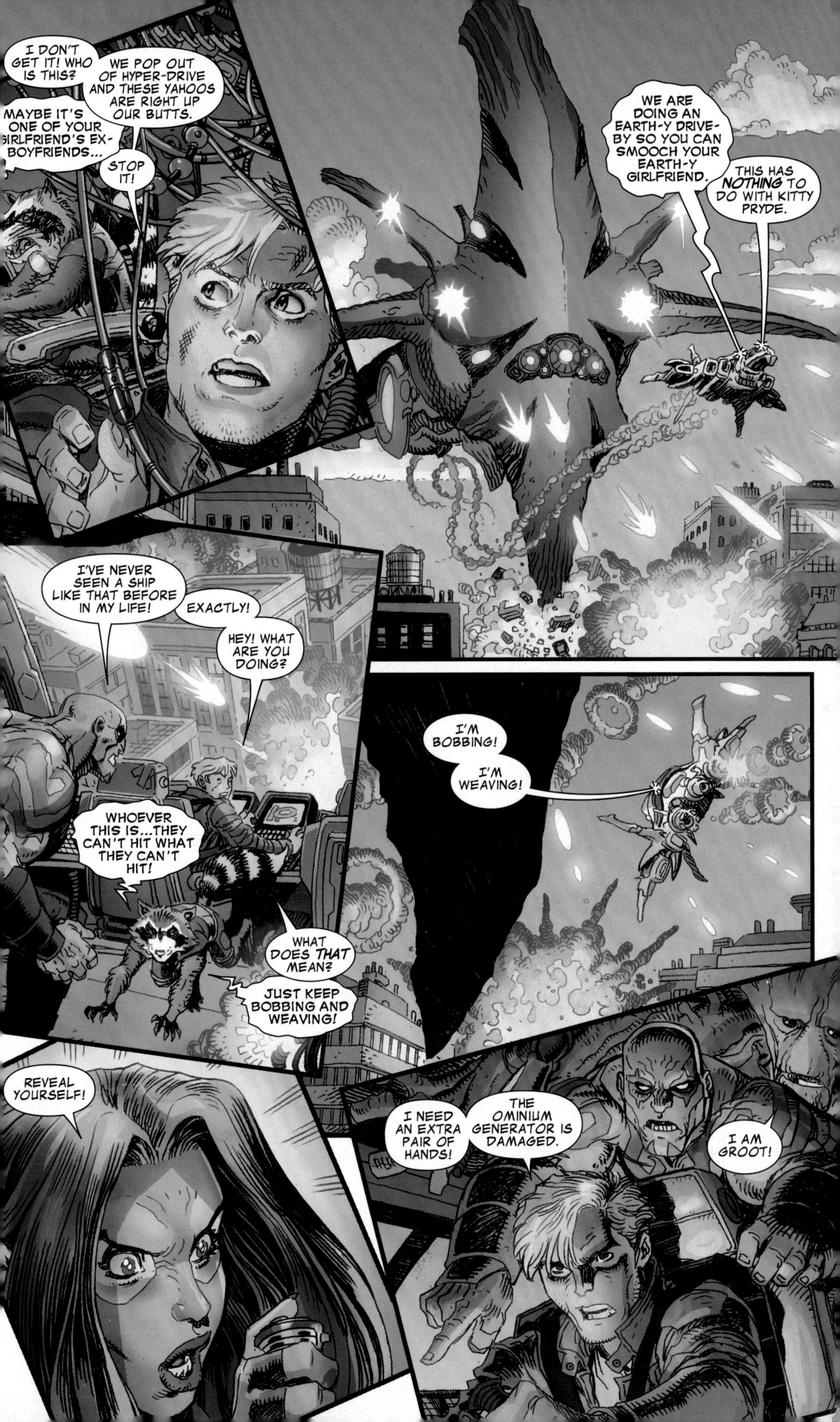
I DON'T GET IT! WHO IS THIS?
WE POP OUT OF HYPER-DRIVE AND THESE YAHOOS ARE RIGHT UP OUR BUTTS.
MAYBE IT'S ONE OF YOUR GIRLFRIEND'S EX-BOYFRIENDS...
STOP IT!
WE ARE DOING AN EARTH-Y DRIVE-BY SO YOU CAN SMOOCH YOUR EARTH-Y GIRLFRIEND.
THIS HAS NOTHING TO DO WITH KITTY PRYDE.
I'VE NEVER SEEN A SHIP LIKE THAT BEFORE IN MY LIFE!
EXACTLY!
HEY! WHAT ARE YOU DOING?
WHOEVER THIS IS...THEY CAN'T HIT WHAT THEY CAN'T HIT!
WHAT DOES THAT MEAN?
JUST KEEP BOBBING AND WEAVING!
I'M BOBBING!
I'M WEAVING!
REVEAL YOURSELF!
I NEED AN EXTRA PAIR OF HANDS!
THE OMINIUM GENERATOR IS DAMAGED.
I AM GROOT!

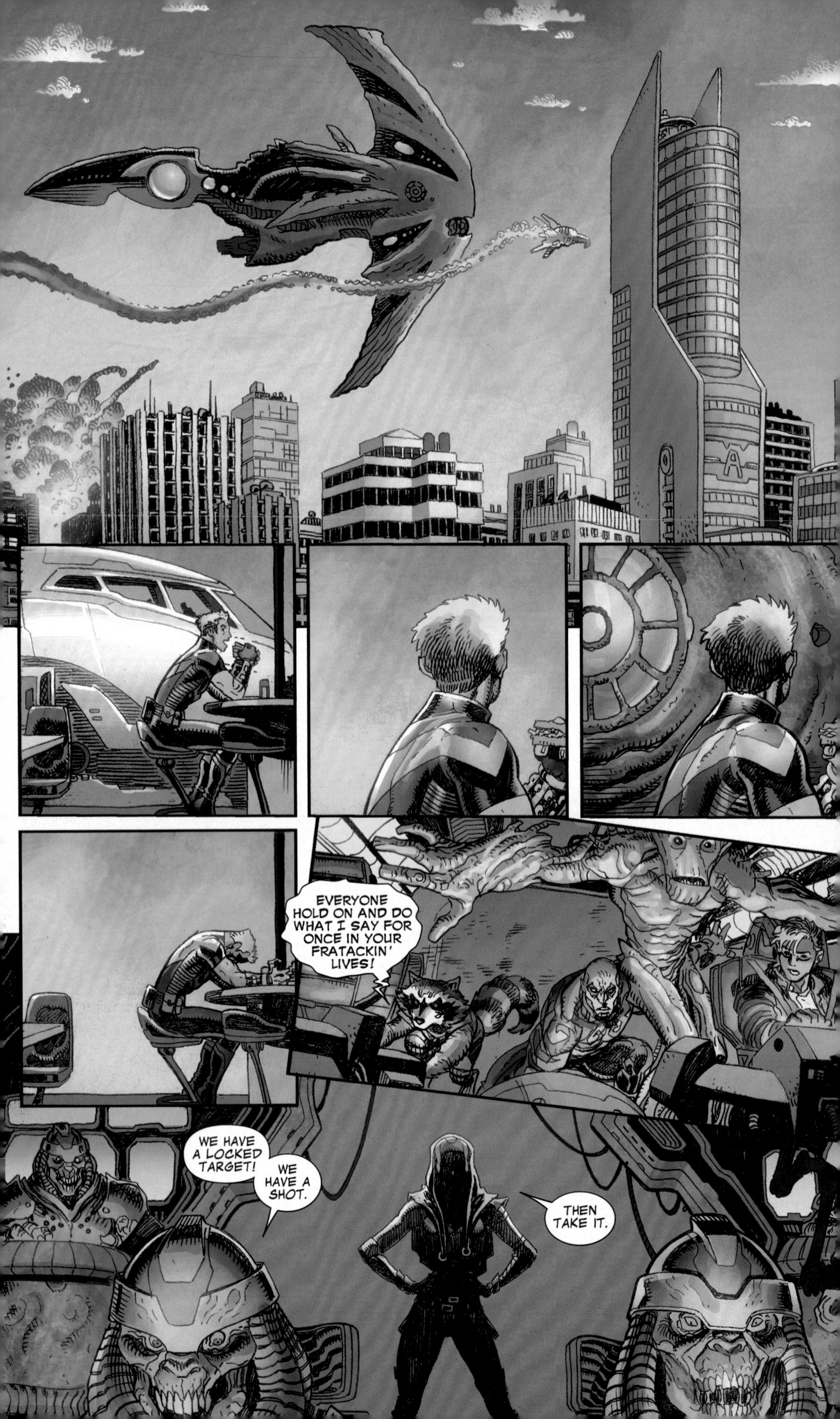
EVERYONE HOLD ON AND DO WHAT I SAY FOR ONCE IN YOUR FRATACKIN' LIVES!
WE HAVE A LOCKED TARGET!
WE HAVE A SHOT.
THEN TAKE IT.

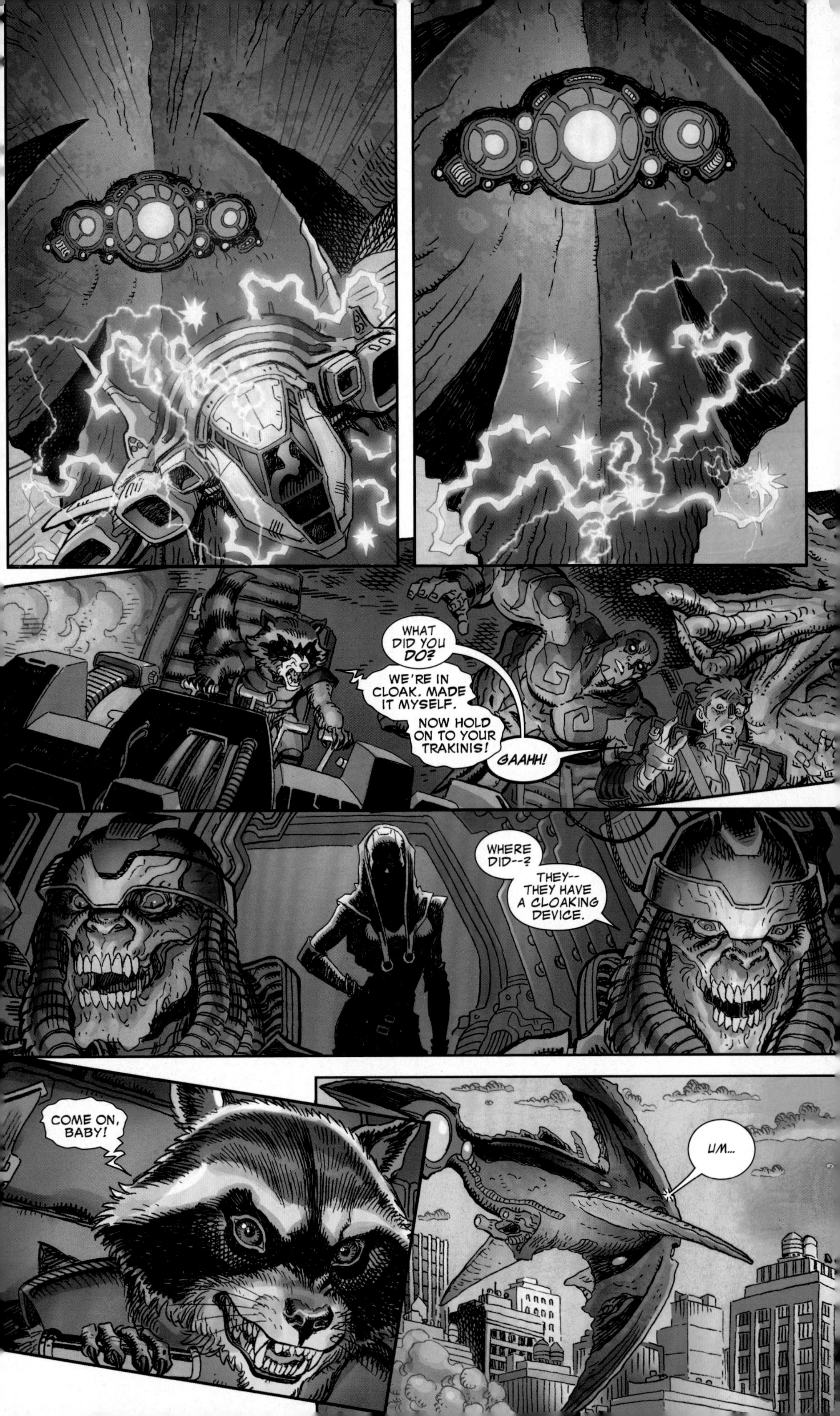
WHAT DID YOU DO?
WE'RE IN CLOAK. MADE IT MYSELF.
NOW HOLD ON TO YOUR TRAKINIS!
GAAHH!
WHERE DID--?
THEY-- THEY HAVE A CLOAKING DEVICE.
COME ON, BABY!
UM...

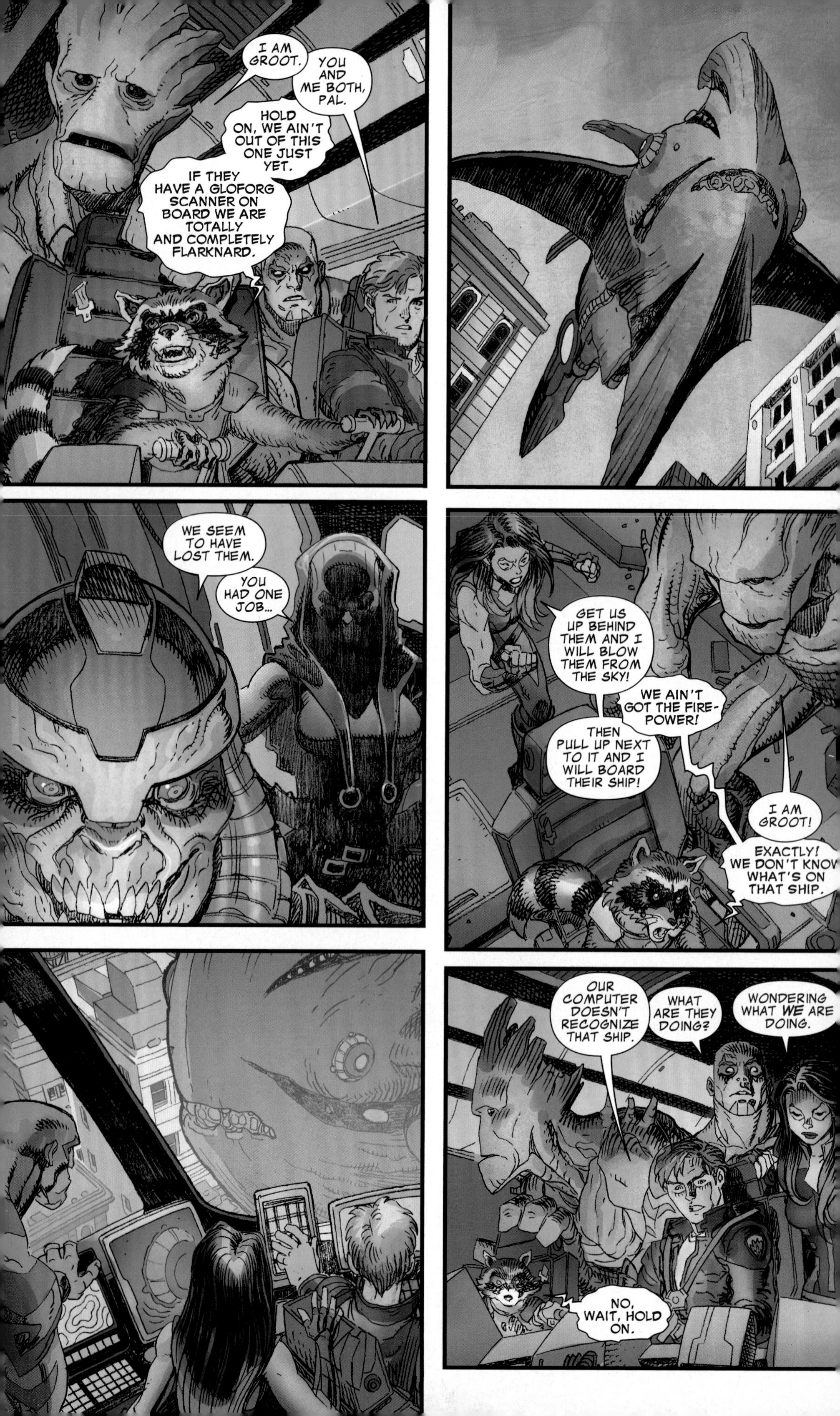
I AM GROOT.
YOU AND ME BOTH, PAL.
HOLD ON, WE AIN'T OUT OF THIS ONE JUST YET.
IF THEY HAVE A GLOFORG SCANNER ON BOARD WE ARE TOTALLY AND COMPLETELY FLARKNARD.
WE SEEM TO HAVE LOST THEM.
YOU HAD ONE JOB...
GET US UP BEHIND THEM AND I WILL BLOW THEM FROM THE SKY!
WE AIN'T GOT THE FIRE-POWER!
THEN PULL UP NEXT TO IT AND I WILL BOARD THEIR SHIP!
I AM GROOT!
EXACTLY! WE DON'T KNOW WHAT'S ON THAT SHIP.
OUR COMPUTER DOESN'T RECOGNIZE THAT SHIP.
WHAT ARE THEY DOING?
WONDERING WHAT WE ARE DOING.
NO, WAIT, HOLD ON.

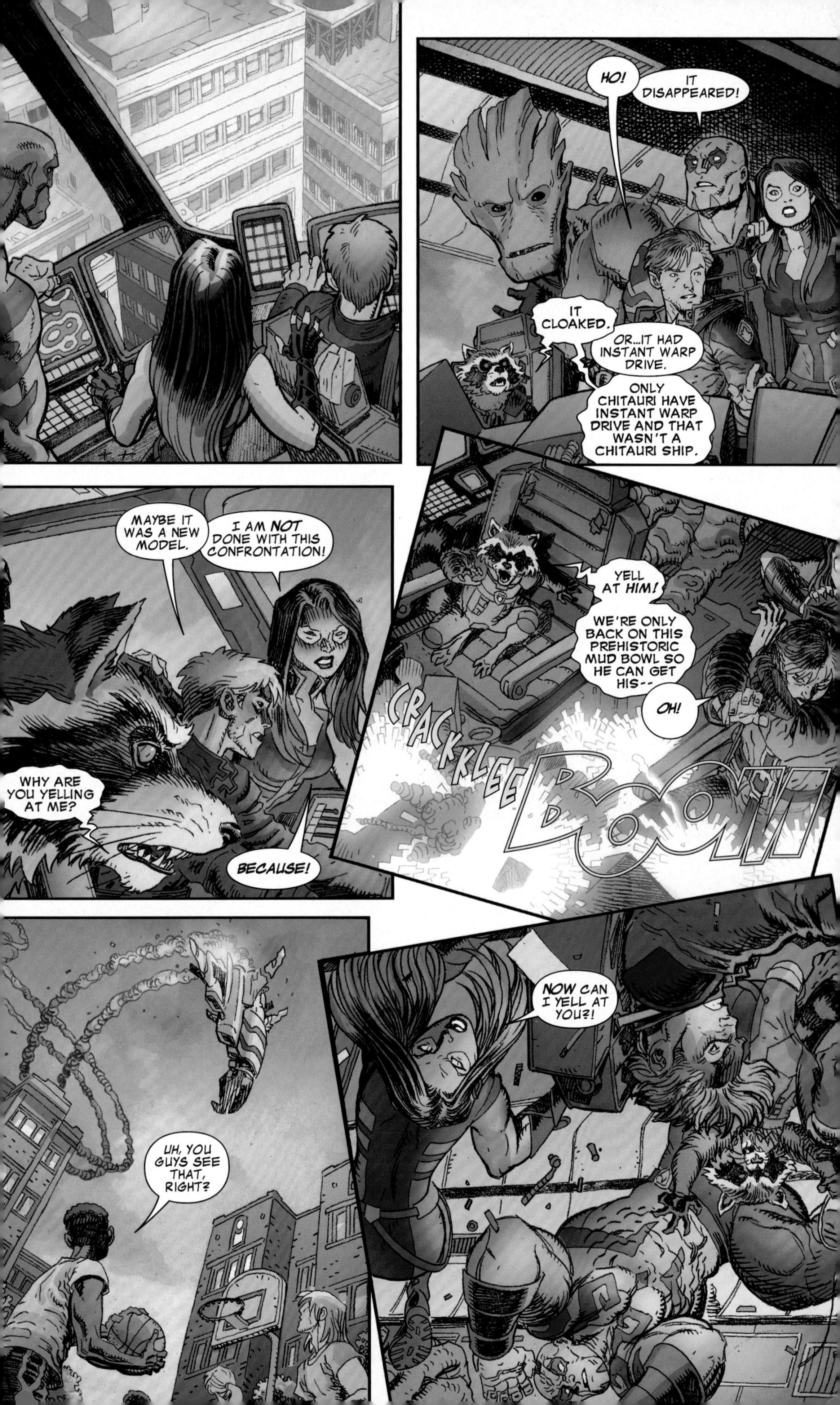
HO!
IT DISAPPEARED!
IT CLOAKED.
OR...IT HAD INSTANT WARP DRIVE.
ONLY CHITAURI HAVE INSTANT WARP DRIVE AND THAT WASN'T A CHITAURI SHIP.
MAYBE IT WAS A NEW MODEL.
I AM NOT DONE WITH THIS CONFRONTATION!
WHY ARE YOU YELLING AT ME?
BECAUSE!
YELL AT HIM!
WE'RE ONLY BACK ON THIS PREHISTORIC MUD BOWL SO HE CAN GET HIS--
OH!
CRACKKLEE BOOM!!
UH, YOU GUYS SEE THAT, RIGHT?
NOW CAN I YELL AT YOU?!

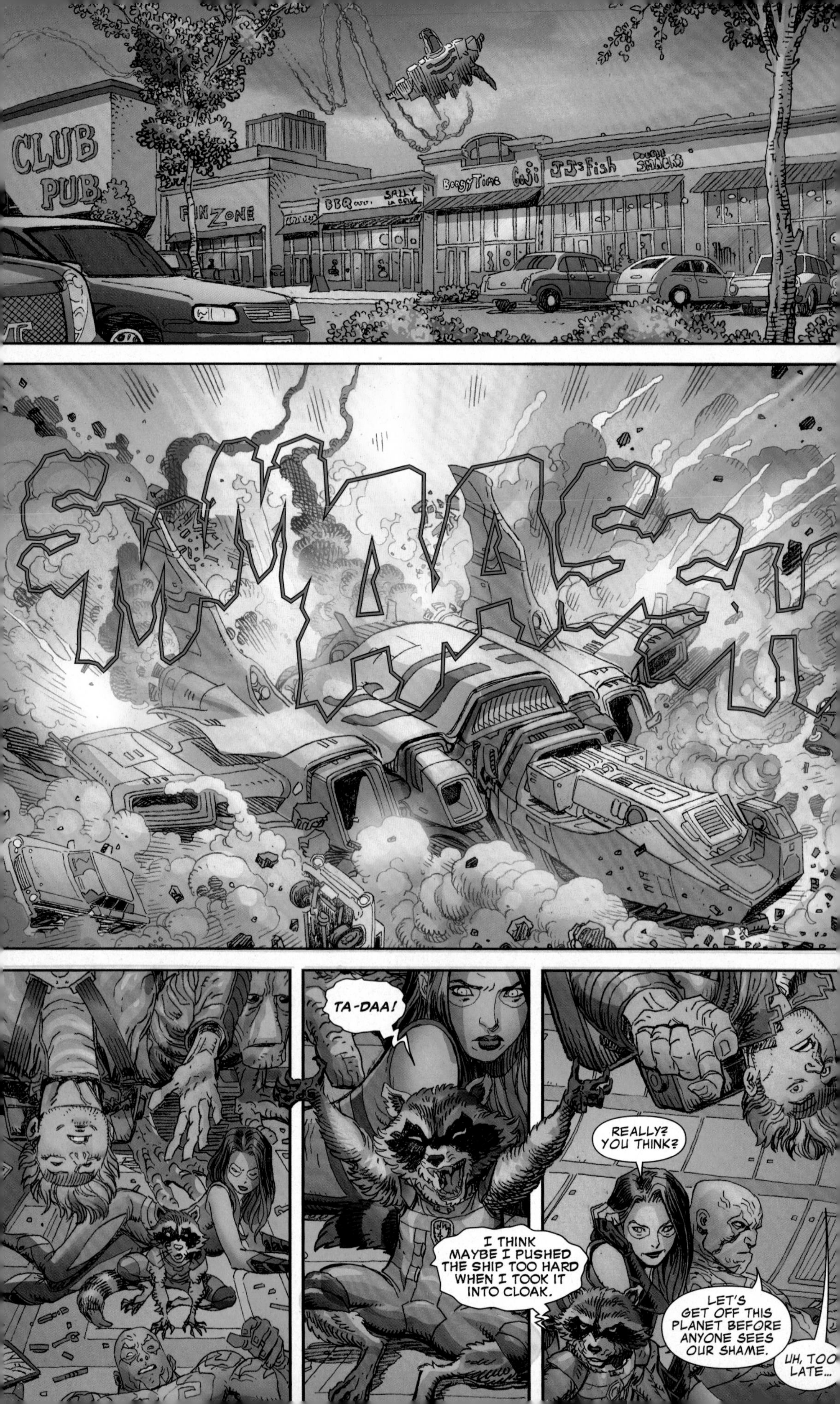

CLUB PUB
FUN ZONE
BBQ
SALLY
BoogyTime
Gaji
JJ's Fish
DOUBLE SNACKS
SMASH
TA-DAA!
I THINK MAYBE I PUSHED THE SHIP TOO HARD WHEN I TOOK IT INTO CLOAK.
REALLY? YOU THINK?
LET'S GET OFF THIS PLANET BEFORE ANYONE SEES OUR SHAME.
UH, TOO LATE...

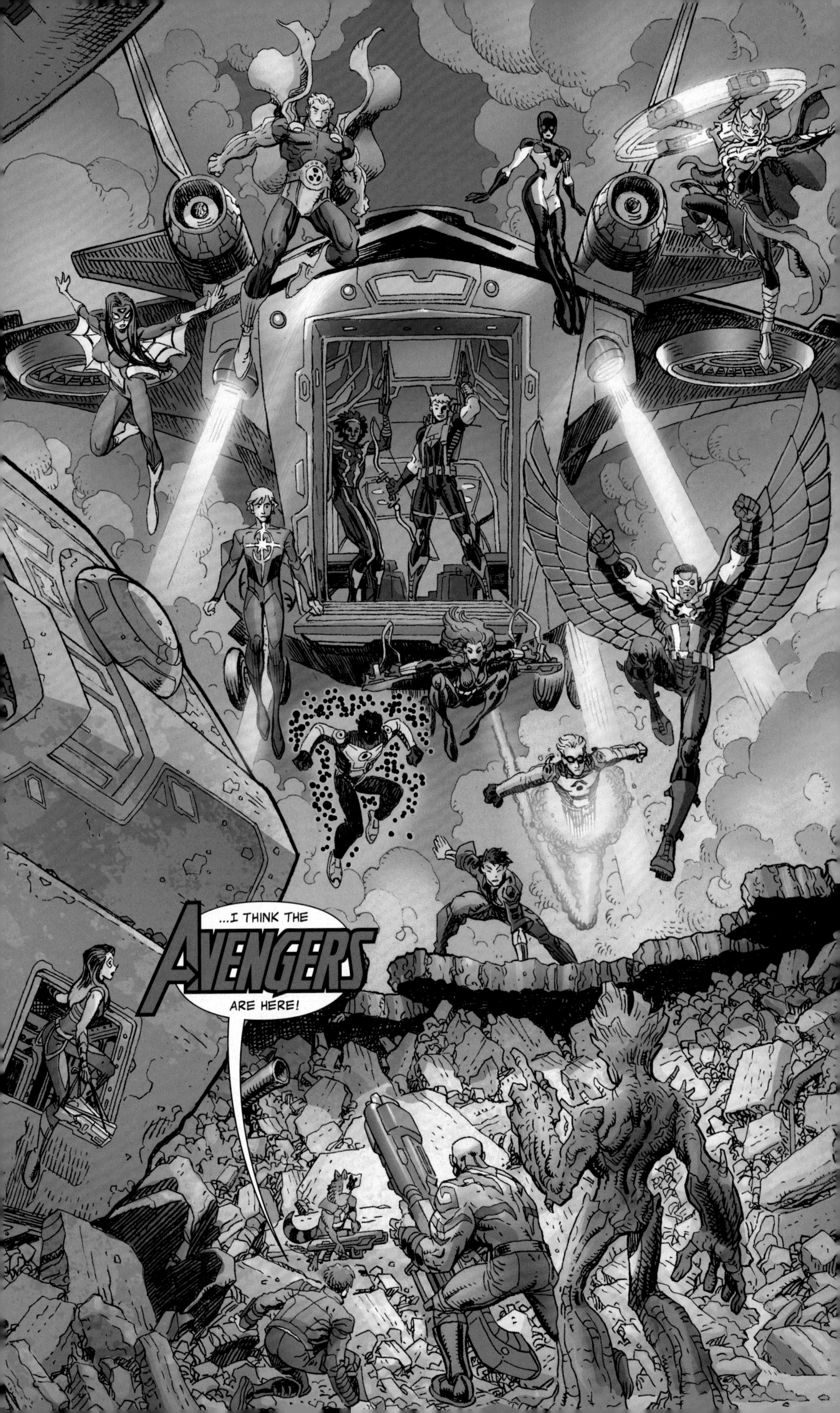
...I THINK THE
AVENGERS
ARE HERE!

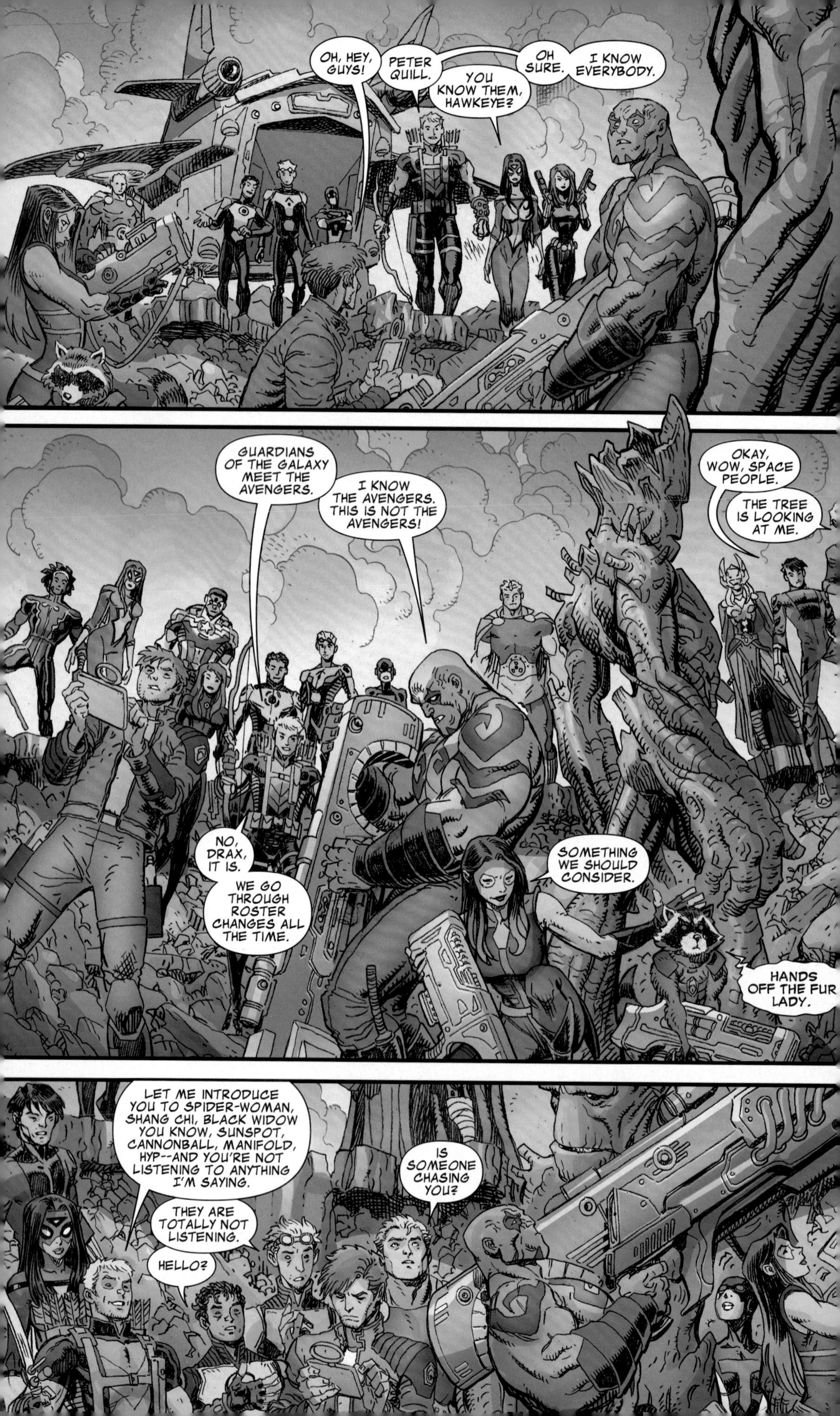
OH, HEY, GUYS!
PETER QUILL.
YOU KNOW THEM, HAWKEYE?
OH SURE.
I KNOW EVERYBODY.
GUARDIANS OF THE GALAXY MEET THE AVENGERS.
I KNOW THE AVENGERS. THIS IS NOT THE AVENGERS!
OKAY, WOW, SPACE PEOPLE.
THE TREE IS LOOKING AT ME.
NO, DRAX, IT IS.
WE GO THROUGH ROSTER CHANGES ALL THE TIME.
SOMETHING WE SHOULD CONSIDER.
HANDS OFF THE FUR LADY.
LET ME INTRODUCE YOU TO SPIDER-WOMAN, SHANG CHI, BLACK WIDOW YOU KNOW, SUNSPOT, CANNONBALL, MANIFOLD, HYP--AND YOU'RE NOT LISTENING TO ANYTHING I'M SAYING.
THEY ARE TOTALLY NOT LISTENING.
HELLO?
IS SOMEONE CHASING YOU?

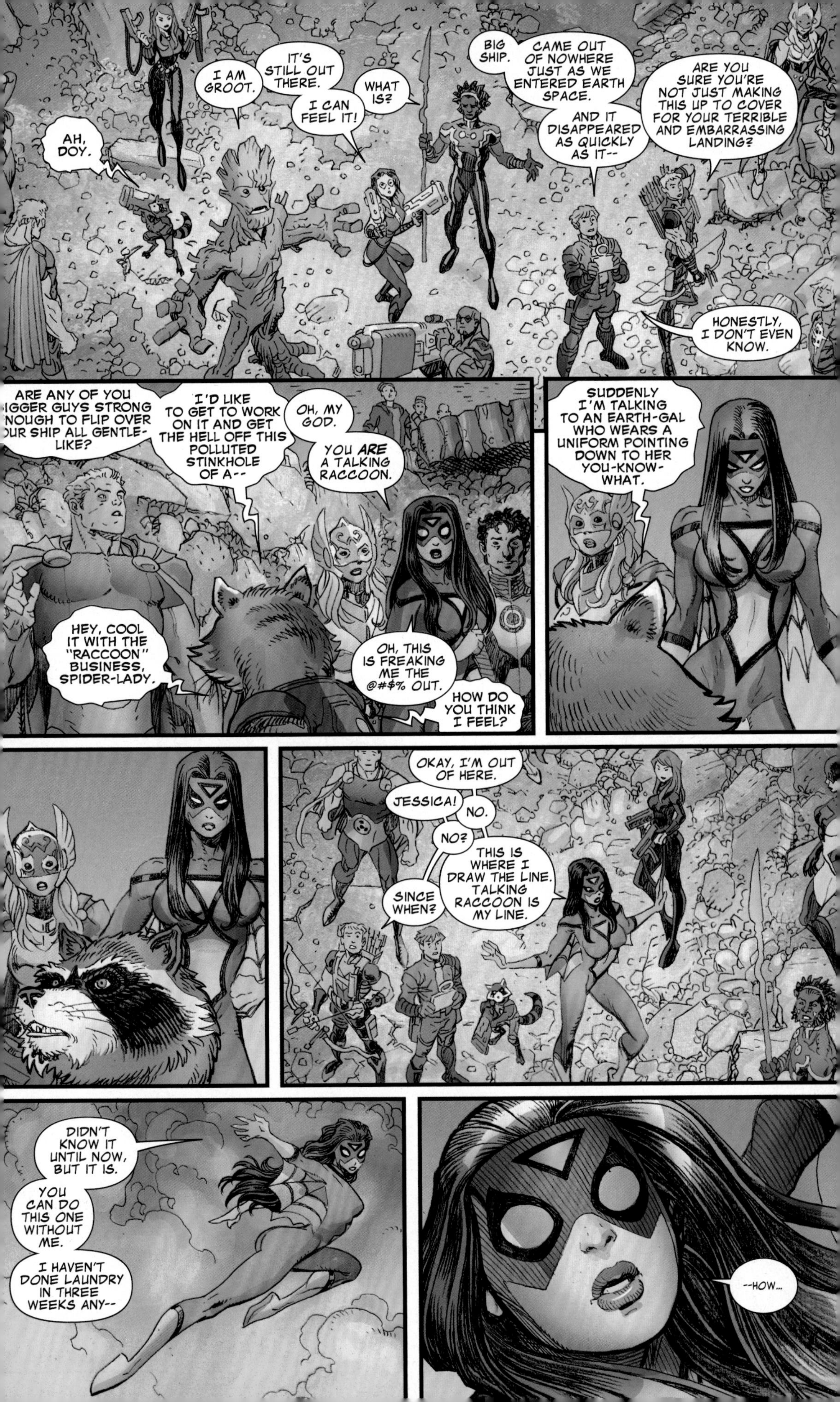

AH, DOY.
I AM GROOT.
IT'S STILL OUT THERE.
I CAN FEEL IT!
WHAT IS?
BIG SHIP.
CAME OUT OF NOWHERE JUST AS WE ENTERED EARTH SPACE.
AND IT DISAPPEARED AS QUICKLY AS IT--
ARE YOU SURE YOU'RE NOT JUST MAKING THIS UP TO COVER FOR YOUR TERRIBLE AND EMBARRASSING LANDING?
HONESTLY, I DON'T EVEN KNOW.
ARE ANY OF YOU BIGGER GUYS STRONG ENOUGH TO FLIP OVER OUR SHIP ALL GENTLE-LIKE?
I'D LIKE TO GET TO WORK ON IT AND GET THE HELL OFF THIS POLLUTED STINKHOLE OF A--
OH, MY GOD.
YOU ARE A TALKING RACCOON.
HEY, COOL IT WITH THE "RACCOON" BUSINESS, SPIDER-LADY.
OH, THIS IS FREAKING ME THE @#$% OUT.
HOW DO YOU THINK I FEEL?
SUDDENLY I'M TALKING TO AN EARTH-GAL WHO WEARS A UNIFORM POINTING DOWN TO HER YOU-KNOW-WHAT.
OKAY, I'M OUT OF HERE.
JESSICA!
NO.
NO?
THIS IS WHERE I DRAW THE LINE. TALKING RACCOON IS MY LINE.
SINCE WHEN?
DIDN'T KNOW IT UNTIL NOW, BUT IT IS.
YOU CAN DO THIS ONE WITHOUT ME.
I HAVEN'T DONE LAUNDRY IN THREE WEEKS ANY--
--HOW...

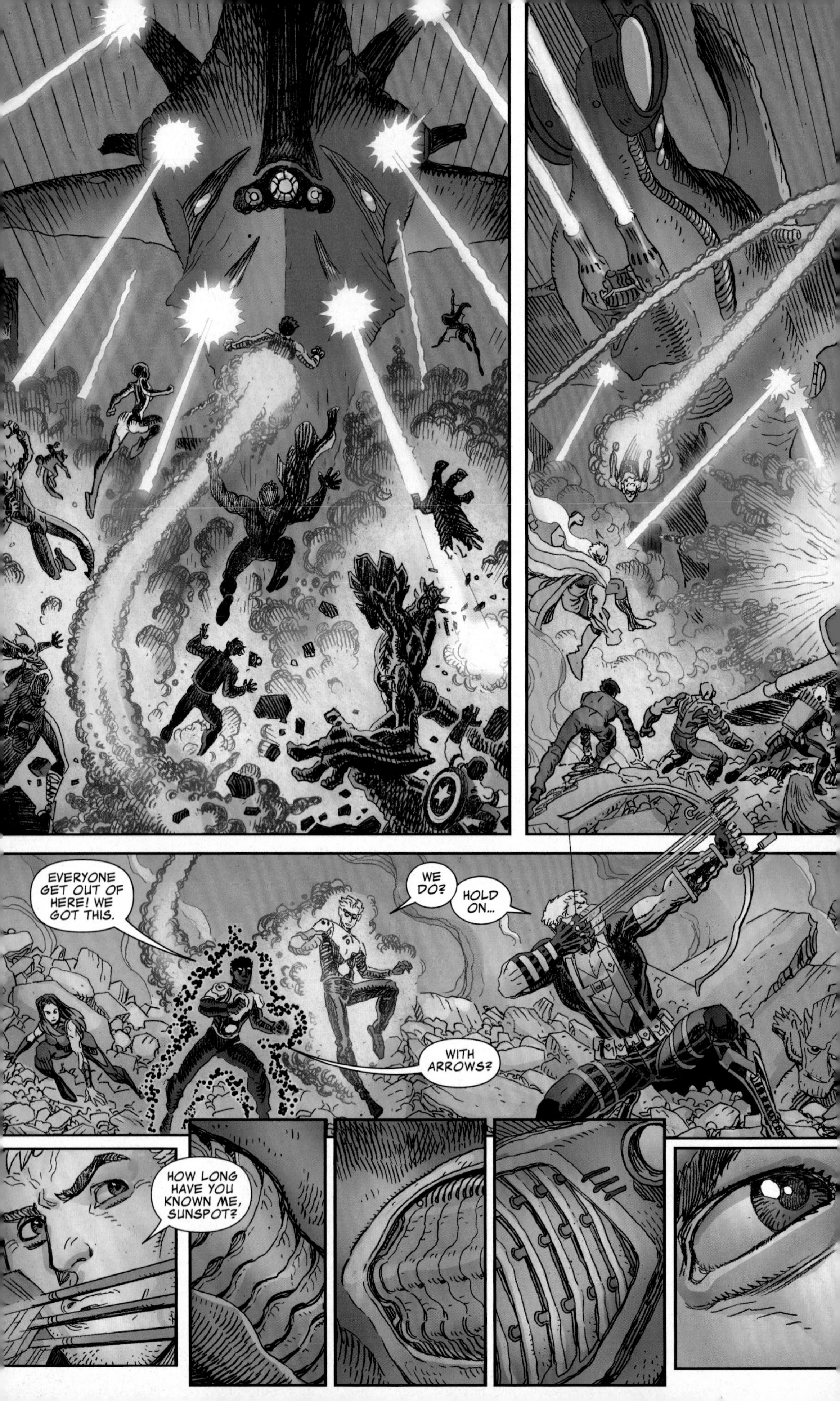
EVERYONE GET OUT OF HERE! WE GOT THIS.
WE DO?
HOLD ON...
WITH ARROWS?
HOW LONG HAVE YOU KNOWN ME, SUNSPOT?

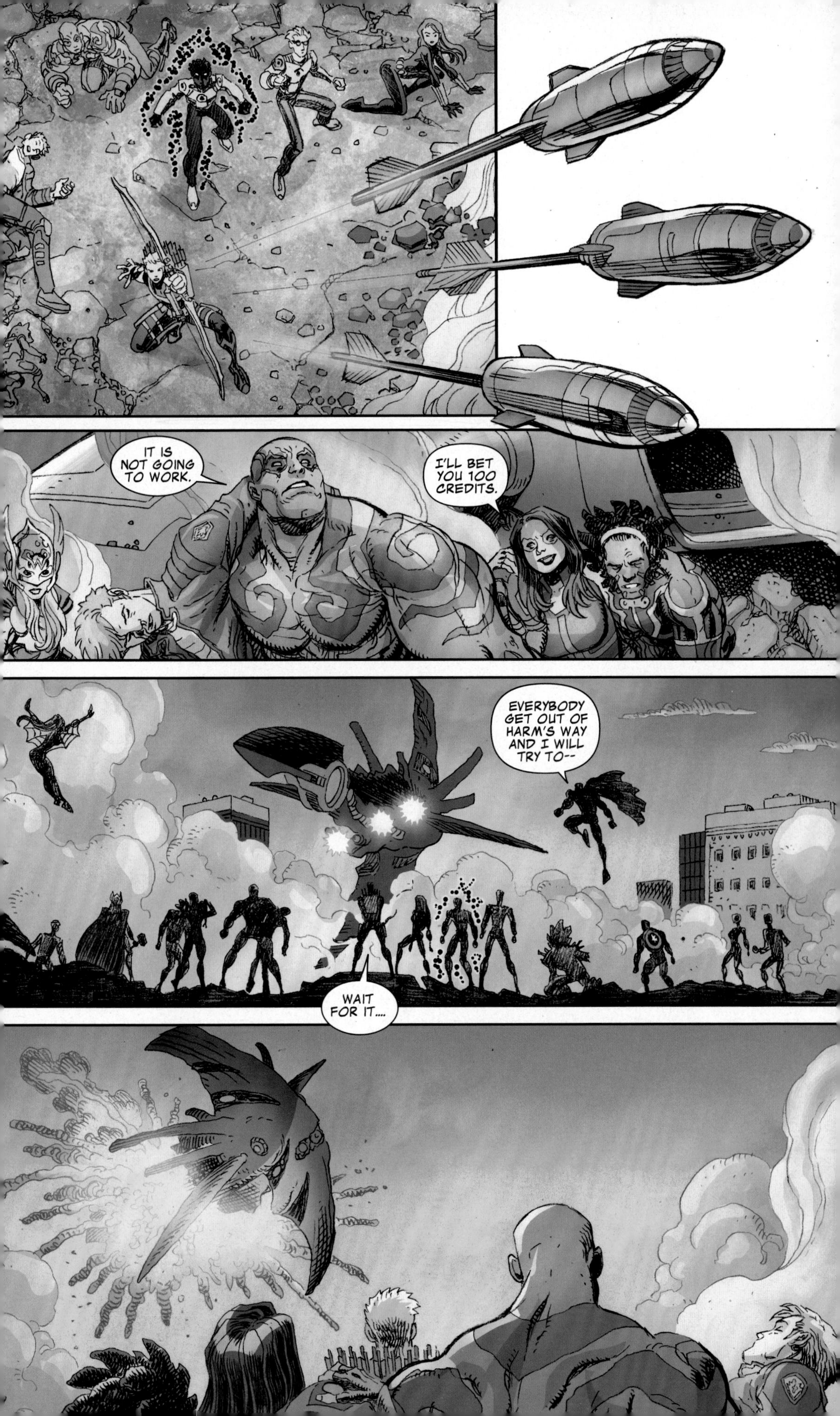
IT IS NOT GOING TO WORK.
I'LL BET YOU 100 CREDITS.
EVERYBODY GET OUT OF HARM'S WAY AND I WILL TRY TO--
WAIT FOR IT....

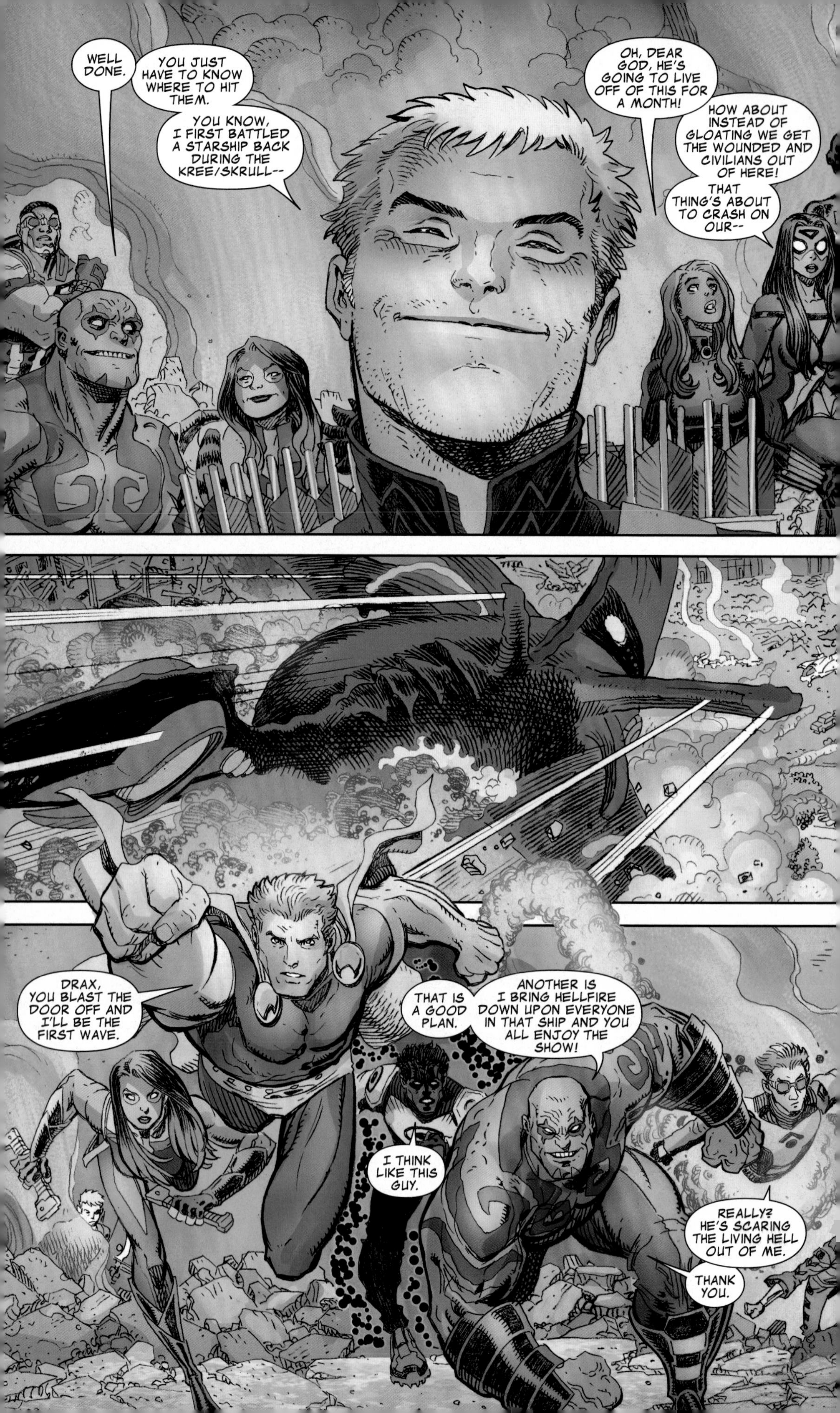
WELL DONE.
YOU JUST HAVE TO KNOW WHERE TO HIT THEM.
YOU KNOW, I FIRST BATTLED A STARSHIP BACK DURING THE KREE/SKRULL--
OH, DEAR GOD, HE'S GOING TO LIVE OFF OF THIS FOR A MONTH!
HOW ABOUT INSTEAD OF GLOATING WE GET THE WOUNDED AND CIVILIANS OUT OF HERE!
THAT THING'S ABOUT TO CRASH ON OUR--
DRAX, YOU BLAST THE DOOR OFF AND I'LL BE THE FIRST WAVE.
THAT IS A GOOD PLAN.
ANOTHER IS I BRING HELLFIRE DOWN UPON EVERYONE IN THAT SHIP AND YOU ALL ENJOY THE SHOW!
I THINK LIKE THIS GUY.
REALLY? HE'S SCARING THE LIVING HELL OUT OF ME.
THANK YOU.

GESUNDHEIT!

HYEZ XYIX SEX GIEGHI CYIGX

CHITAURI!

MIGEY IE MEIGH XE EX MIXX

UGH!

WHASGOINON?

ALIEN BATTLE IN A STRIP MALL. YOU KNOW, SAME OL'.

NO, FOOLISH EARTHER-BABY! CHITAURI! THAT IS WHO CHALLENGES US.

OKAY, GEEZ, YOU DON'T HAVE TO BE A JERK ABOUT IT.

XGM

THIS ESCALATED QUICKLY.

I WAS JUST THINKING THAT.

WHO LEADS YOU DEMONS? WHO IS YOUR MASTER?!

YOO-HOO!

BOOM!

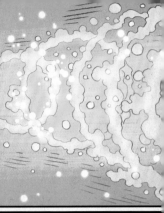

AND *THAT'S* HOW YOU BAKE A--HEY!

WHAT IS THIS? WHO ARE THESE, UM, PEOPLE?

I DON'T KNOW WHAT THAT MEANS.

I KNO THAT

CHITAURI.

ALIENS.

HAVE AT THEE!

SEE, I COULD NEVER PULL OFF A "HAVE AT THEE." NOT IN A MILLION YEARS.

WHAT DID YOU DO TO START THIS, STAR-LORD?

I PROMISE YOU, WE DIDN'T DO ANYTHING.

SOMETHING HAPPENED!

THEY JUMPED US. THERE'S NO OTHER WAY TO PUT IT.

I AM...

...GROOT...

TELL ME!

WHY ARE YOU HERE?!

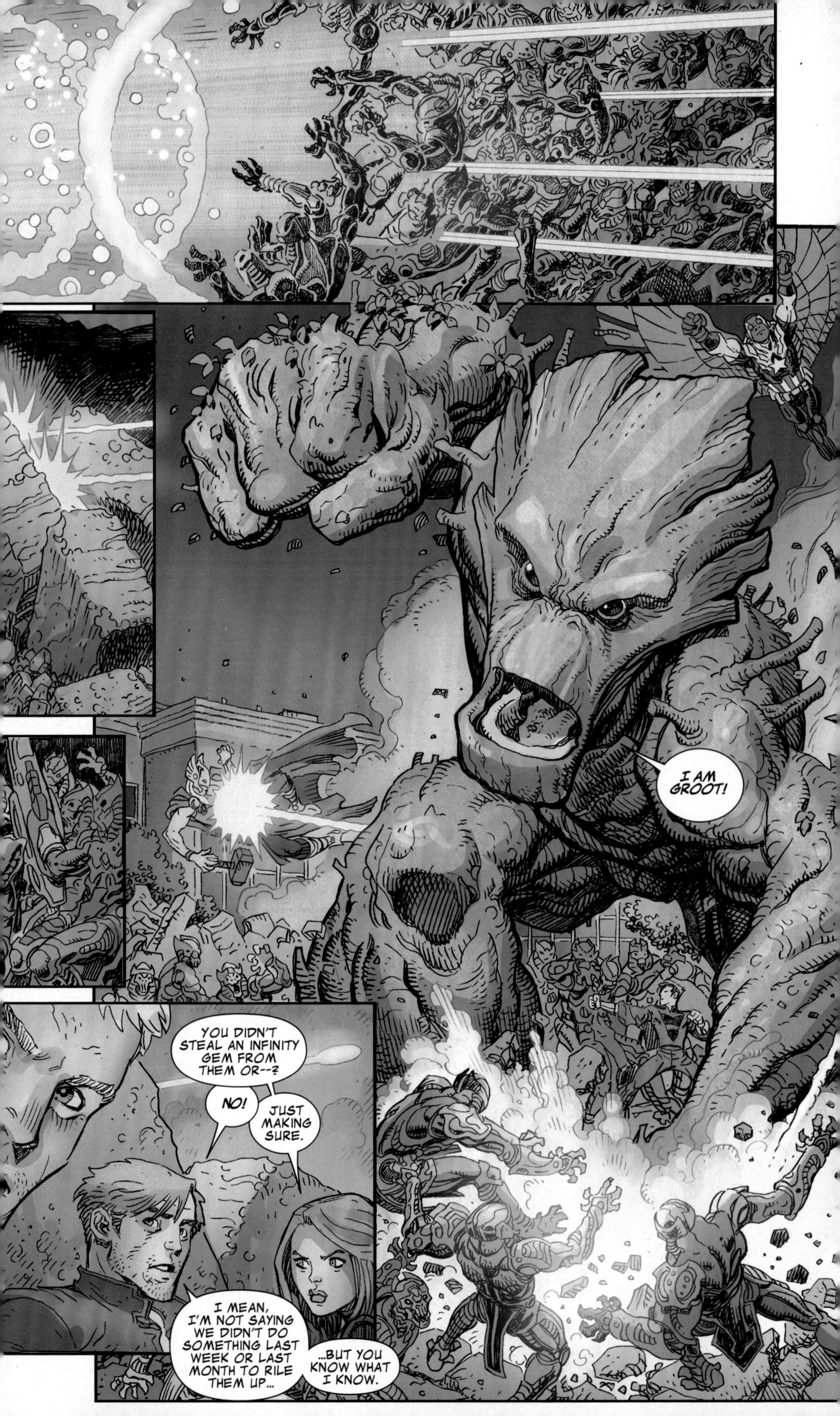
I AM GROOT!
YOU DIDN'T STEAL AN INFINITY GEM FROM THEM OR--?
NO!
JUST MAKING SURE.
I MEAN, I'M NOT SAYING WE DIDN'T DO SOMETHING LAST WEEK OR LAST MONTH TO RILE THEM UP...
...BUT YOU KNOW WHAT I KNOW.

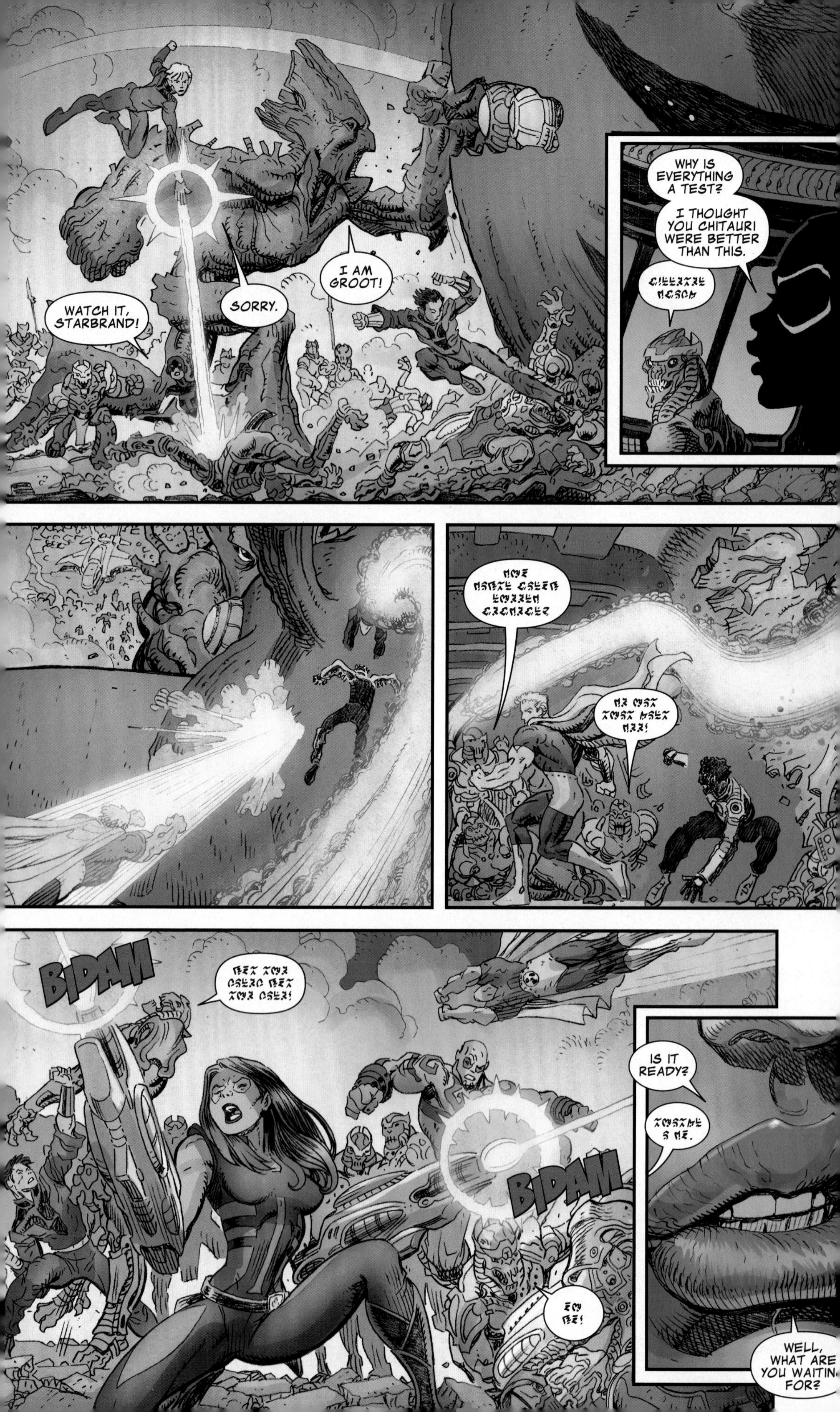
WATCH IT, STARBRAND!
SORRY.
I AM GROOT!
WHY IS EVERYTHING A TEST?
I THOUGHT YOU CHITAURI WERE BETTER THAN THIS.
BIDAM
BIDAM
IS IT READY?
WELL, WHAT ARE YOU WAITIN FOR?

HA!EN
!E CASTA!
!TE NE CELTC
ROROCNER!

BIDAM
BIDAM

OICEZ
EEKA OICEZ
EKOOZT

GRIE!
NAPE

UM...

ARE THEY
RETREATING?

HYPERION!
STARBRAND!
HELP THEM!

NOW.

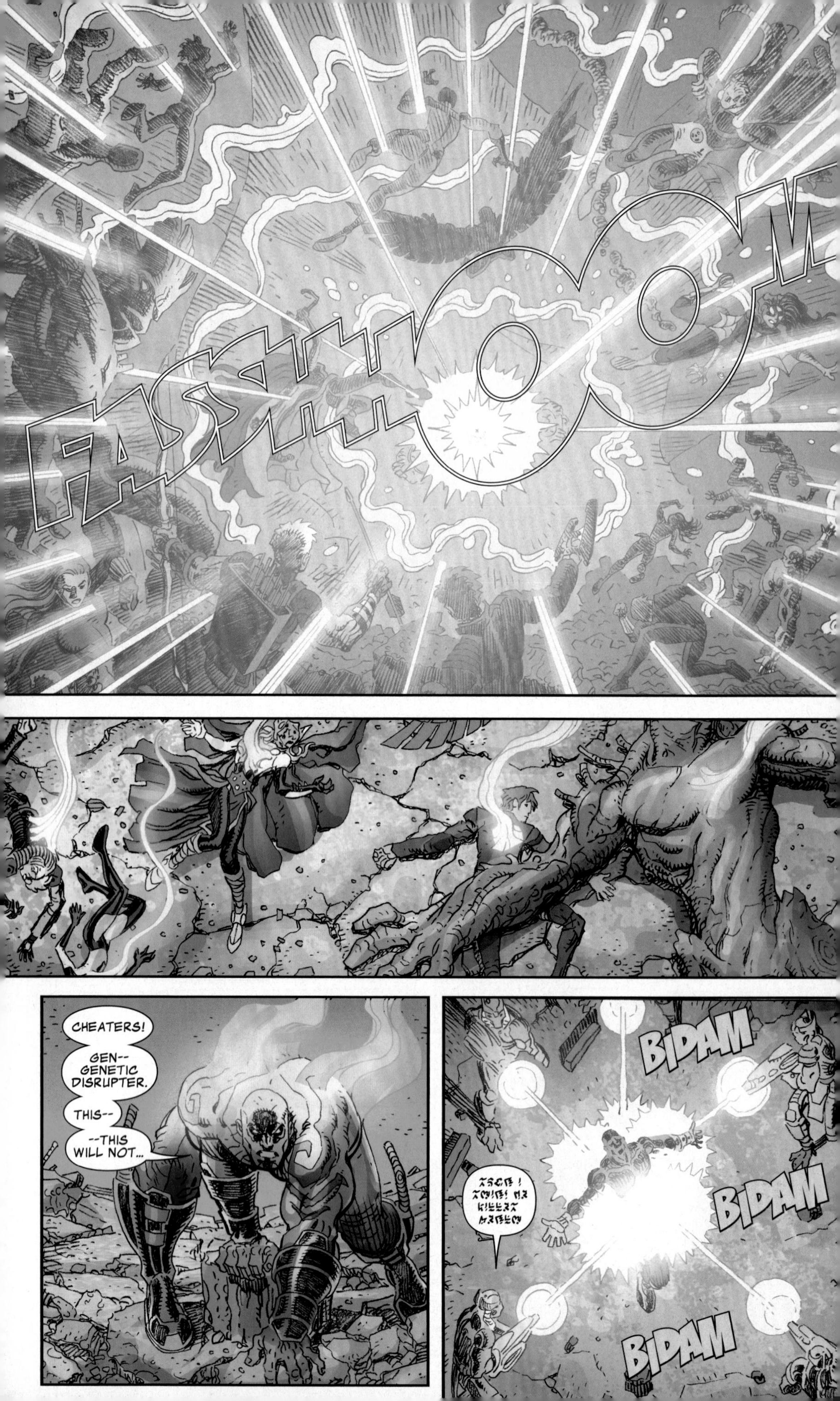
FASHHOOM
CHEATERS!
GEN-- GENETIC DISRUPTER.
THIS--
--THIS WILL NOT...
BIDAM
BIDAM
BIDAM

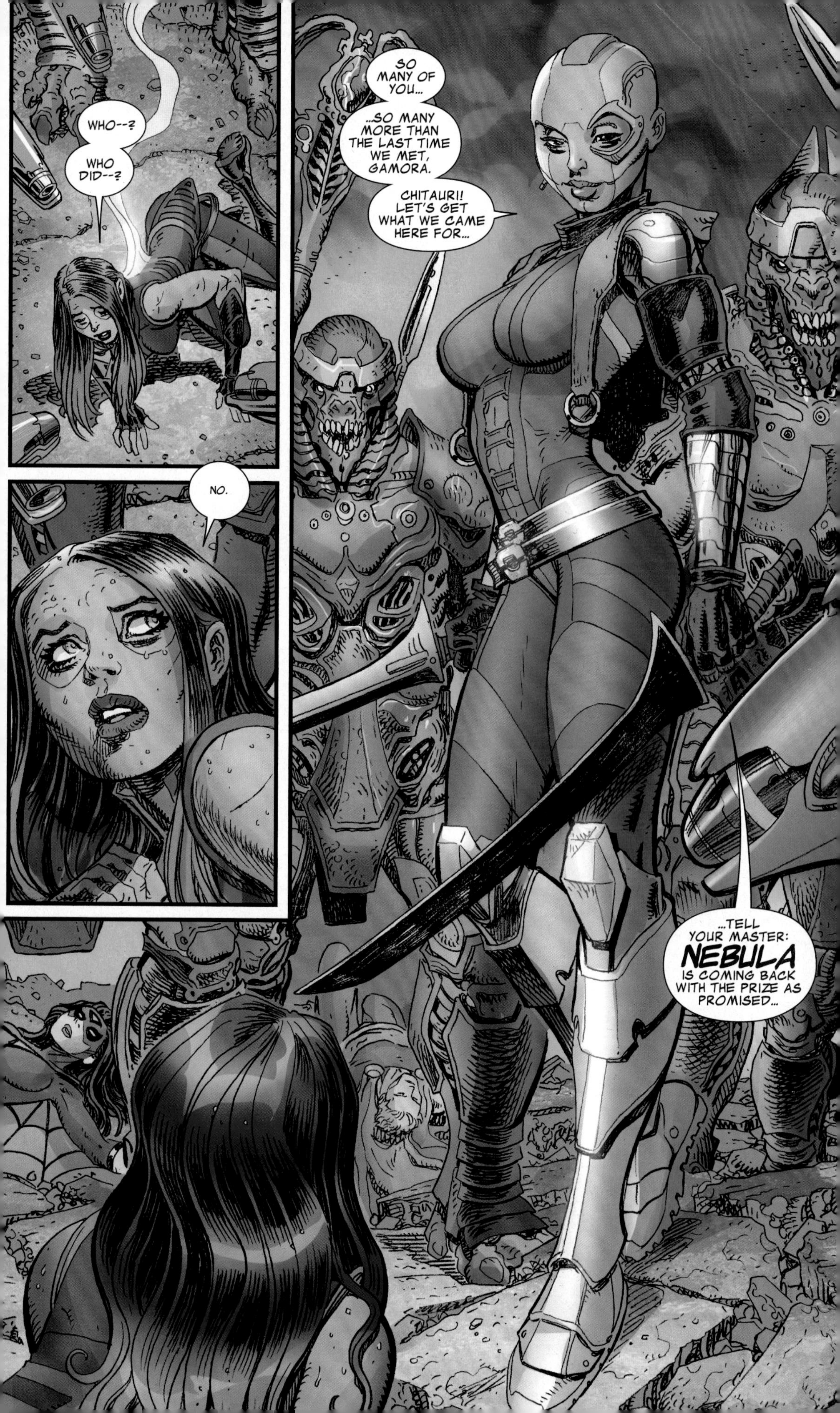
WHO--?
WHO DID--?
SO MANY OF YOU...
...SO MANY MORE THAN THE LAST TIME WE MET, GAMORA.
CHITAURI! LET'S GET WHAT WE CAME HERE FOR...
NO.
...TELL YOUR MASTER: NEBULA IS COMING BACK WITH THE PRIZE AS PROMISED...

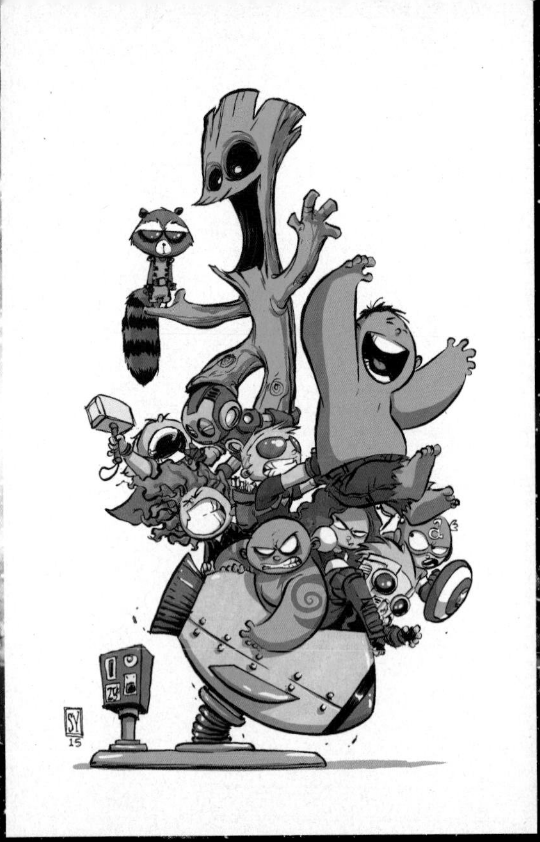

GUARDIANS TEAM-UP #1 VARIANT
BY SKOTTIE YOUNG

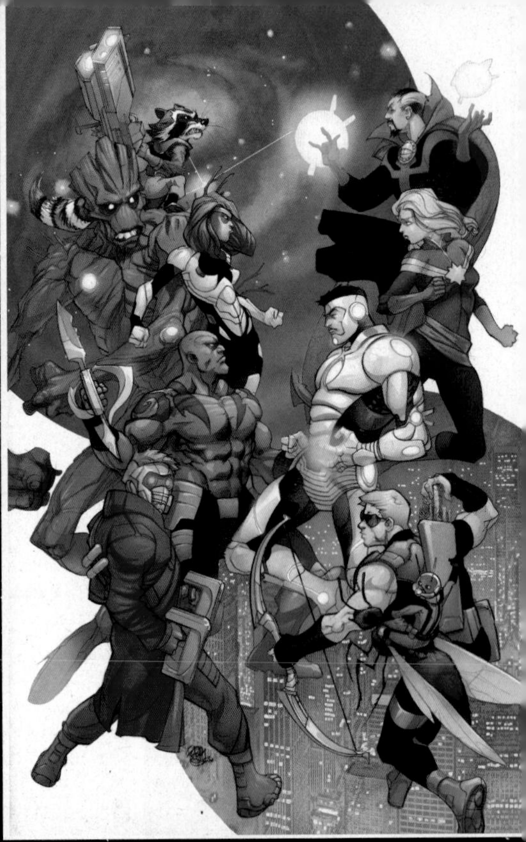

GUARDIANS TEAM-UP #1 VARIANT
BY PASQUAL FERRY & JEAN-FRANCOIS BEAULIEU

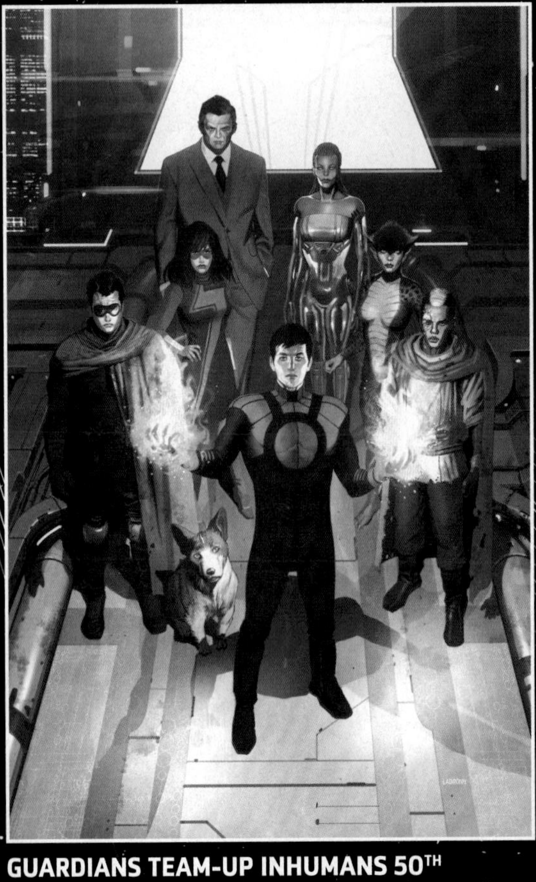

GUARDIANS TEAM-UP INHUMANS 50TH ANNIVERSARY #1 VARIANT BY JOSÉ LADRÖNN

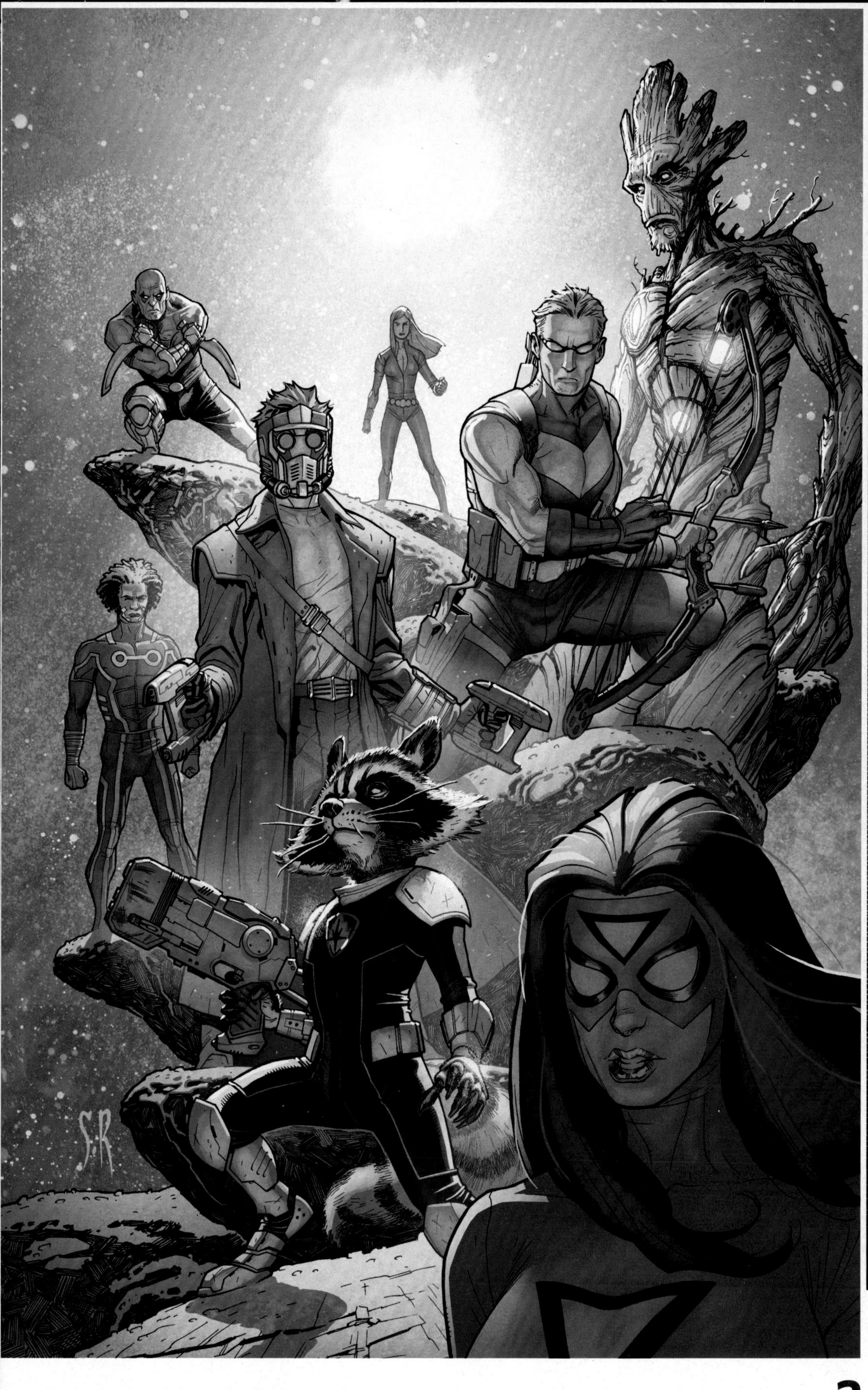
S.R

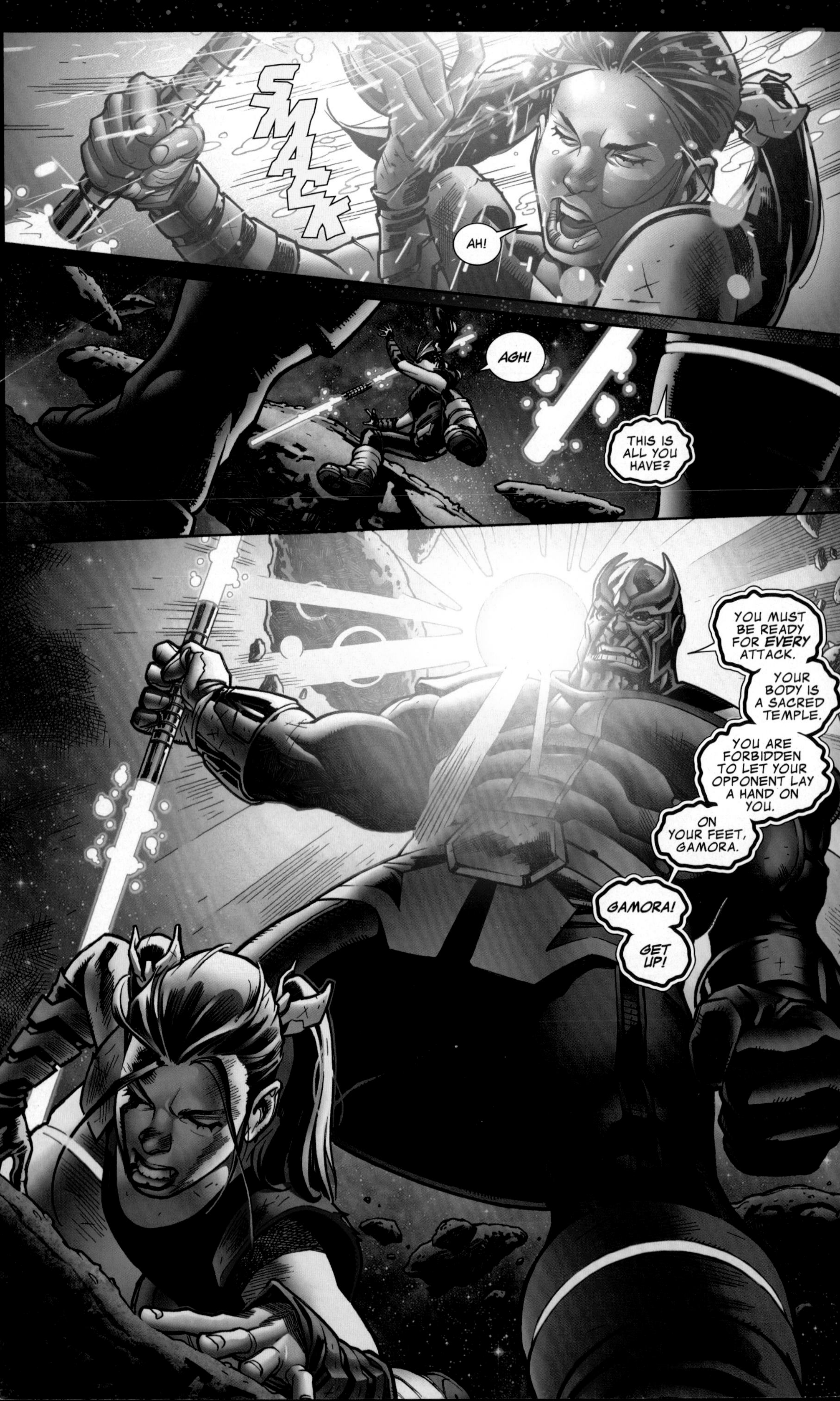
SMACK
AH!
AGH!
THIS IS ALL YOU HAVE?
YOU MUST BE READY FOR *EVERY* ATTACK.
YOUR BODY IS A SACRED TEMPLE.
YOU ARE FORBIDDEN TO LET YOUR OPPONENT LAY A HAND ON YOU.
ON YOUR FEET, GAMORA.
GAMORA!
GET UP!

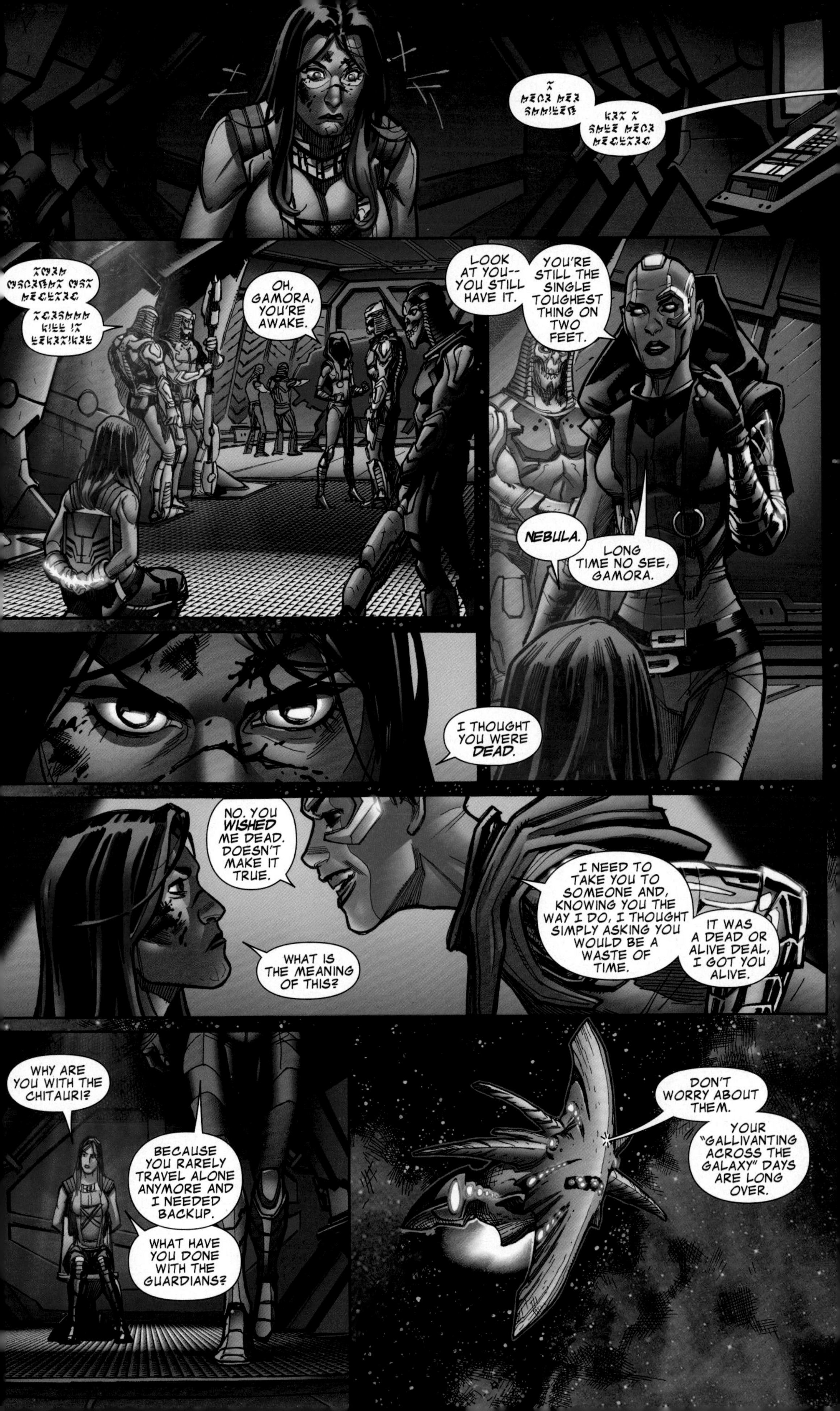
OH, GAMORA, YOU'RE AWAKE.
LOOK AT YOU-- YOU STILL HAVE IT.
YOU'RE STILL THE SINGLE TOUGHEST THING ON TWO FEET.
NEBULA.
LONG TIME NO SEE, GAMORA.
I THOUGHT YOU WERE DEAD.
NO. YOU WISHED ME DEAD. DOESN'T MAKE IT TRUE.
WHAT IS THE MEANING OF THIS?
I NEED TO TAKE YOU TO SOMEONE AND, KNOWING YOU THE WAY I DO, I THOUGHT SIMPLY ASKING YOU WOULD BE A WASTE OF TIME.
IT WAS A DEAD OR ALIVE DEAL, I GOT YOU ALIVE.
WHY ARE YOU WITH THE CHITAURI?
BECAUSE YOU RARELY TRAVEL ALONE ANYMORE AND I NEEDED BACKUP.
WHAT HAVE YOU DONE WITH THE GUARDIANS?
DON'T WORRY ABOUT THEM.
YOUR "GALLIVANTING ACROSS THE GALAXY" DAYS ARE LONG OVER.

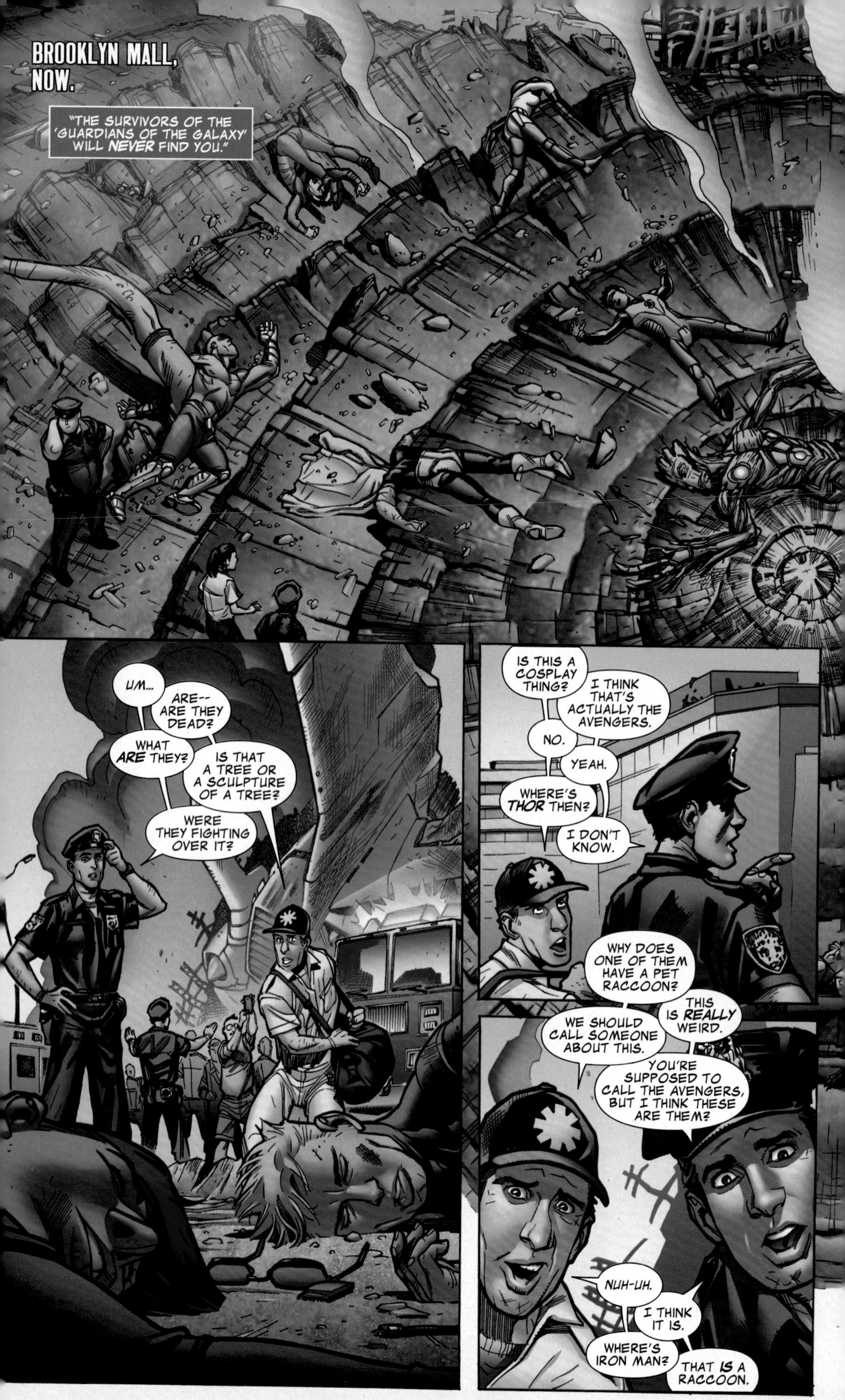
BROOKLYN MALL, NOW.
"THE SURVIVORS OF THE 'GUARDIANS OF THE GALAXY' WILL NEVER FIND YOU."
UM...
ARE-- ARE THEY DEAD?
WHAT ARE THEY?
IS THAT A TREE OR A SCULPTURE OF A TREE?
WERE THEY FIGHTING OVER IT?
IS THIS A COSPLAY THING?
I THINK THAT'S ACTUALLY THE AVENGERS.
NO.
YEAH.
WHERE'S THOR THEN?
I DON'T KNOW.
WHY DOES ONE OF THEM HAVE A PET RACCOON?
WE SHOULD CALL SOMEONE ABOUT THIS.
THIS IS REALLY WEIRD.
YOU'RE SUPPOSED TO CALL THE AVENGERS, BUT I THINK THESE ARE THEM?
NUH-UH.
I THINK IT IS.
WHERE'S IRON MAN?
THAT IS A RACCOON.

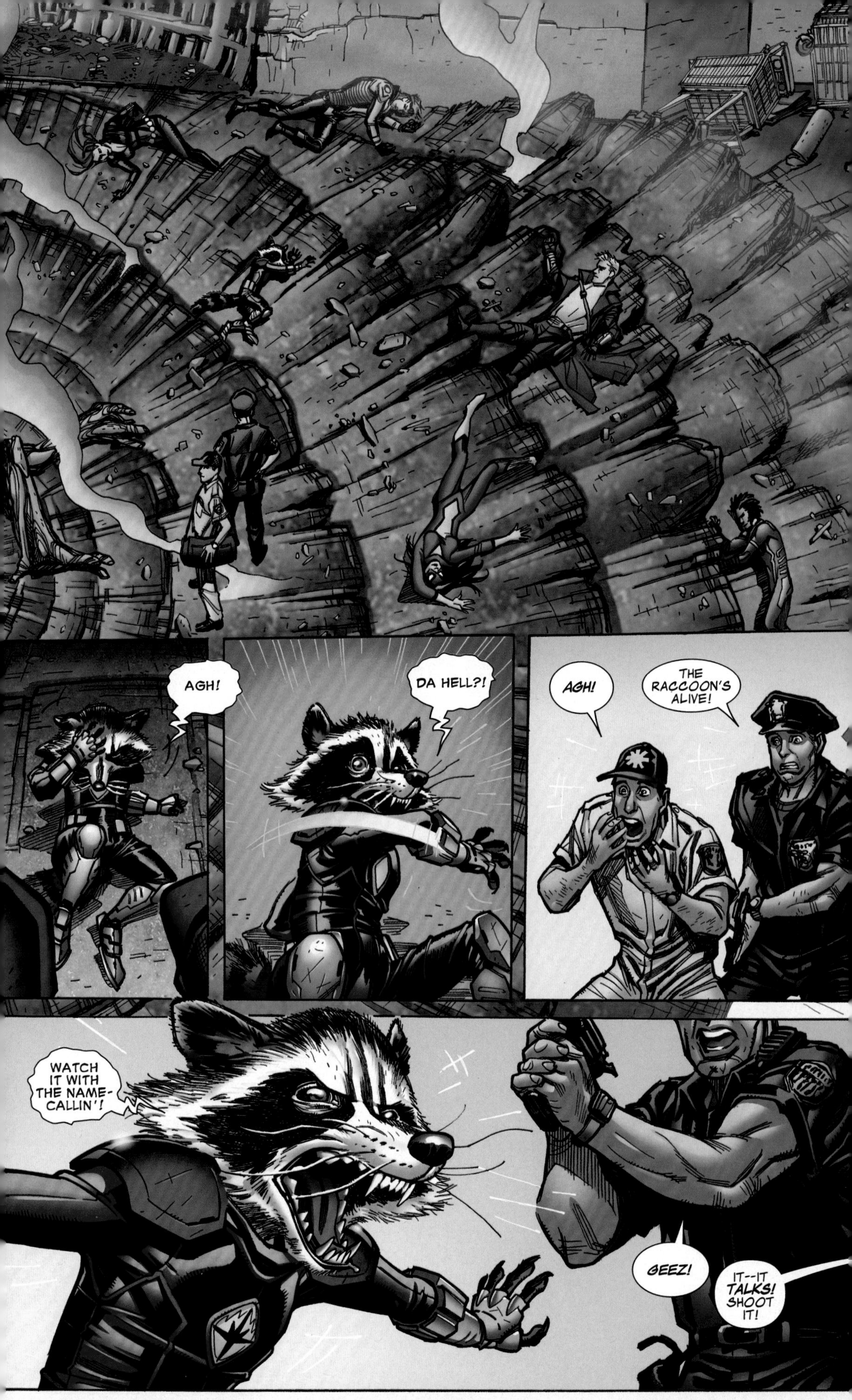
AGH!
DA HELL?!
AGH!
THE RACCOON'S ALIVE!
WATCH IT WITH THE NAME-CALLIN'!
GEEZ!
IT--IT TALKS! SHOOT IT!

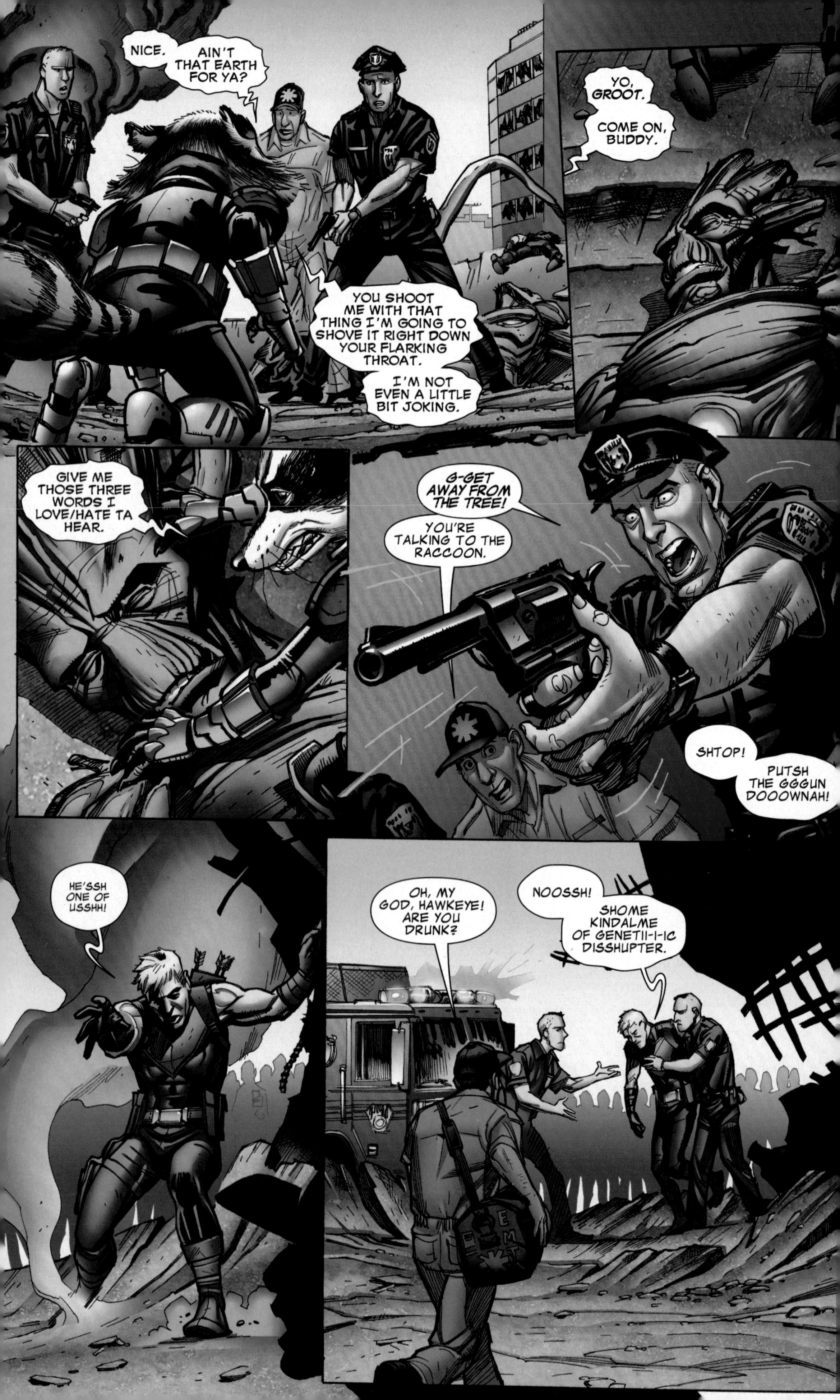
NICE.
AIN'T THAT EARTH FOR YA?
YO, GROOT.
COME ON, BUDDY.
YOU SHOOT ME WITH THAT THING I'M GOING TO SHOVE IT RIGHT DOWN YOUR FLARKING THROAT.
I'M NOT EVEN A LITTLE BIT JOKING.
GIVE ME THOSE THREE WORDS I LOVE/HATE TA HEAR.
G-GET AWAY FROM THE TREE!
YOU'RE TALKING TO THE RACCOON.
SHTOP!
PUTSH THE GGGUN DOOOWNAH!
HE'SSH ONE OF USSHH!
OH, MY GOD, HAWKEYE! ARE YOU DRUNK?
NOOSSH!
SHOME KINDALME OF GENETII-I-IC DISSHUPTER.

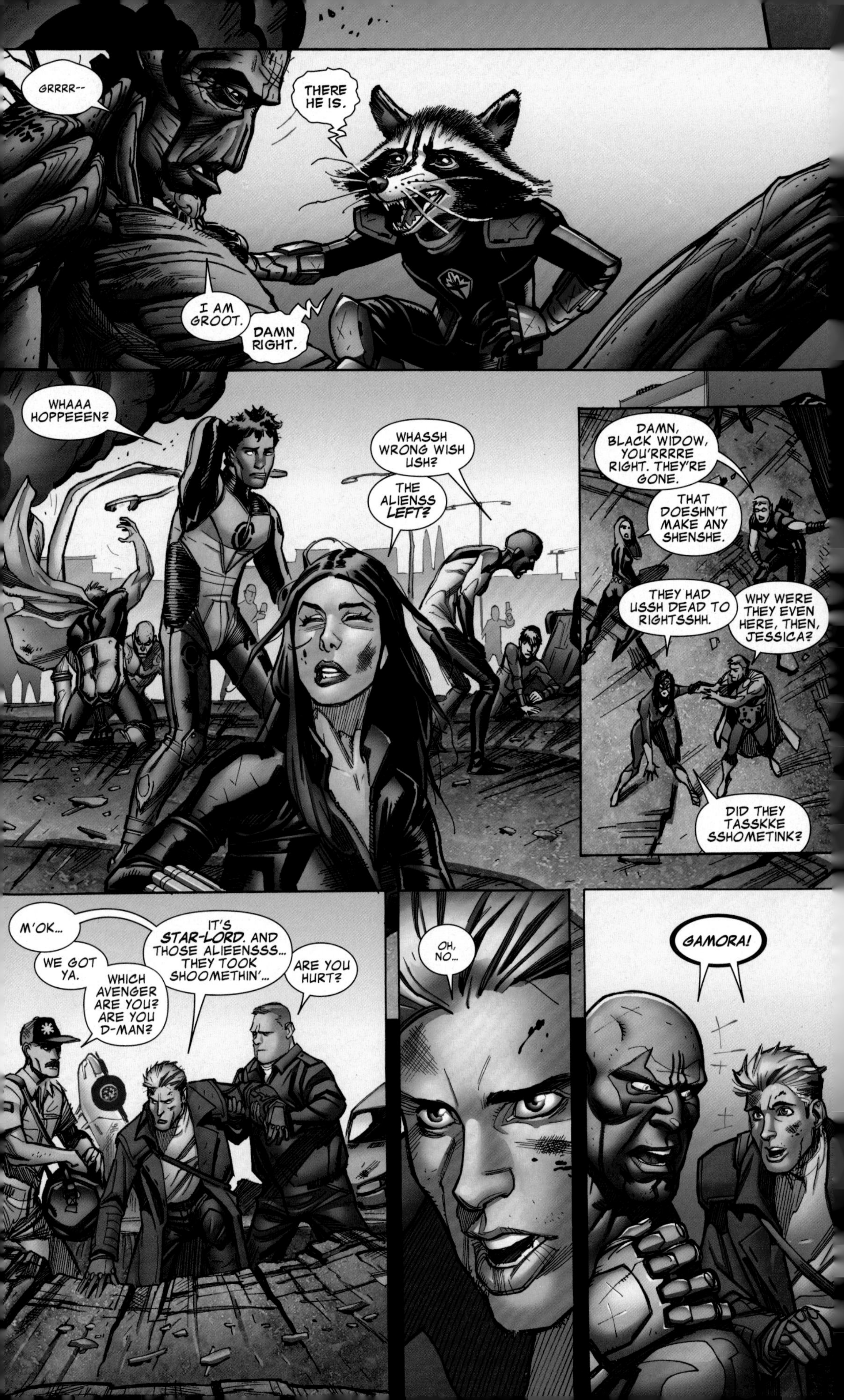
GRRRR--
THERE HE IS.
I AM GROOT.
DAMN RIGHT.
WHAAA HOPPEEEN?
WHASSH WRONG WISH USH?
THE ALIENSS LEFT?
DAMN, BLACK WIDOW, YOU'RRRRE RIGHT. THEY'RE GONE.
THAT DOESHN'T MAKE ANY SHENSHE.
THEY HAD USSH DEAD TO RIGHTSSHH.
WHY WERE THEY EVEN HERE, THEN, JESSICA?
DID THEY TASSKKE SSHOMETINK?
M'OK...
WE GOT YA.
WHICH AVENGER ARE YOU? ARE YOU D-MAN?
IT'S STAR-LORD. AND THOSE ALIEENSSS... THEY TOOK SHOOMETHIN'...
ARE YOU HURT?
OH, NO...
GAMORA!

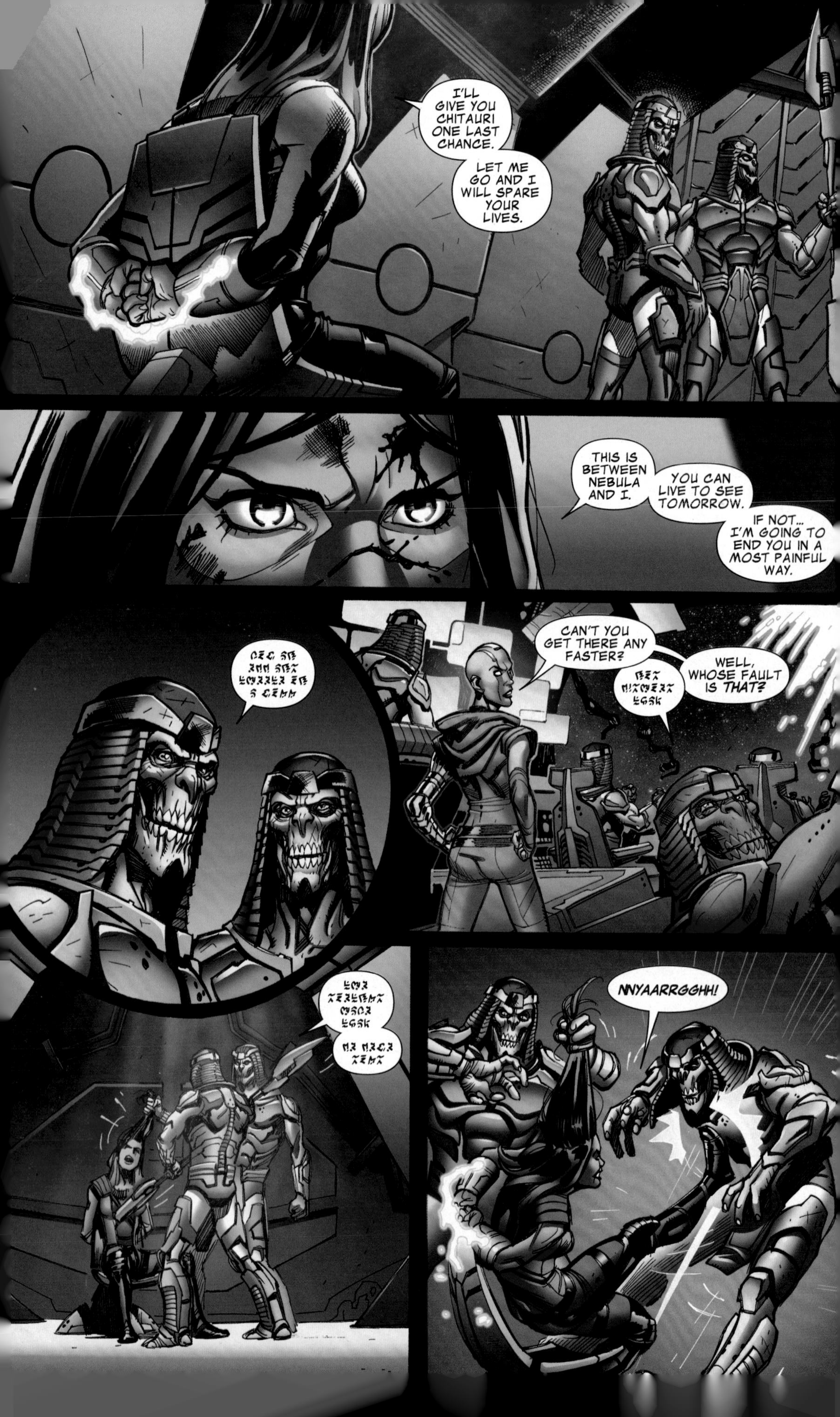
I'LL GIVE YOU CHITAURI ONE LAST CHANCE.
LET ME GO AND I WILL SPARE YOUR LIVES.
THIS IS BETWEEN NEBULA AND I.
YOU CAN LIVE TO SEE TOMORROW.
IF NOT... I'M GOING TO END YOU IN A MOST PAINFUL WAY.
CAN'T YOU GET THERE ANY FASTER?
WELL, WHOSE FAULT IS *THAT?*
NNYAARRGGHH!

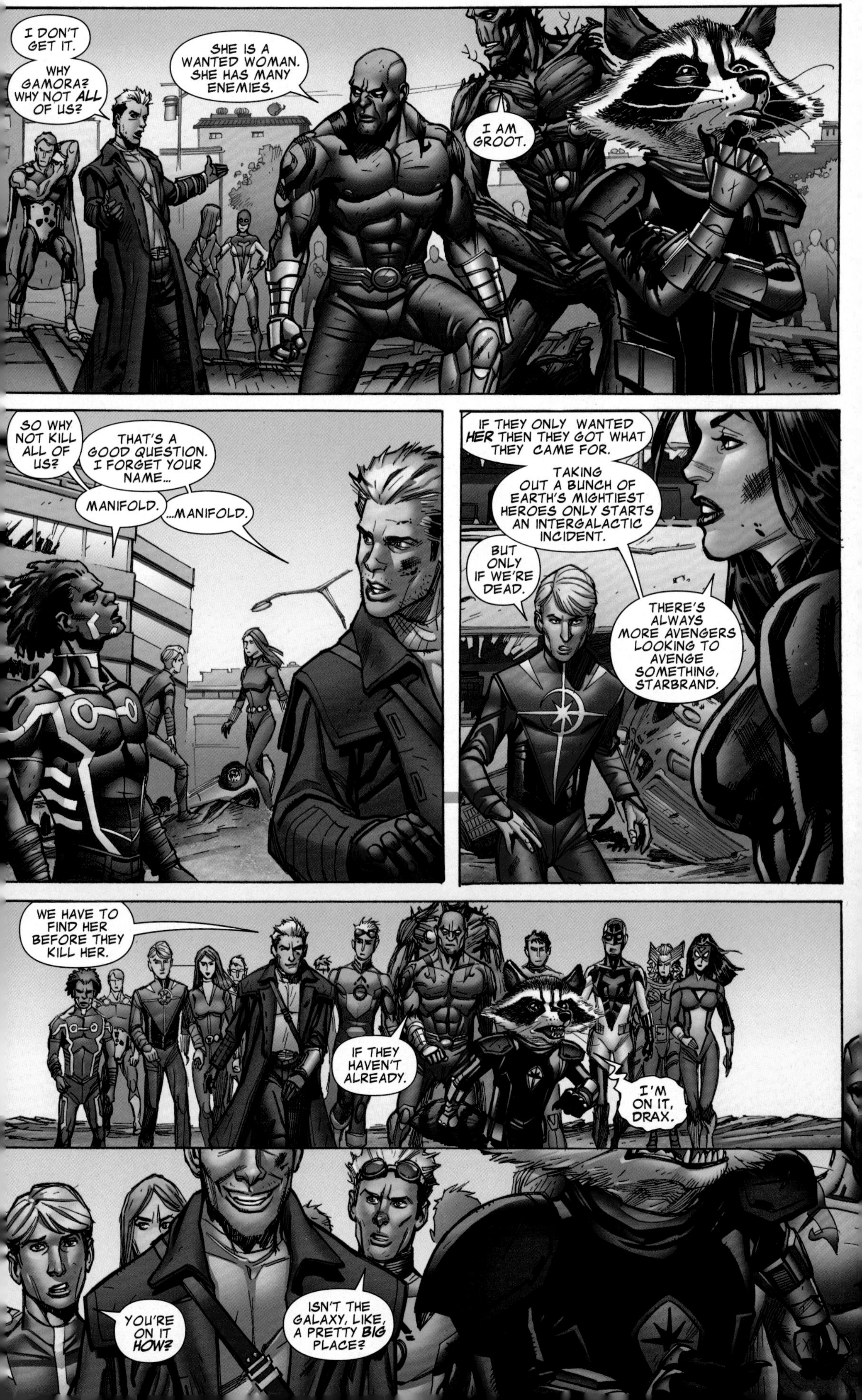
I DON'T GET IT.
WHY GAMORA? WHY NOT ALL OF US?
SHE IS A WANTED WOMAN. SHE HAS MANY ENEMIES.
I AM GROOT.
SO WHY NOT KILL ALL OF US?
THAT'S A GOOD QUESTION. I FORGET YOUR NAME...
MANIFOLD.
...MANIFOLD.
IF THEY ONLY WANTED HER THEN THEY GOT WHAT THEY CAME FOR.
TAKING OUT A BUNCH OF EARTH'S MIGHTIEST HEROES ONLY STARTS AN INTERGALACTIC INCIDENT.
BUT ONLY IF WE'RE DEAD.
THERE'S ALWAYS MORE AVENGERS LOOKING TO AVENGE SOMETHING, STARBRAND.
WE HAVE TO FIND HER BEFORE THEY KILL HER.
IF THEY HAVEN'T ALREADY.
I'M ON IT, DRAX.
YOU'RE ON IT HOW?
ISN'T THE GALAXY, LIKE, A PRETTY BIG PLACE?

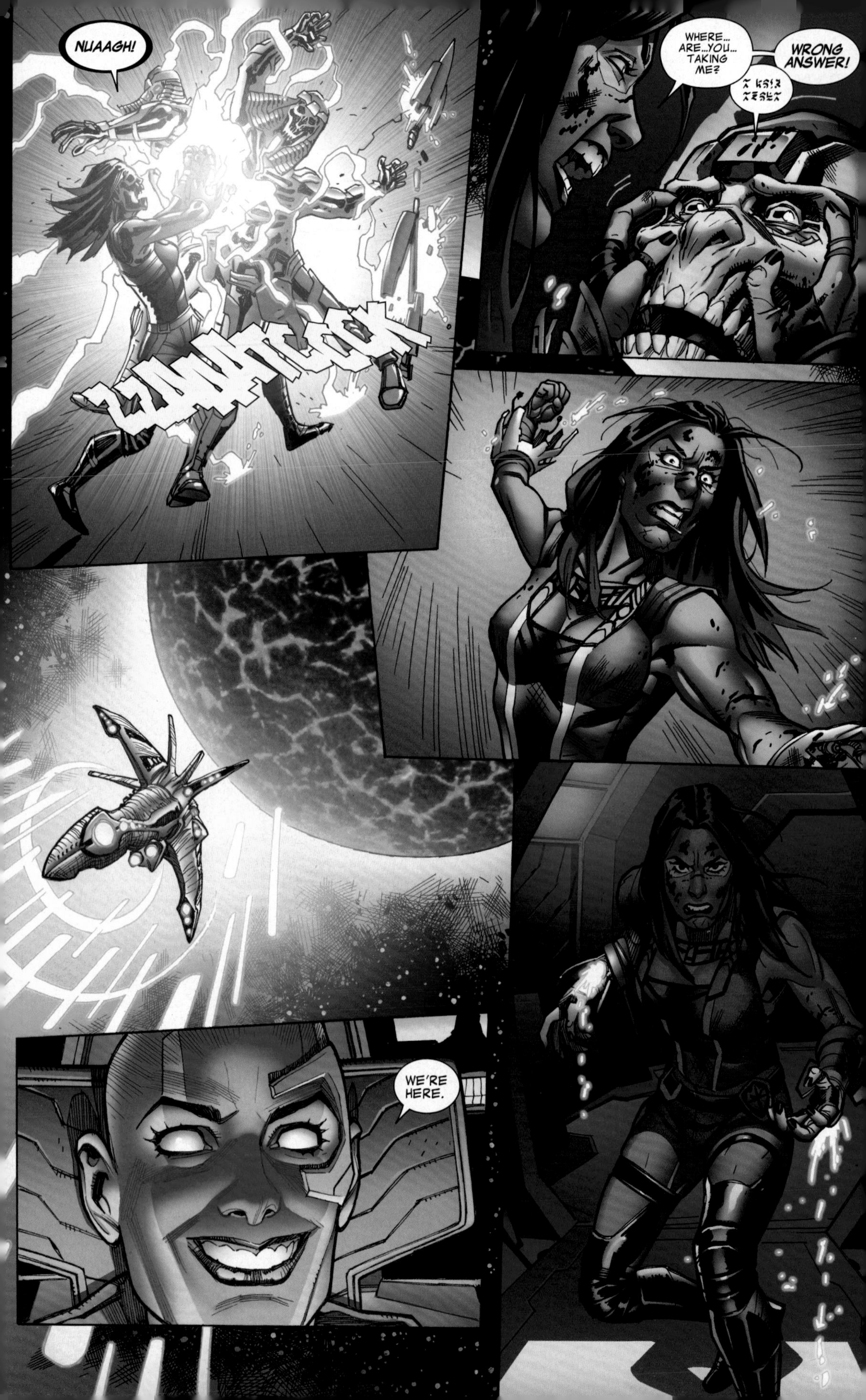
NUAAGH!
ZZAAKKOOK
WHERE... ARE...YOU... TAKING ME?
WRONG ANSWER!
WE'RE HERE.

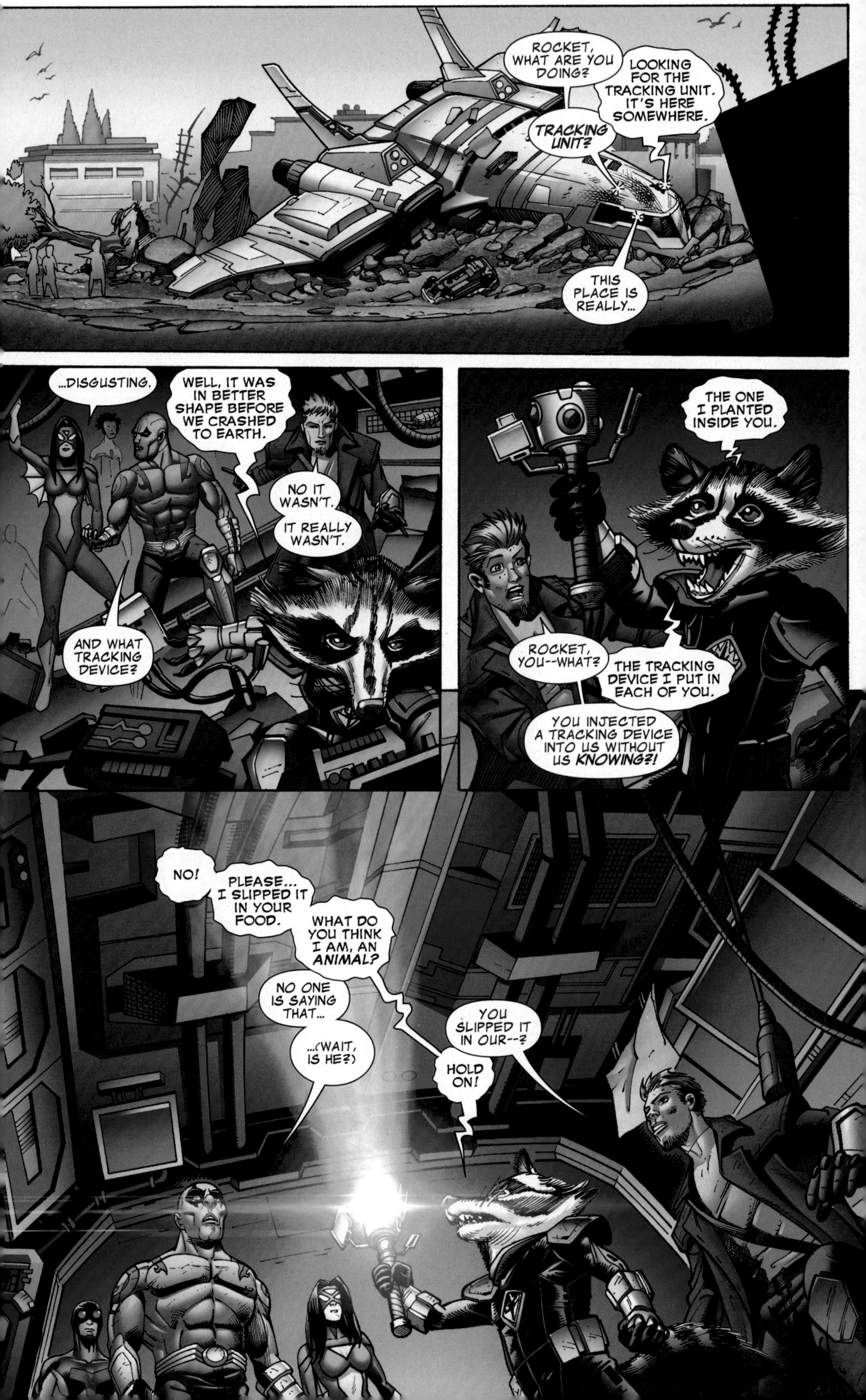
ROCKET, WHAT ARE YOU DOING?
LOOKING FOR THE TRACKING UNIT. IT'S HERE SOMEWHERE.
TRACKING UNIT?
THIS PLACE IS REALLY...
...DISGUSTING.
WELL, IT WAS IN BETTER SHAPE BEFORE WE CRASHED TO EARTH.
NO IT WASN'T.
IT REALLY WASN'T.
AND WHAT TRACKING DEVICE?
THE ONE I PLANTED INSIDE YOU.
ROCKET, YOU--WHAT?
THE TRACKING DEVICE I PUT IN EACH OF YOU.
YOU INJECTED A TRACKING DEVICE INTO US WITHOUT US KNOWING?!
NO!
PLEASE... I SLIPPED IT IN YOUR FOOD.
WHAT DO YOU THINK I AM, AN ANIMAL?
NO ONE IS SAYING THAT...
...(WAIT, IS HE?)
YOU SLIPPED IT IN OUR--?
HOLD ON!

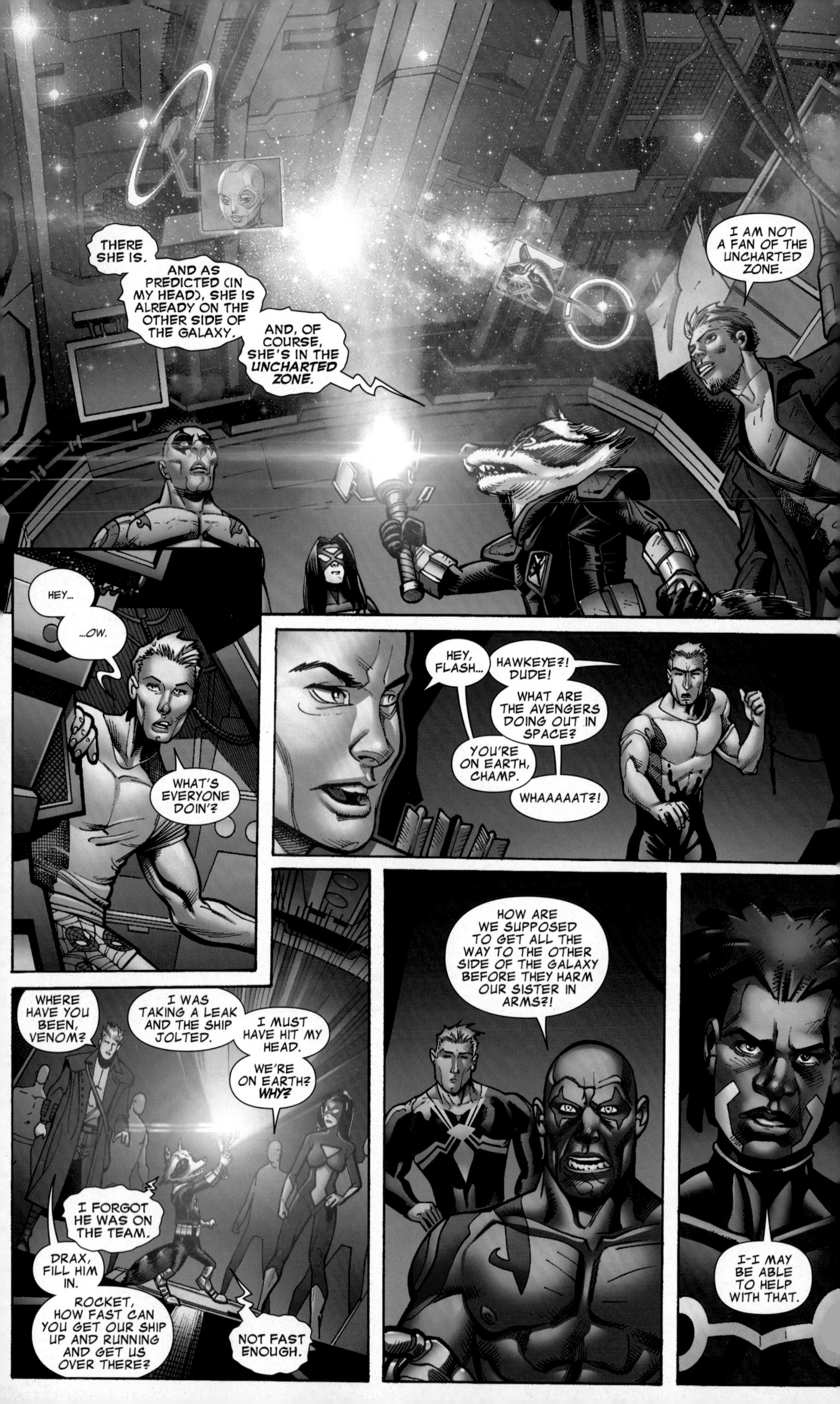

THERE SHE IS.
AND AS PREDICTED (IN MY HEAD), SHE IS ALREADY ON THE OTHER SIDE OF THE GALAXY.
AND, OF COURSE, SHE'S IN THE UNCHARTED ZONE.
I AM NOT A FAN OF THE UNCHARTED ZONE.
HEY...
...OW.
WHAT'S EVERYONE DOIN'?
HEY, FLASH...
HAWKEYE?! DUDE!
WHAT ARE THE AVENGERS DOING OUT IN SPACE?
YOU'RE ON EARTH, CHAMP.
WHAAAAAT?!
WHERE HAVE YOU BEEN, VENOM?
I WAS TAKING A LEAK AND THE SHIP JOLTED.
I MUST HAVE HIT MY HEAD.
WE'RE ON EARTH? WHY?
I FORGOT HE WAS ON THE TEAM.
DRAX, FILL HIM IN.
ROCKET, HOW FAST CAN YOU GET OUR SHIP UP AND RUNNING AND GET US OVER THERE?
NOT FAST ENOUGH.
HOW ARE WE SUPPOSED TO GET ALL THE WAY TO THE OTHER SIDE OF THE GALAXY BEFORE THEY HARM OUR SISTER IN ARMS?!
I-I MAY BE ABLE TO HELP WITH THAT.

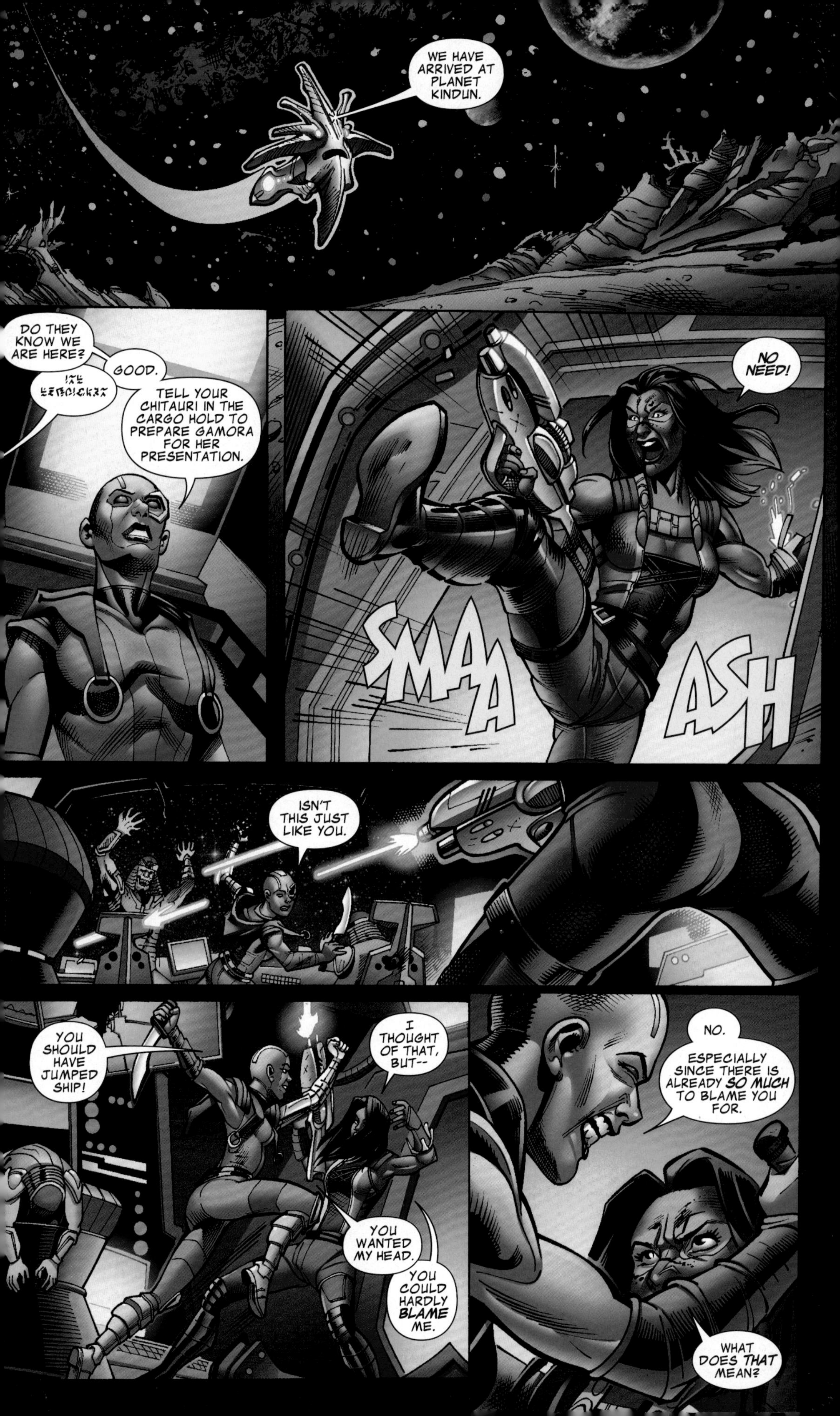
WE HAVE ARRIVED AT PLANET KINDUN.
DO THEY KNOW WE ARE HERE?
GOOD.
TELL YOUR CHITAURI IN THE CARGO HOLD TO PREPARE GAMORA FOR HER PRESENTATION.
NO NEED!
SMAAASH
ISN'T THIS JUST LIKE YOU.
YOU SHOULD HAVE JUMPED SHIP!
I THOUGHT OF THAT, BUT--
YOU WANTED MY HEAD.
YOU COULD HARDLY BLAME ME.
NO.
ESPECIALLY SINCE THERE IS ALREADY SO MUCH TO BLAME YOU FOR.
WHAT DOES THAT MEAN?

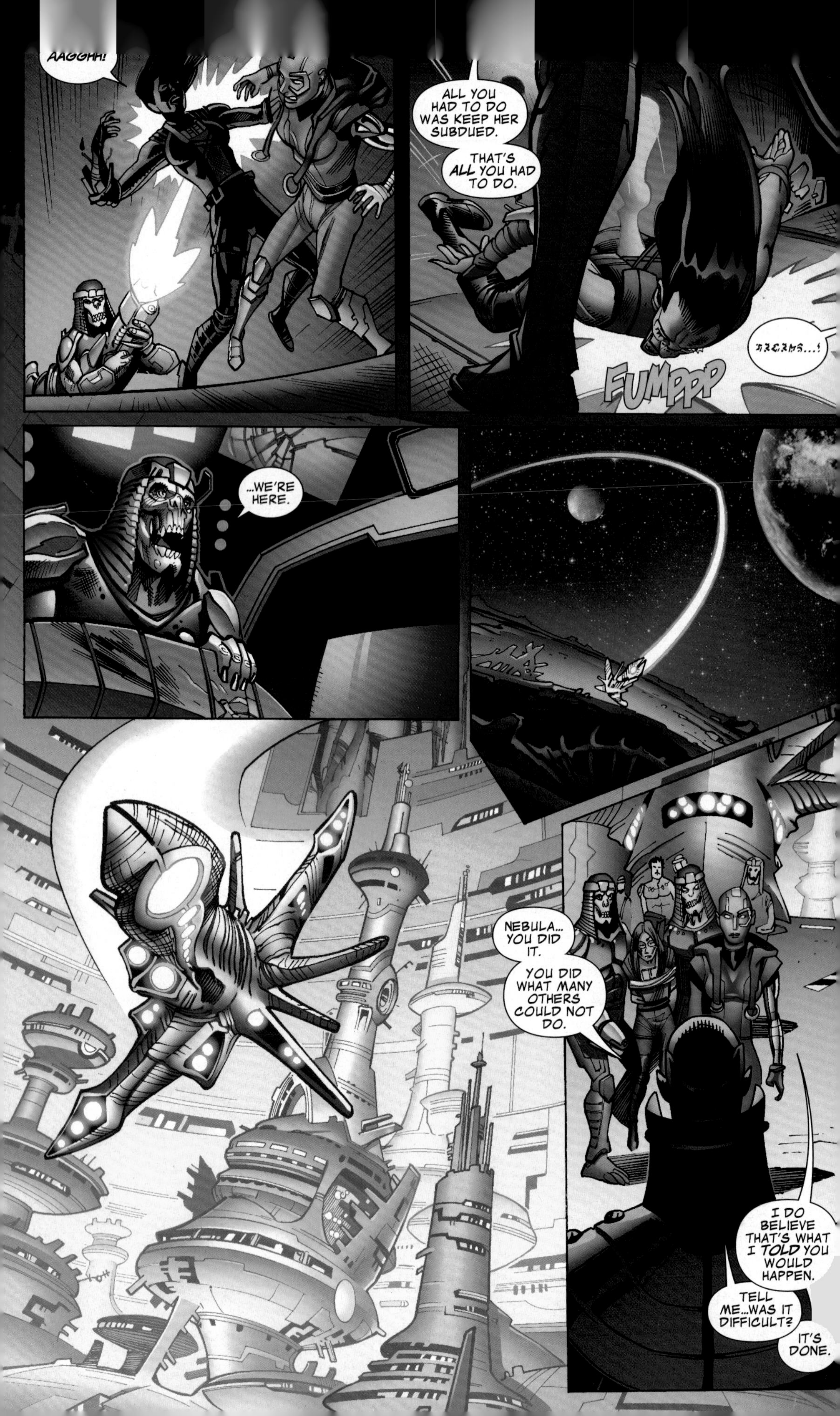
AAGGHH!
ALL YOU HAD TO DO WAS KEEP HER SUBDUED.
THAT'S ALL YOU HAD TO DO.
FUMPPP
...WE'RE HERE.
NEBULA... YOU DID IT.
YOU DID WHAT MANY OTHERS COULD NOT DO.
I DO BELIEVE THAT'S WHAT I TOLD YOU WOULD HAPPEN.
TELL ME...WAS IT DIFFICULT?
IT'S DONE.

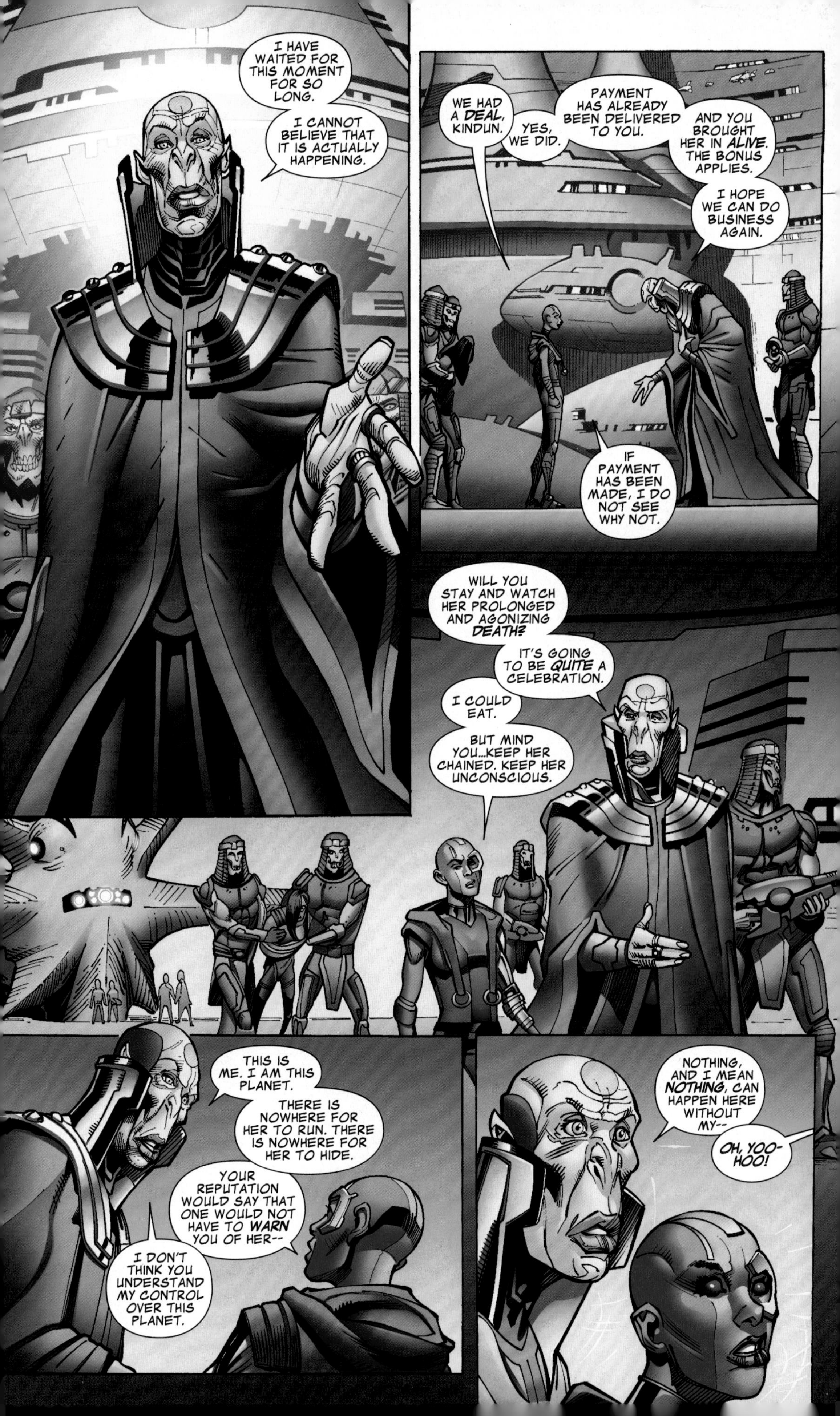

I HAVE WAITED FOR THIS MOMENT FOR SO LONG.
I CANNOT BELIEVE THAT IT IS ACTUALLY HAPPENING.
WE HAD A DEAL, KINDUN.
YES, WE DID.
PAYMENT HAS ALREADY BEEN DELIVERED TO YOU.
AND YOU BROUGHT HER IN ALIVE. THE BONUS APPLIES.
I HOPE WE CAN DO BUSINESS AGAIN.
IF PAYMENT HAS BEEN MADE, I DO NOT SEE WHY NOT.
WILL YOU STAY AND WATCH HER PROLONGED AND AGONIZING DEATH?
IT'S GOING TO BE QUITE A CELEBRATION.
I COULD EAT.
BUT MIND YOU...KEEP HER CHAINED. KEEP HER UNCONSCIOUS.
THIS IS ME. I AM THIS PLANET.
THERE IS NOWHERE FOR HER TO RUN. THERE IS NOWHERE FOR HER TO HIDE.
YOUR REPUTATION WOULD SAY THAT ONE WOULD NOT HAVE TO WARN YOU OF HER--
I DON'T THINK YOU UNDERSTAND MY CONTROL OVER THIS PLANET.
NOTHING, AND I MEAN NOTHING, CAN HAPPEN HERE WITHOUT MY--
OH, YOO-HOO!

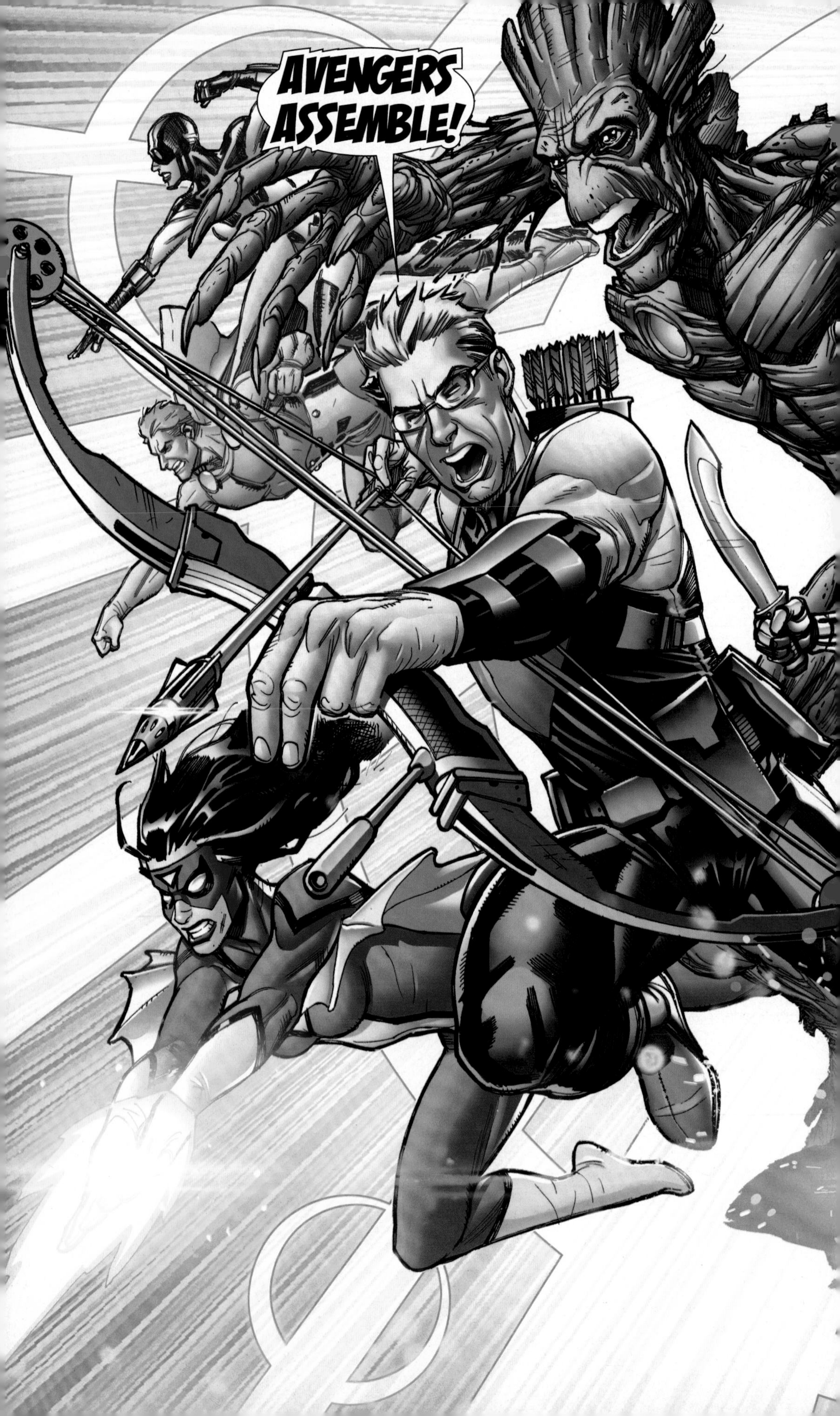
AVENGERS ASSEMBLE!

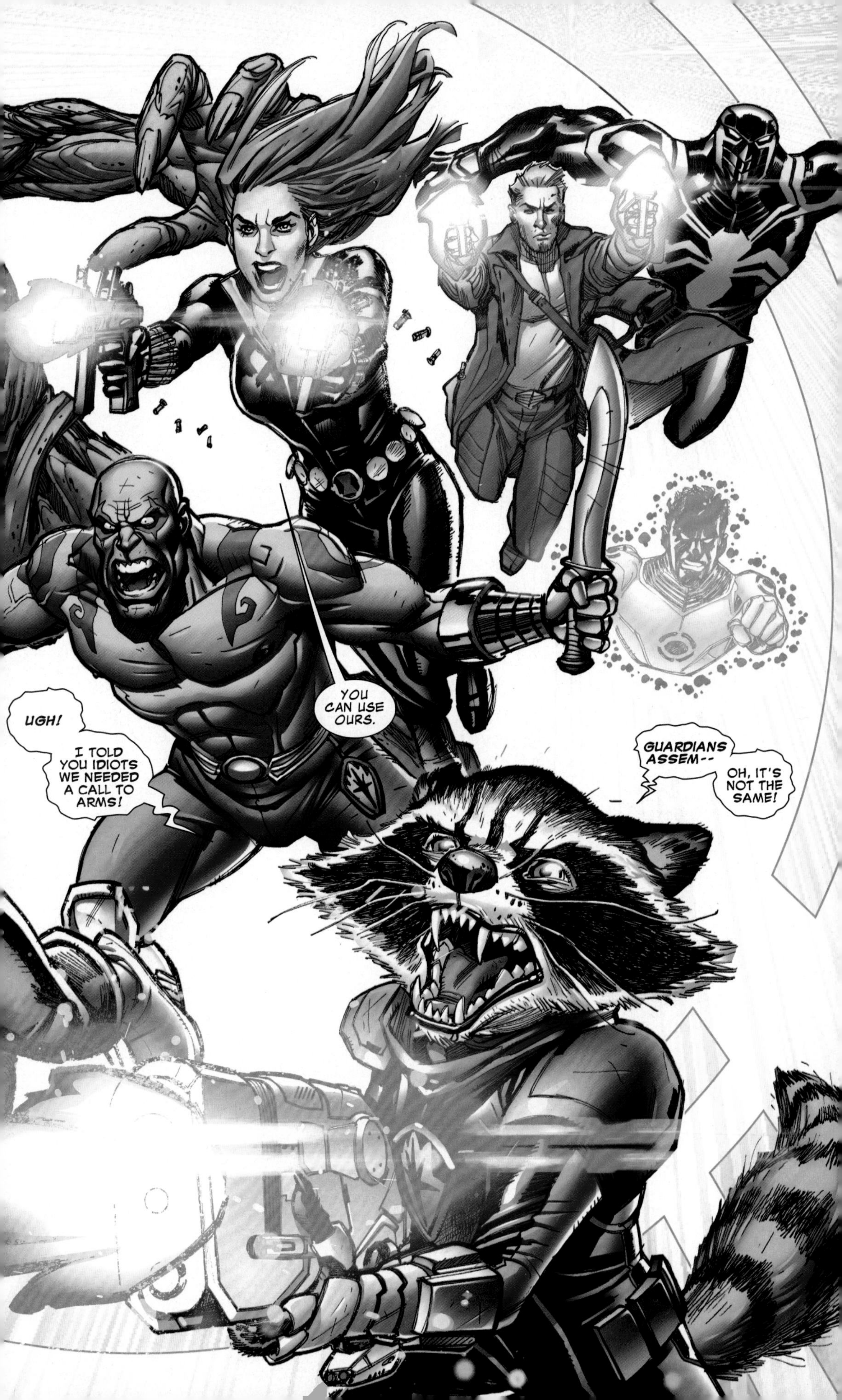
UGH!
I TOLD YOU IDIOTS WE NEEDED A CALL TO ARMS!
YOU CAN USE OURS.
GUARDIANS ASSEM--
OH, IT'S NOT THE SAME!

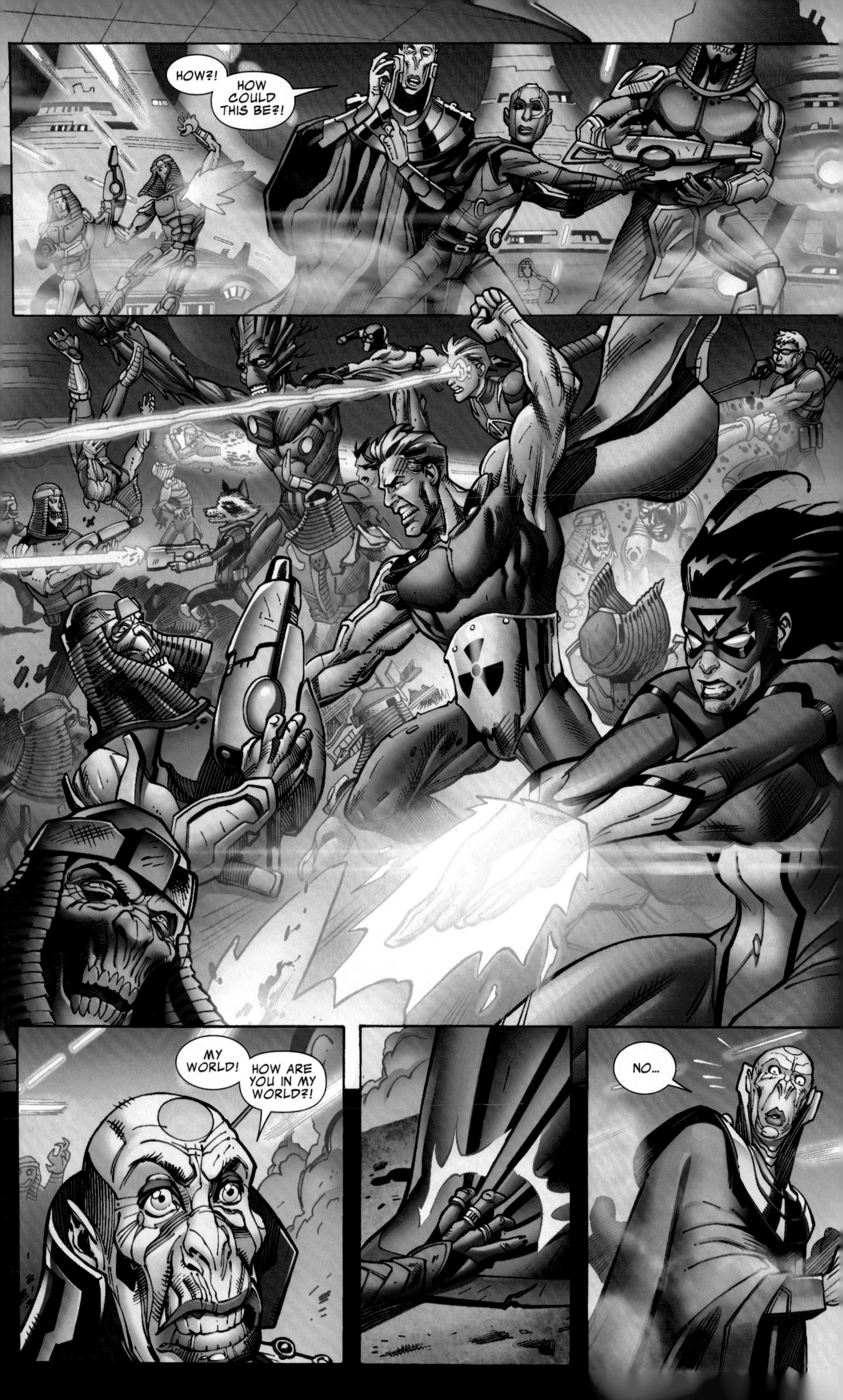
HOW?!
HOW COULD THIS BE?!
MY WORLD!
HOW ARE YOU IN MY WORLD?!
NO...

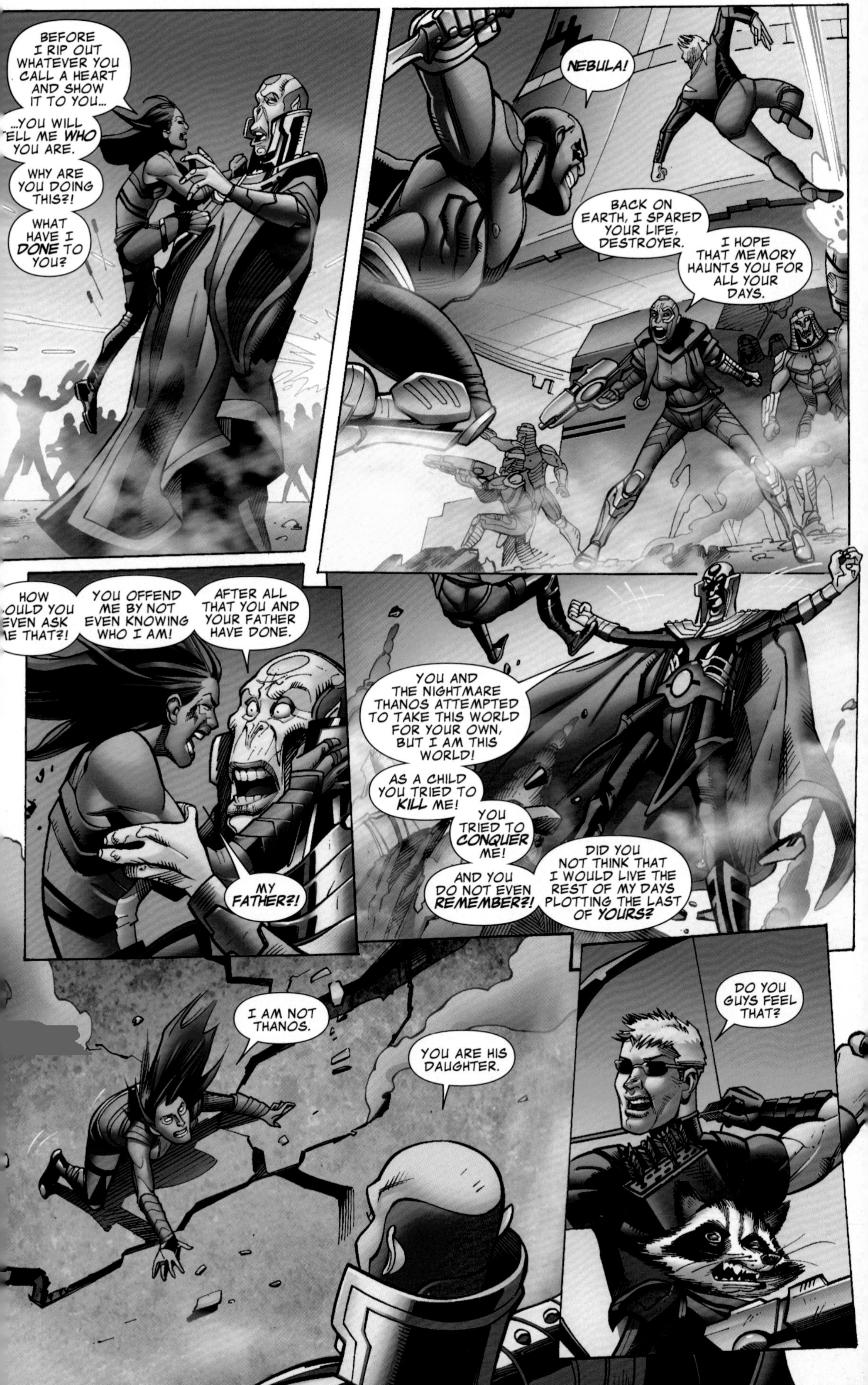
BEFORE I RIP OUT WHATEVER YOU CALL A HEART AND SHOW IT TO YOU...
...YOU WILL ELL ME WHO YOU ARE.
WHY ARE YOU DOING THIS?!
WHAT HAVE I DONE TO YOU?
NEBULA!
BACK ON EARTH, I SPARED YOUR LIFE, DESTROYER.
I HOPE THAT MEMORY HAUNTS YOU FOR ALL YOUR DAYS.
HOW OULD YOU EVEN ASK E THAT?!
YOU OFFEND ME BY NOT EVEN KNOWING WHO I AM!
AFTER ALL THAT YOU AND YOUR FATHER HAVE DONE.
MY FATHER?!
YOU AND THE NIGHTMARE THANOS ATTEMPTED TO TAKE THIS WORLD FOR YOUR OWN, BUT I AM THIS WORLD!
AS A CHILD YOU TRIED TO KILL ME!
YOU TRIED TO CONQUER ME!
AND YOU DO NOT EVEN REMEMBER?!
DID YOU NOT THINK THAT I WOULD LIVE THE REST OF MY DAYS PLOTTING THE LAST OF YOURS?
I AM NOT THANOS.
YOU ARE HIS DAUGHTER.
DO YOU GUYS FEEL THAT?

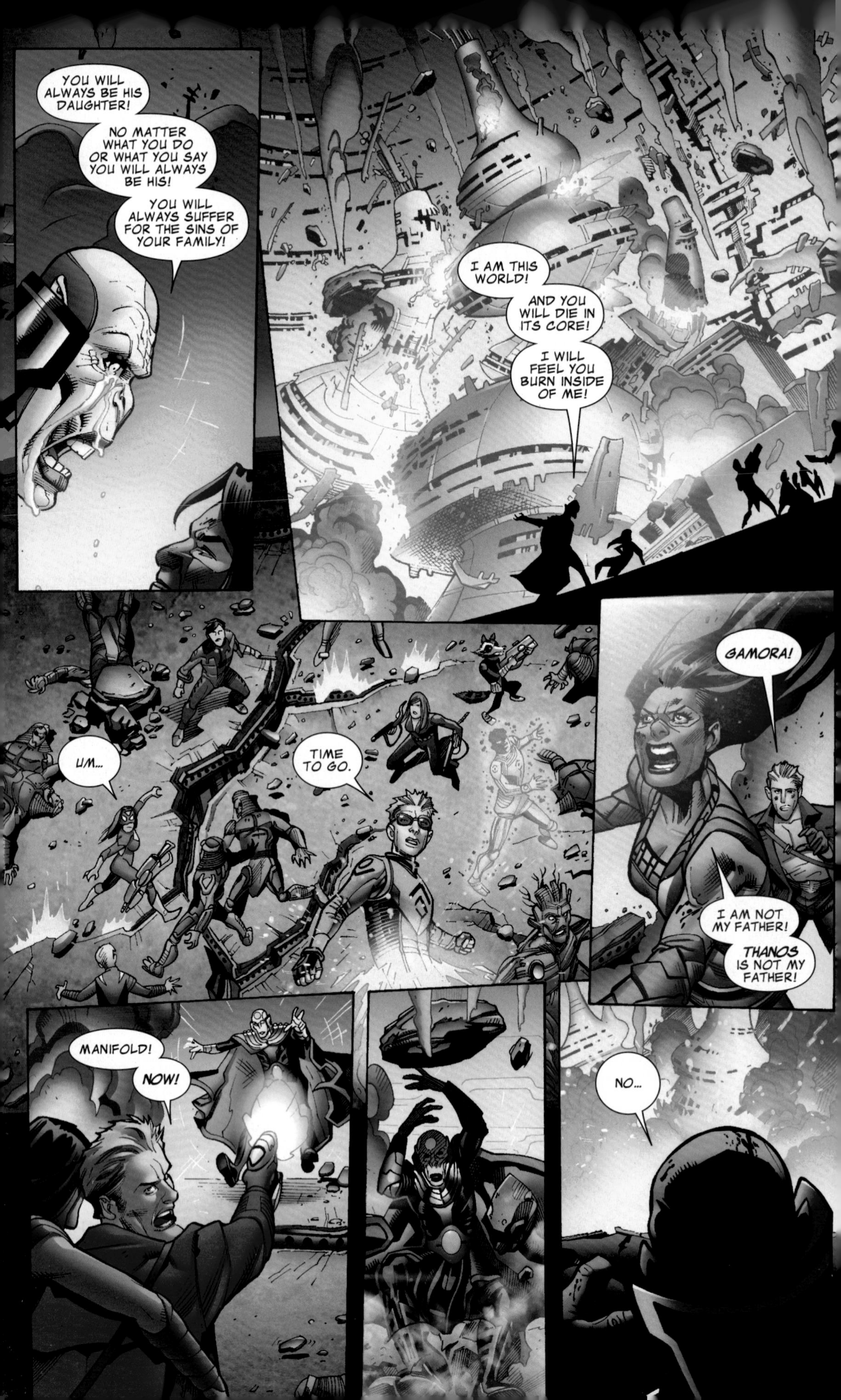
YOU WILL ALWAYS BE HIS DAUGHTER!
NO MATTER WHAT YOU DO OR WHAT YOU SAY YOU WILL ALWAYS BE HIS!
YOU WILL ALWAYS SUFFER FOR THE SINS OF YOUR FAMILY!
I AM THIS WORLD!
AND YOU WILL DIE IN ITS CORE!
I WILL FEEL YOU BURN INSIDE OF ME!
UM...
TIME TO GO.
GAMORA!
I AM NOT MY FATHER!
THANOS IS NOT MY FATHER!
MANIFOLD!
NOW!
NO...

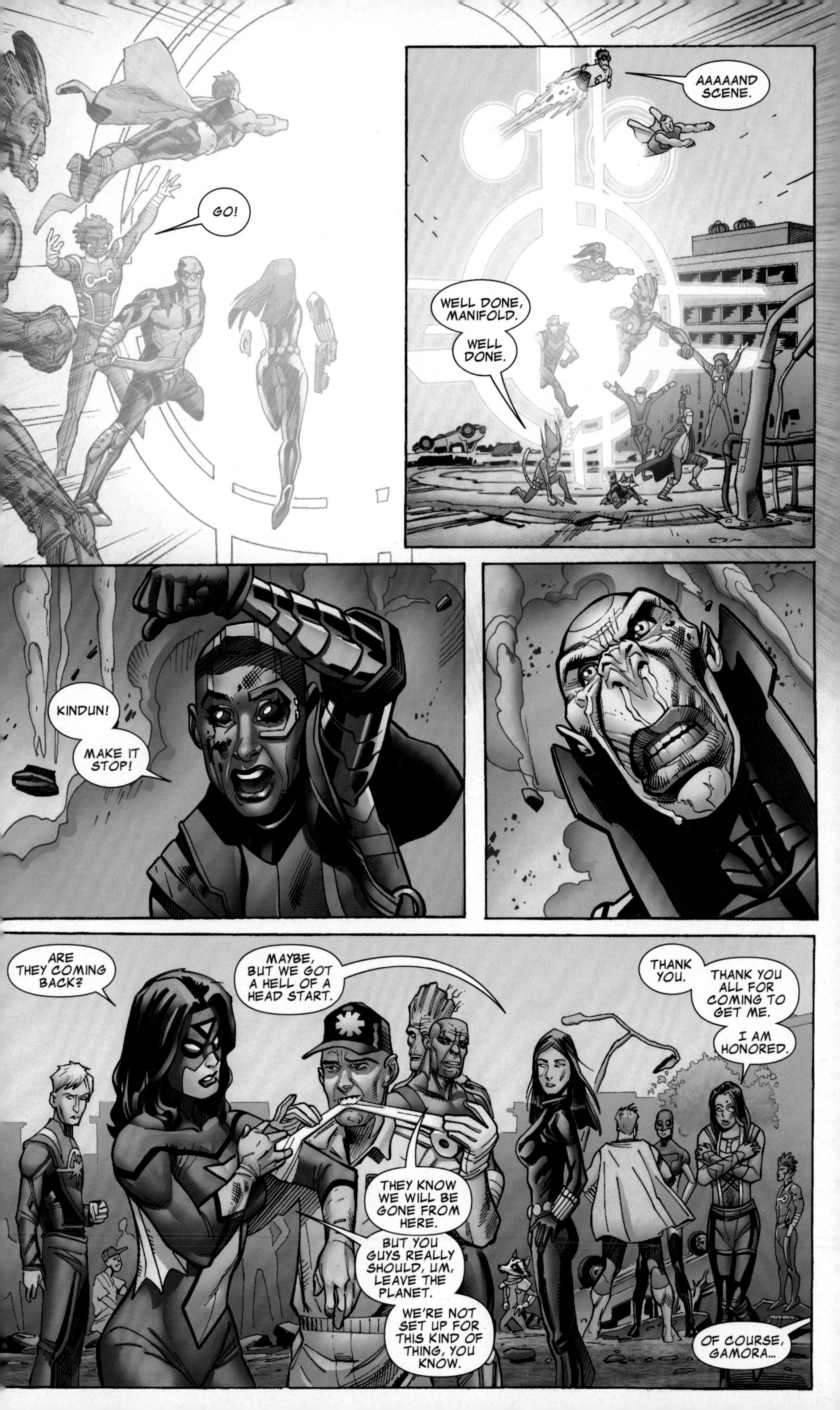
GO!
AAAAAND SCENE.
WELL DONE, MANIFOLD.
WELL DONE.
KINDUN!
MAKE IT STOP!
ARE THEY COMING BACK?
MAYBE, BUT WE GOT A HELL OF A HEAD START.
THEY KNOW WE WILL BE GONE FROM HERE.
BUT YOU GUYS REALLY SHOULD, UM, LEAVE THE PLANET.
WE'RE NOT SET UP FOR THIS KIND OF THING, YOU KNOW.
THANK YOU.
THANK YOU ALL FOR COMING TO GET ME.
I AM HONORED.
OF COURSE, GAMORA...

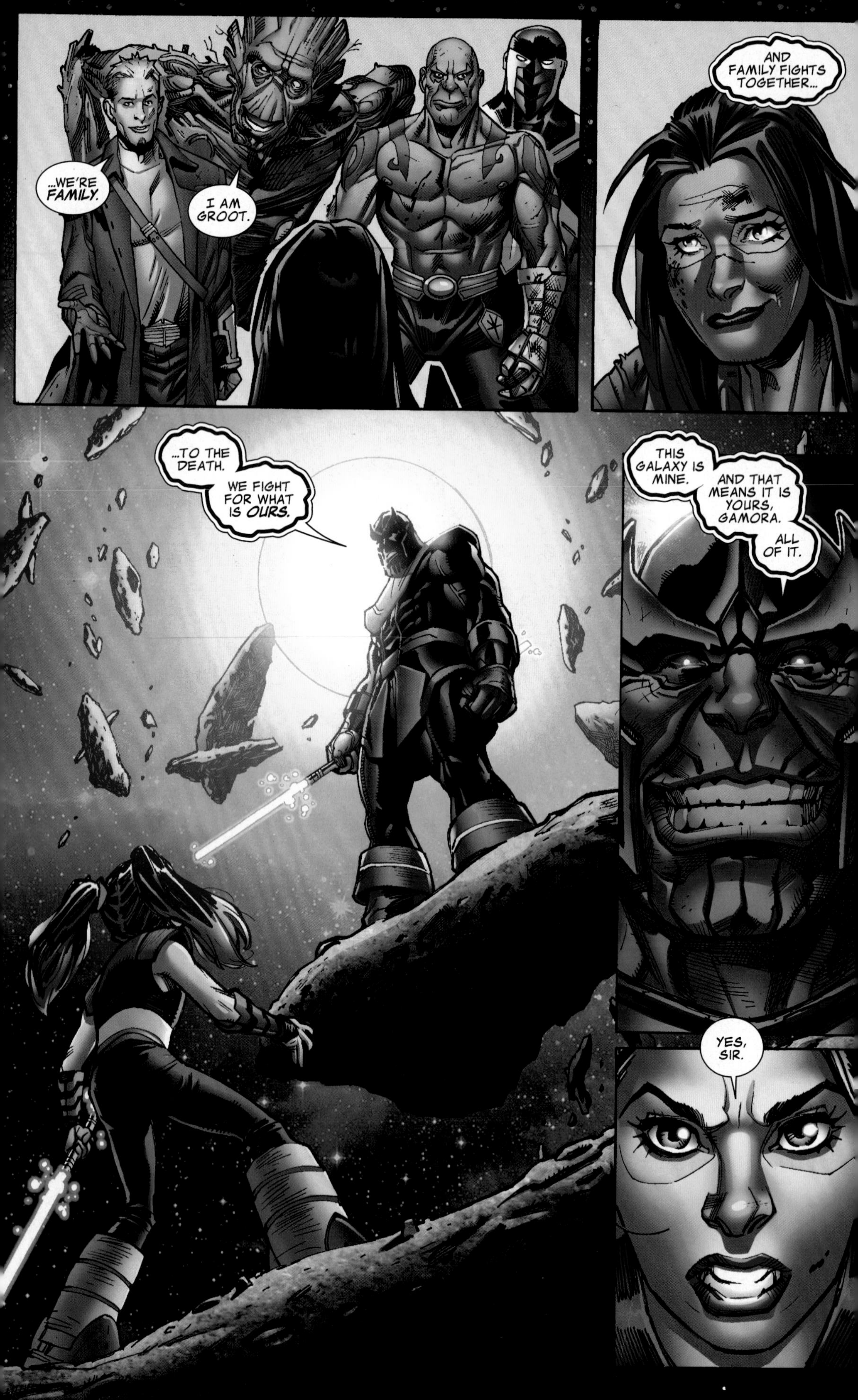
...WE'RE FAMILY.
I AM GROOT.
AND FAMILY FIGHTS TOGETHER...
...TO THE DEATH.
WE FIGHT FOR WHAT IS OURS.
THIS GALAXY IS MINE.
AND THAT MEANS IT IS YOURS, GAMORA.
ALL OF IT.
YES, SIR.

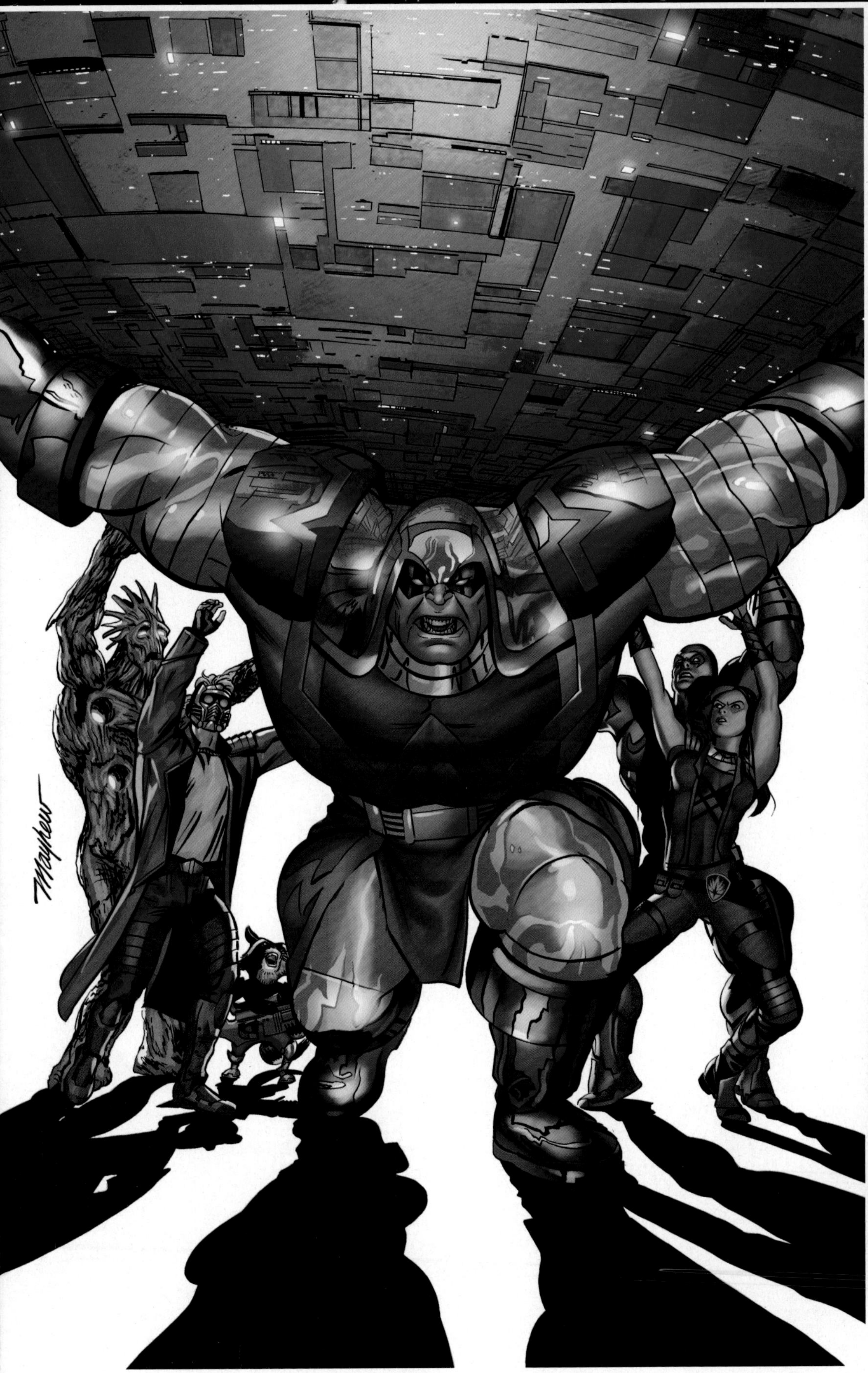
Mayhew

GUARDIANS OF THE GALAXY & X-MEN

THE BLACK VORTEX

CHAPTER 6

Previously in *The Black Vortex*...

Billions of years ago, an ancient race named the Viscardi were gifted an object of immense cosmic power by a Celestial. This artifact, known as the Black Vortex, transformed the user, imbuing them with cosmic energy. However, the power of this object caused the Viscardi to turn on each other, annihilating their own race from within.

When the sadistic Mister Knife, also known as J'Son, Peter Quill's father, managed to obtain the Black Vortex, Peter and Kitty Pryde stole the artifact and recruited the Guardians of the Galaxy and the X-Men to help battle Mister Knife. Gamora, the elder Beast, and Angel chose to submit to the Vortex and the three cosmically enhanced heroes took the artifact and sped off with a new mission—to reshape the universe in their image. However, they were ambushed by Ronan the Accuser, who stole the Black Vortex from them. In retaliation for this, Gamora, Beast, and Angel began to lay waste to the Kree homeworld, Hala, while Ronan, Star-Lord, Storm and Jean Grey can do nothing but watch...

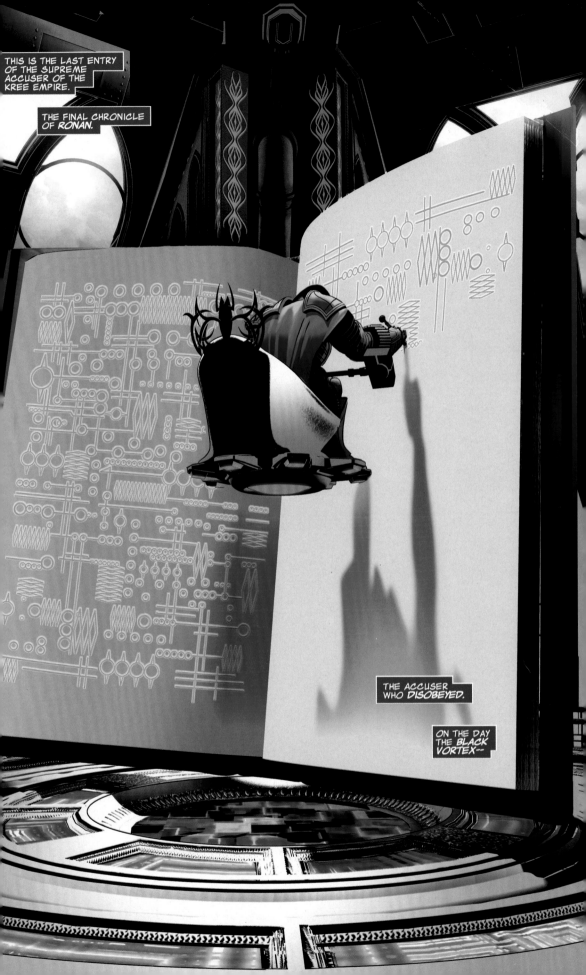

THIS IS THE LAST ENTRY OF THE SUPREME ACCUSER OF THE KREE EMPIRE.

THE FINAL CHRONICLE OF RONAN.

THE ACCUSER WHO *DISOBEYED*.

ON THE DAY THE *BLACK VORTEX*--

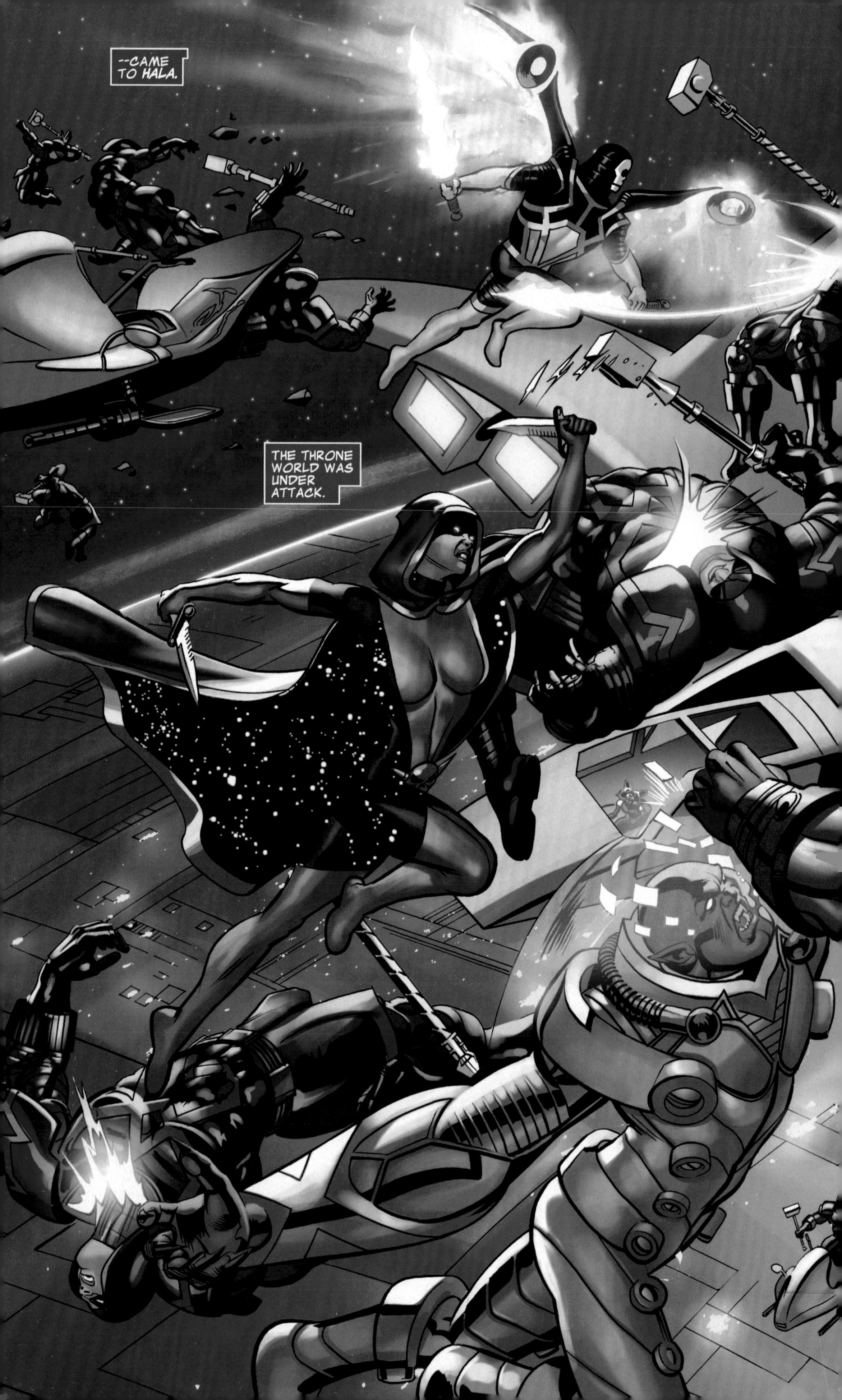
--CAME TO HALA.
THE THRONE WORLD WAS UNDER ATTACK.

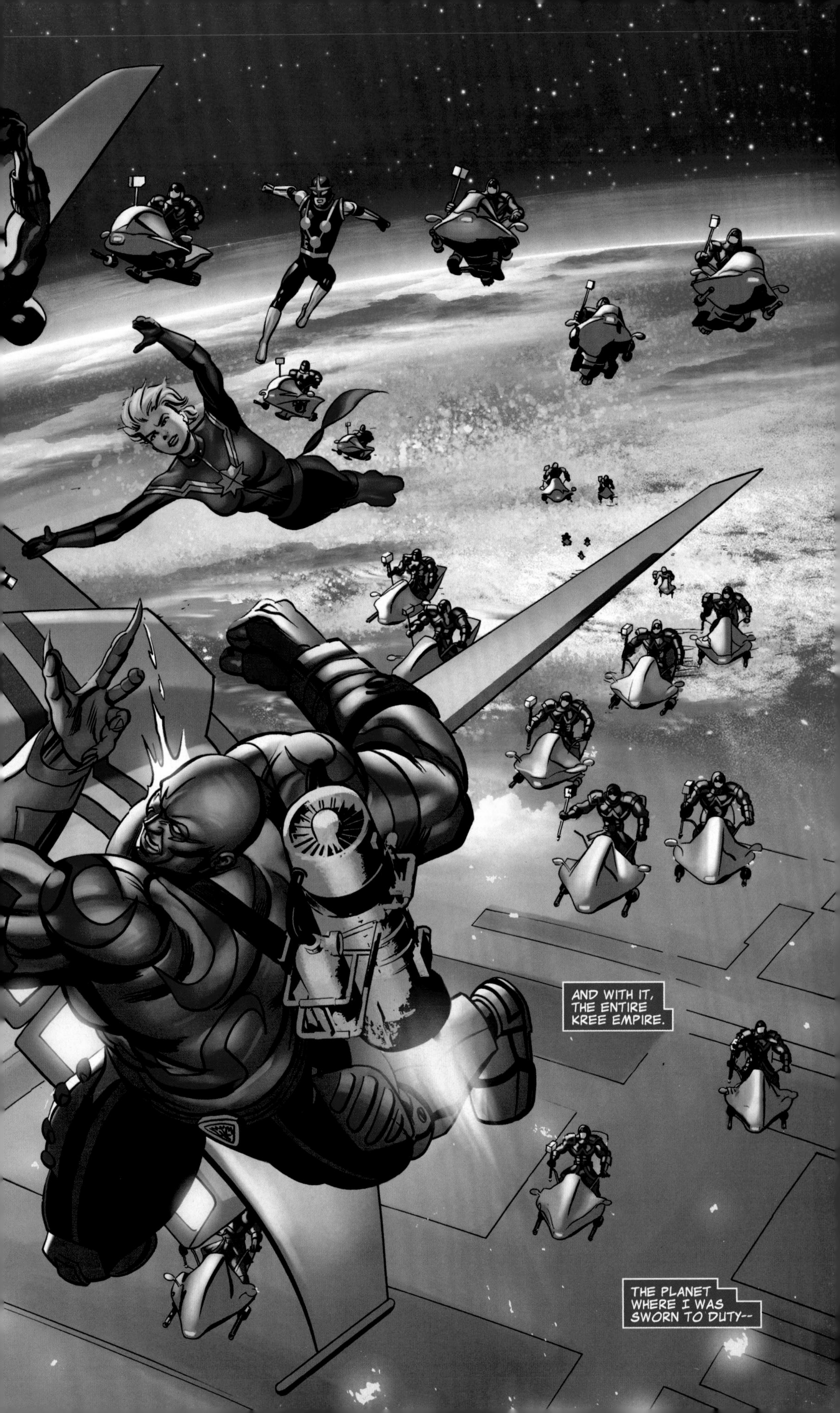
AND WITH IT, THE ENTIRE KREE EMPIRE.
THE PLANET WHERE I WAS SWORN TO DUTY--

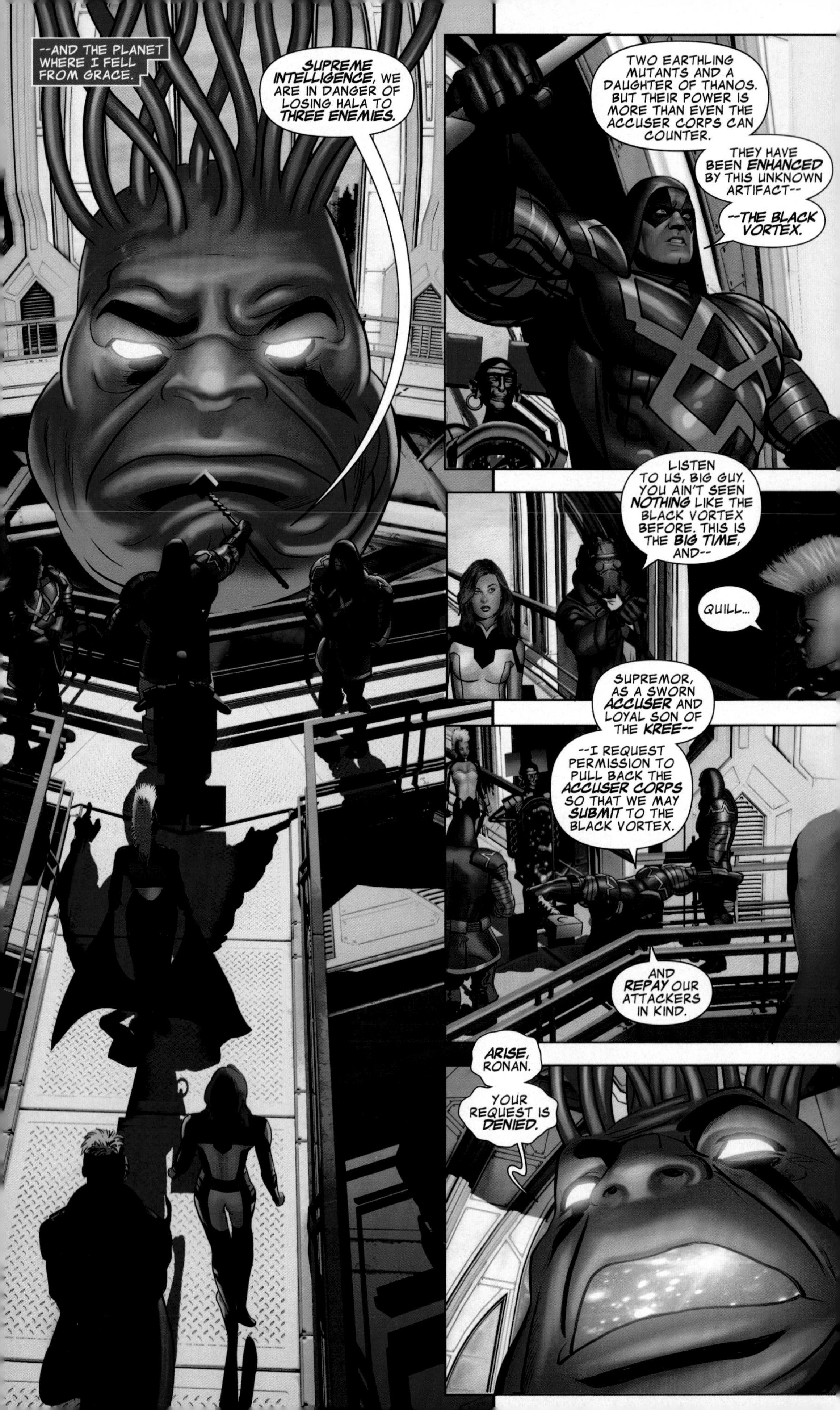
--AND THE PLANET WHERE I FELL FROM GRACE.
SUPREME INTELLIGENCE, WE ARE IN DANGER OF LOSING HALA TO THREE ENEMIES.
TWO EARTHLING MUTANTS AND A DAUGHTER OF THANOS. BUT THEIR POWER IS MORE THAN EVEN THE ACCUSER CORPS CAN COUNTER.
THEY HAVE BEEN ENHANCED BY THIS UNKNOWN ARTIFACT--
--THE BLACK VORTEX.
LISTEN TO US, BIG GUY. YOU AIN'T SEEN NOTHING LIKE THE BLACK VORTEX BEFORE. THIS IS THE BIG TIME, AND--
QUILL...
SUPREMOR, AS A SWORN ACCUSER AND LOYAL SON OF THE KREE--
--I REQUEST PERMISSION TO PULL BACK THE ACCUSER CORPS SO THAT WE MAY SUBMIT TO THE BLACK VORTEX.
AND REPAY OUR ATTACKERS IN KIND.
ARISE, RONAN.
YOUR REQUEST IS DENIED.

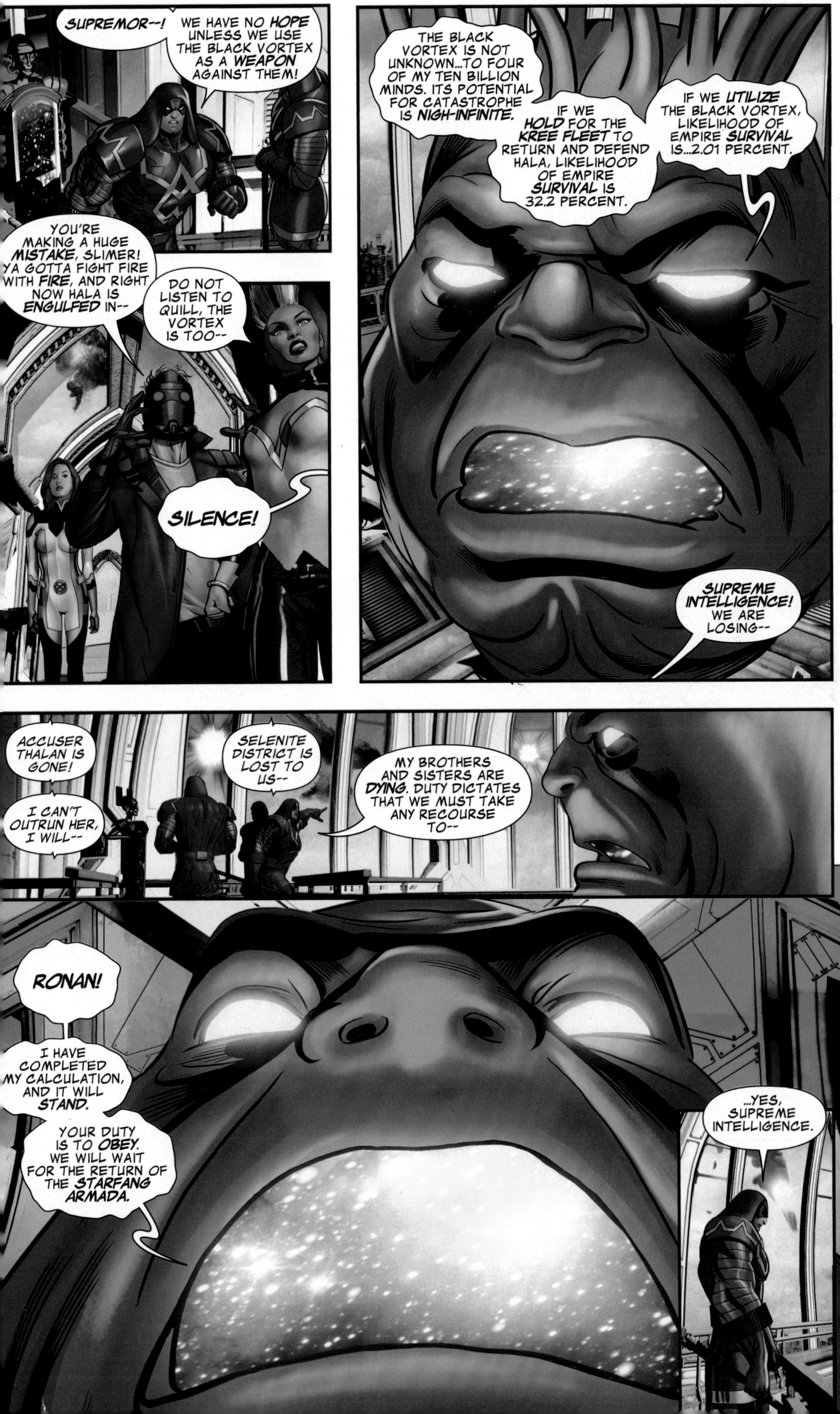
SUPREMOR--!
WE HAVE NO HOPE UNLESS WE USE THE BLACK VORTEX AS A WEAPON AGAINST THEM!
YOU'RE MAKING A HUGE MISTAKE, SLIMER! YA GOTTA FIGHT FIRE WITH FIRE, AND RIGHT NOW HALA IS ENGULFED IN--
DO NOT LISTEN TO QUILL, THE VORTEX IS TOO--
SILENCE!
THE BLACK VORTEX IS NOT UNKNOWN...TO FOUR OF MY TEN BILLION MINDS. ITS POTENTIAL FOR CATASTROPHE IS NIGH-INFINITE.
IF WE HOLD FOR THE KREE FLEET TO RETURN AND DEFEND HALA, LIKELIHOOD OF EMPIRE SURVIVAL IS 32.2 PERCENT.
IF WE UTILIZE THE BLACK VORTEX, LIKELIHOOD OF EMPIRE SURVIVAL IS...2.01 PERCENT.
SUPREME INTELLIGENCE! WE ARE LOSING--
ACCUSER THALAN IS GONE!
I CAN'T OUTRUN HER, I WILL--
SELENITE DISTRICT IS LOST TO US--
MY BROTHERS AND SISTERS ARE DYING. DUTY DICTATES THAT WE MUST TAKE ANY RECOURSE TO--
RONAN!
I HAVE COMPLETED MY CALCULATION, AND IT WILL STAND.
YOUR DUTY IS TO OBEY. WE WILL WAIT FOR THE RETURN OF THE STARFANG ARMADA.
...YES, SUPREME INTELLIGENCE.

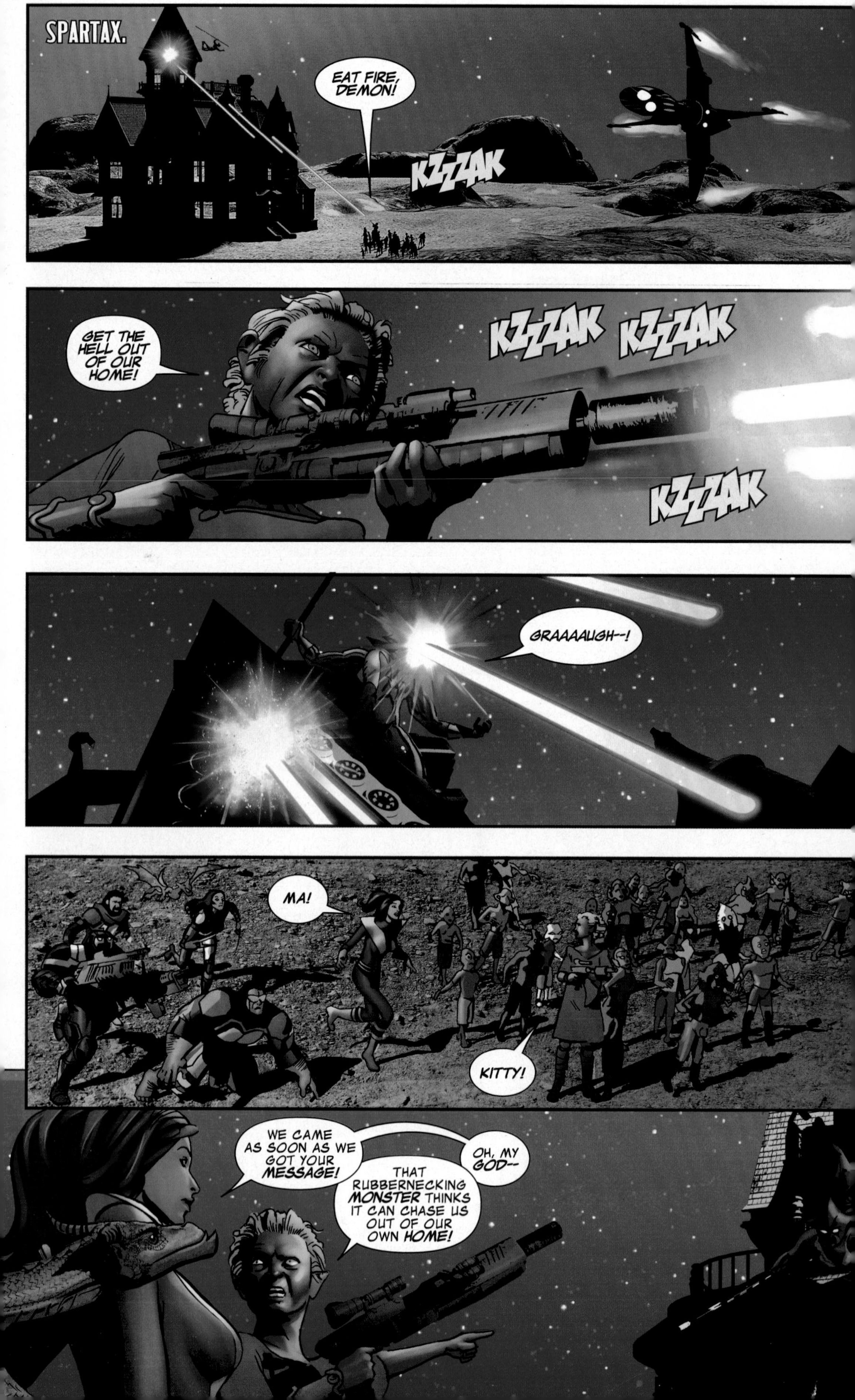
SPARTAX.
EAT FIRE, DEMON!
KZZZAK
GET THE HELL OUT OF OUR HOME!
KZZZAK KZZZAK
KZZZAK
GRAAAAUGH--!
MA!
KITTY!
WE CAME AS SOON AS WE GOT YOUR MESSAGE!
OH, MY GOD--
THAT RUBBERNECKING MONSTER THINKS IT CAN CHASE US OUT OF OUR OWN HOME!

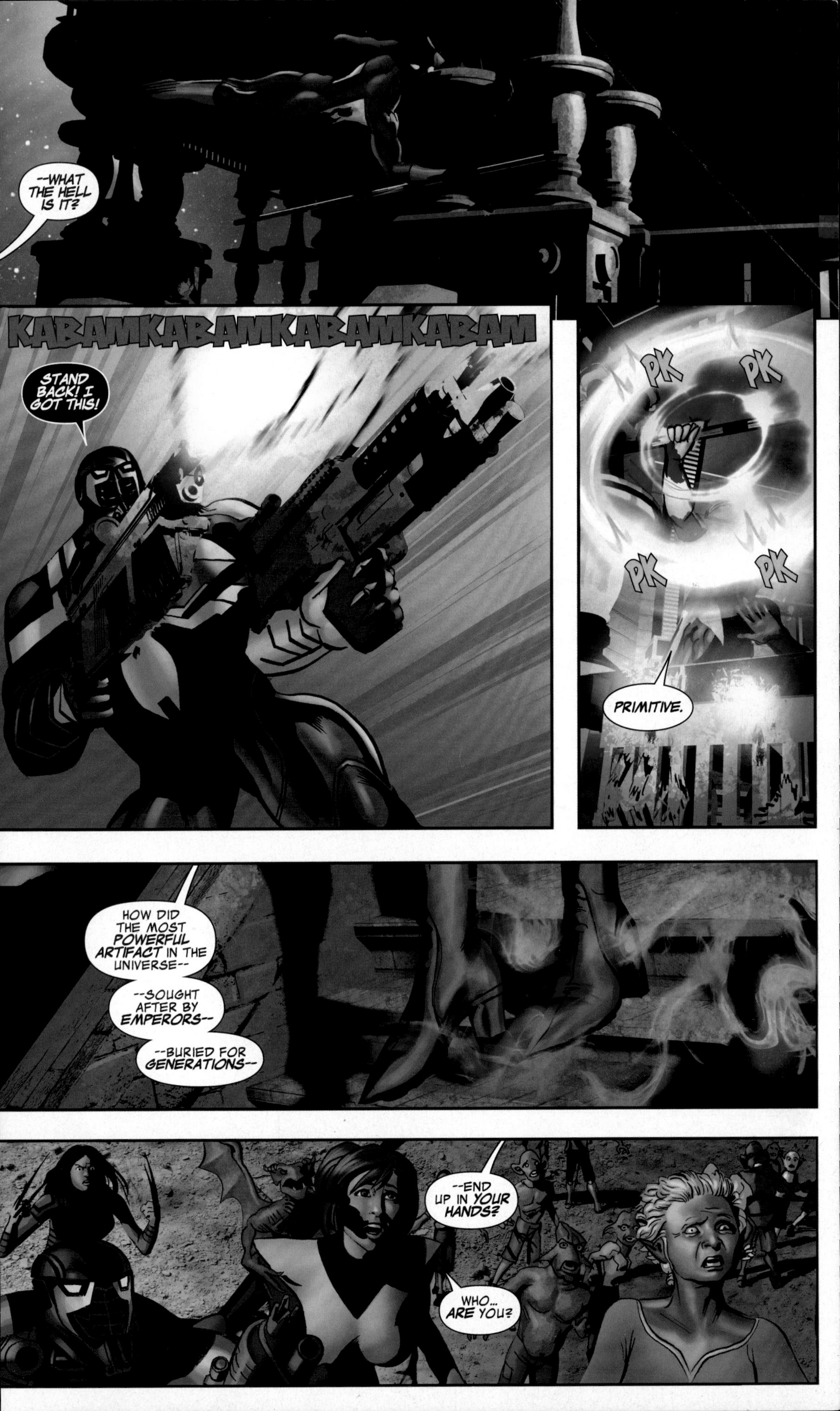
--WHAT THE HELL IS IT?
KABAMKABAMKABAMKABAM
STAND BACK! I GOT THIS!
PK
PK
PK
PK
PRIMITIVE.
HOW DID THE MOST POWERFUL ARTIFACT IN THE UNIVERSE--
--SOUGHT AFTER BY EMPERORS--
--BURIED FOR GENERATIONS--
--END UP IN YOUR HANDS?
WHO... ARE YOU?

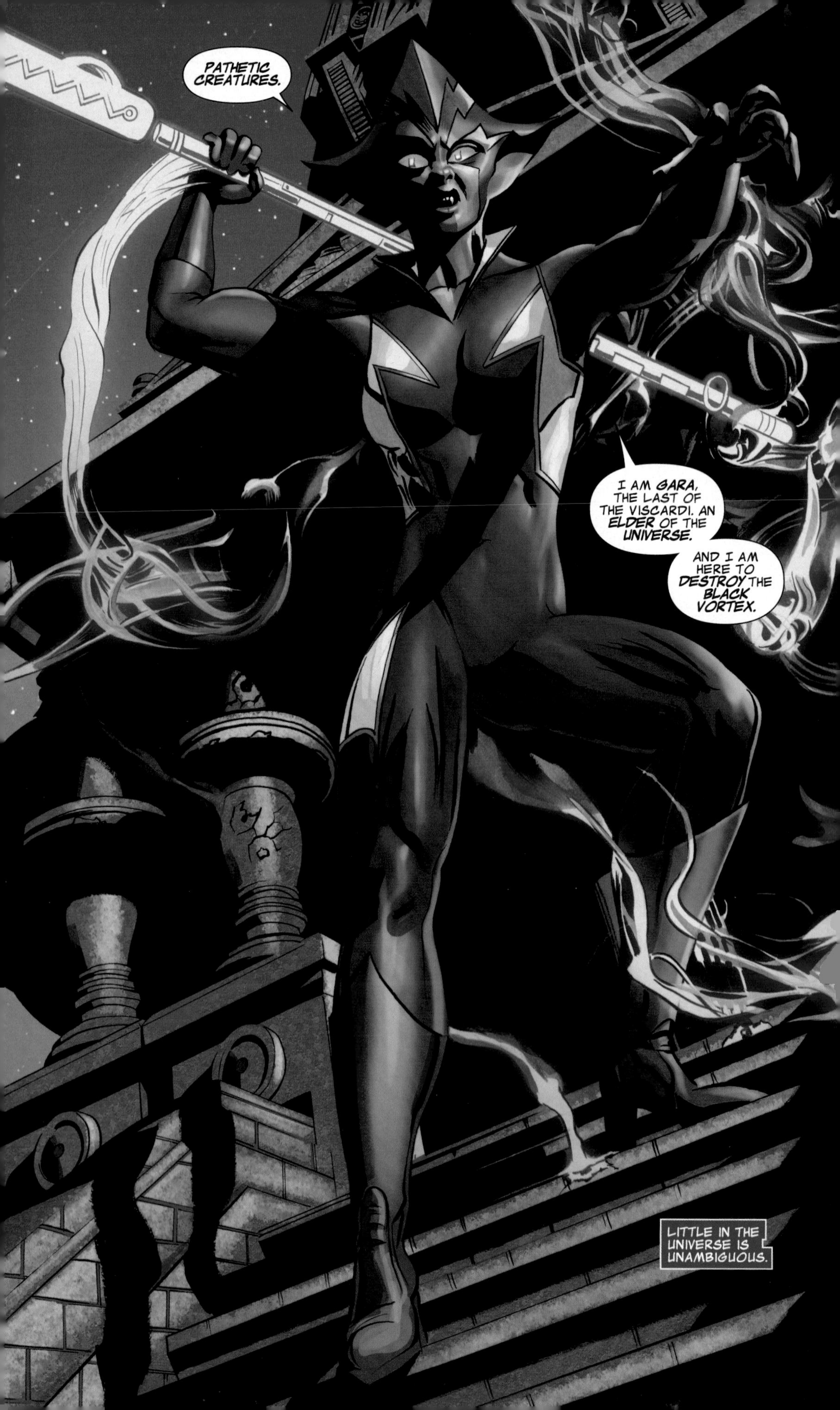
PATHETIC CREATURES.
I AM GARA, THE LAST OF THE VISCARDI. AN ELDER OF THE UNIVERSE.
AND I AM HERE TO DESTROY THE BLACK VORTEX.
LITTLE IN THE UNIVERSE IS UNAMBIGUOUS.

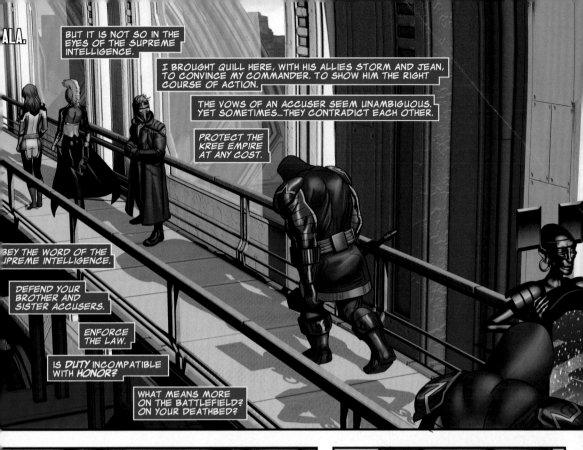

ALA.

BUT IT IS NOT SO IN THE EYES OF THE SUPREME INTELLIGENCE.

I BROUGHT QUILL HERE, WITH HIS ALLIES STORM AND JEAN, TO CONVINCE MY COMMANDER. TO SHOW HIM THE RIGHT COURSE OF ACTION.

THE VOWS OF AN ACCUSER SEEM UNAMBIGUOUS. YET SOMETIMES...THEY CONTRADICT EACH OTHER.

PROTECT THE KREE EMPIRE AT ANY COST.

BEY THE WORD OF THE UPREME INTELLIGENCE.

DEFEND YOUR BROTHER AND SISTER ACCUSERS.

ENFORCE THE LAW.

IS DUTY INCOMPATIBLE WITH HONOR?

WHAT MEANS MORE ON THE BATTLEFIELD? ON YOUR DEATHBED?

HEY, BIG GUY.

I NEED TO KNOW. IF YOU HAD THE CHANCE...

...WOULD YOU REALLY DO IT? SUBMIT?

RIGHT.

WELL, LUCKY FOR YOU, I DON'T MIND EMBARRASSING MYSELF FOR A GOOD CAUSE.

JUST BE READY TO MAKE YOUR MOVE, OKAY?

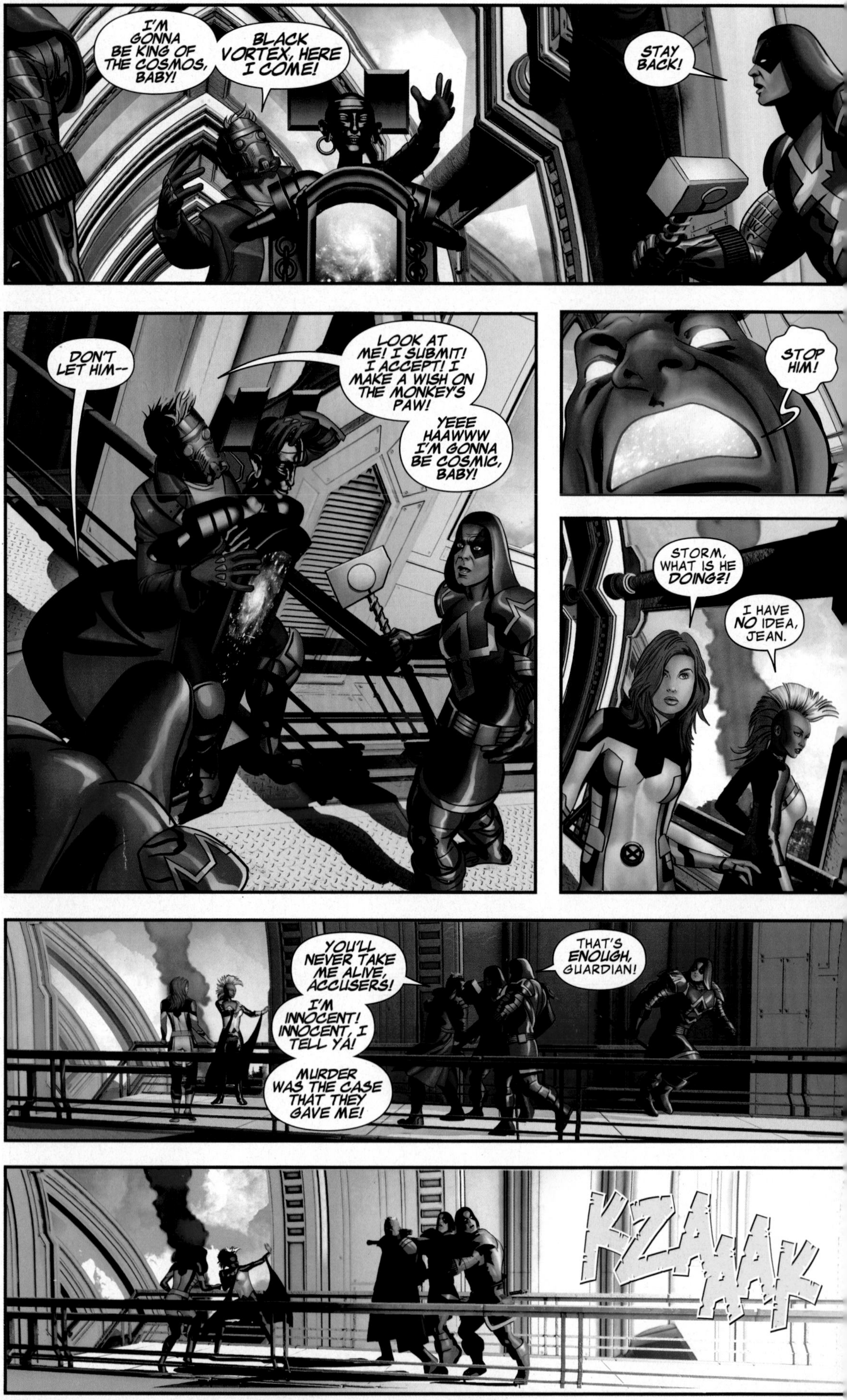
I'M GONNA BE KING OF THE COSMOS, BABY!
BLACK VORTEX, HERE I COME!
STAY BACK!
DON'T LET HIM--
LOOK AT ME! I SUBMIT! I ACCEPT! I MAKE A WISH ON THE MONKEY'S PAW!
YEEE HAAWWW I'M GONNA BE COSMIC, BABY!
STOP HIM!
STORM, WHAT IS HE DOING?!
I HAVE NO IDEA, JEAN.
YOU'LL NEVER TAKE ME ALIVE, ACCUSERS!
I'M INNOCENT! INNOCENT, I TELL YA!
MURDER WAS THE CASE THAT THEY GAVE ME!
THAT'S ENOUGH, GUARDIAN!
KZAAAK

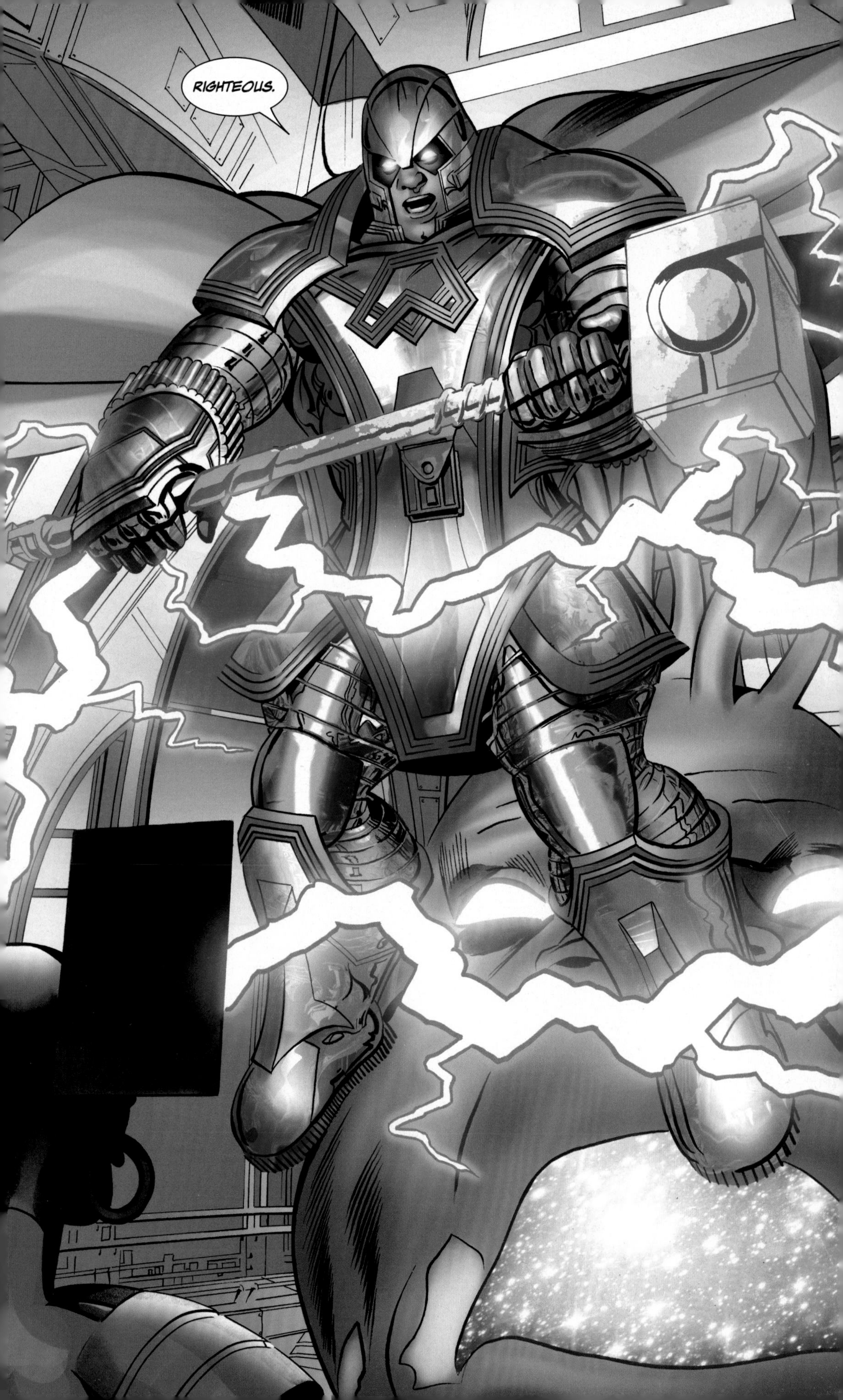
RIGHTEOUS.

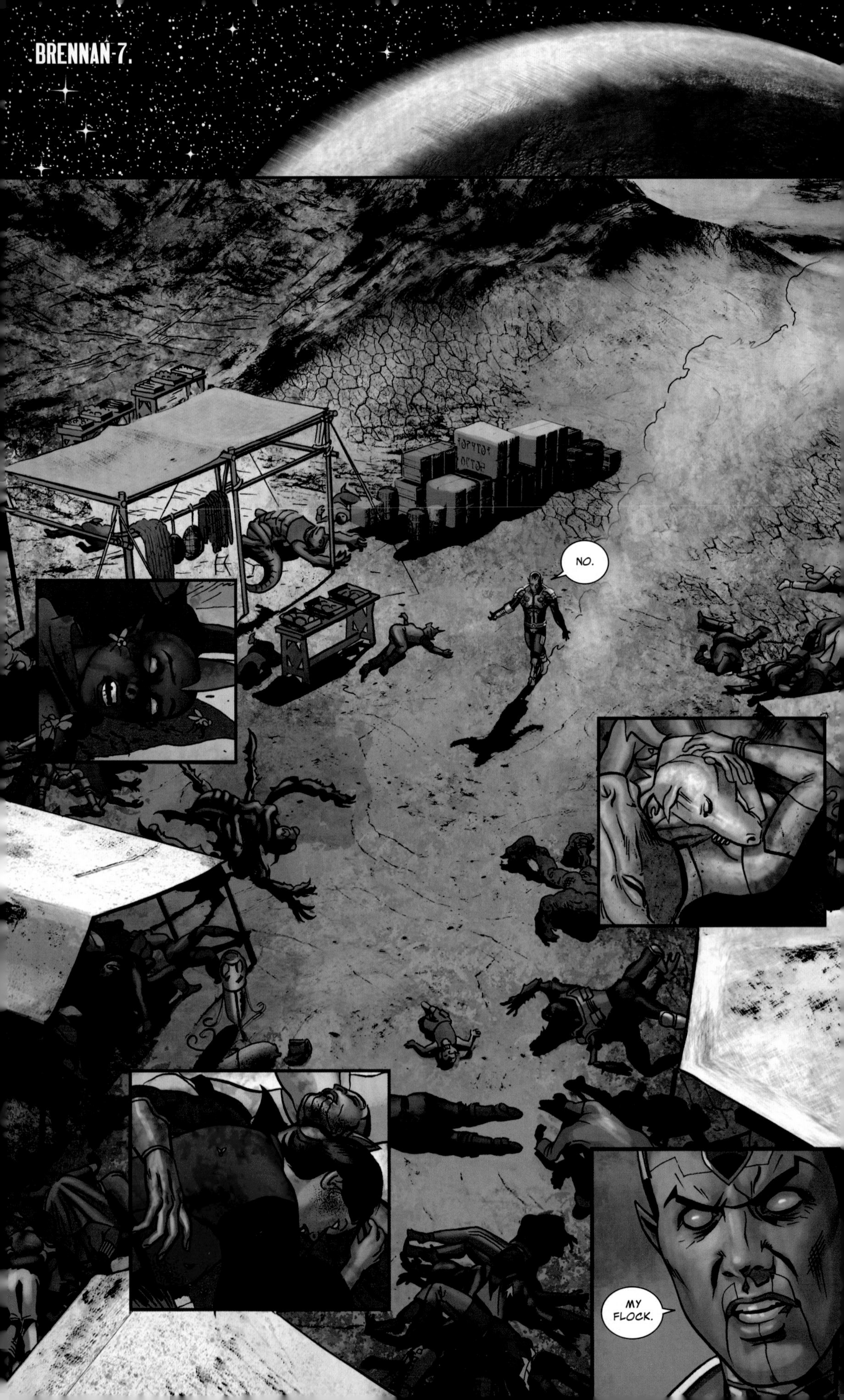
BRENNAN-7.
NO.
MY FLOCK.

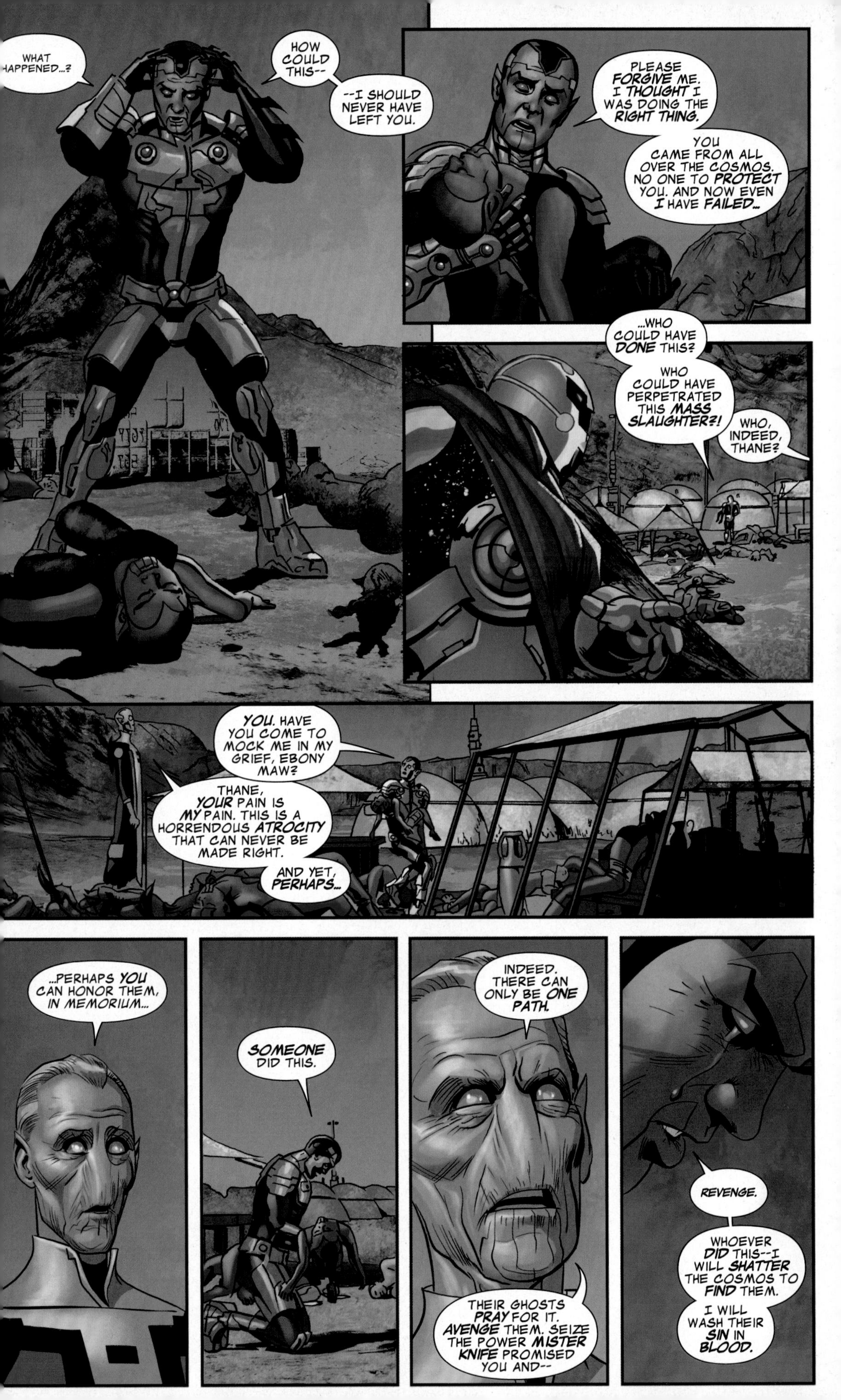
WHAT HAPPENED...?
HOW COULD THIS--
--I SHOULD NEVER HAVE LEFT YOU.
PLEASE FORGIVE ME. I THOUGHT I WAS DOING THE RIGHT THING.
YOU CAME FROM ALL OVER THE COSMOS. NO ONE TO PROTECT YOU. AND NOW EVEN I HAVE FAILED...
...WHO COULD HAVE DONE THIS?
WHO COULD HAVE PERPETRATED THIS MASS SLAUGHTER?!
WHO, INDEED, THANE?
YOU. HAVE YOU COME TO MOCK ME IN MY GRIEF, EBONY MAW?
THANE, YOUR PAIN IS MY PAIN. THIS IS A HORRENDOUS ATROCITY THAT CAN NEVER BE MADE RIGHT.
AND YET, PERHAPS...
...PERHAPS YOU CAN HONOR THEM, IN MEMORIUM...
SOMEONE DID THIS.
INDEED. THERE CAN ONLY BE ONE PATH.
THEIR GHOSTS PRAY FOR IT. AVENGE THEM. SEIZE THE POWER MISTER KNIFE PROMISED YOU AND--
REVENGE.
WHOEVER DID THIS--I WILL SHATTER THE COSMOS TO FIND THEM.
I WILL WASH THEIR SIN IN BLOOD.

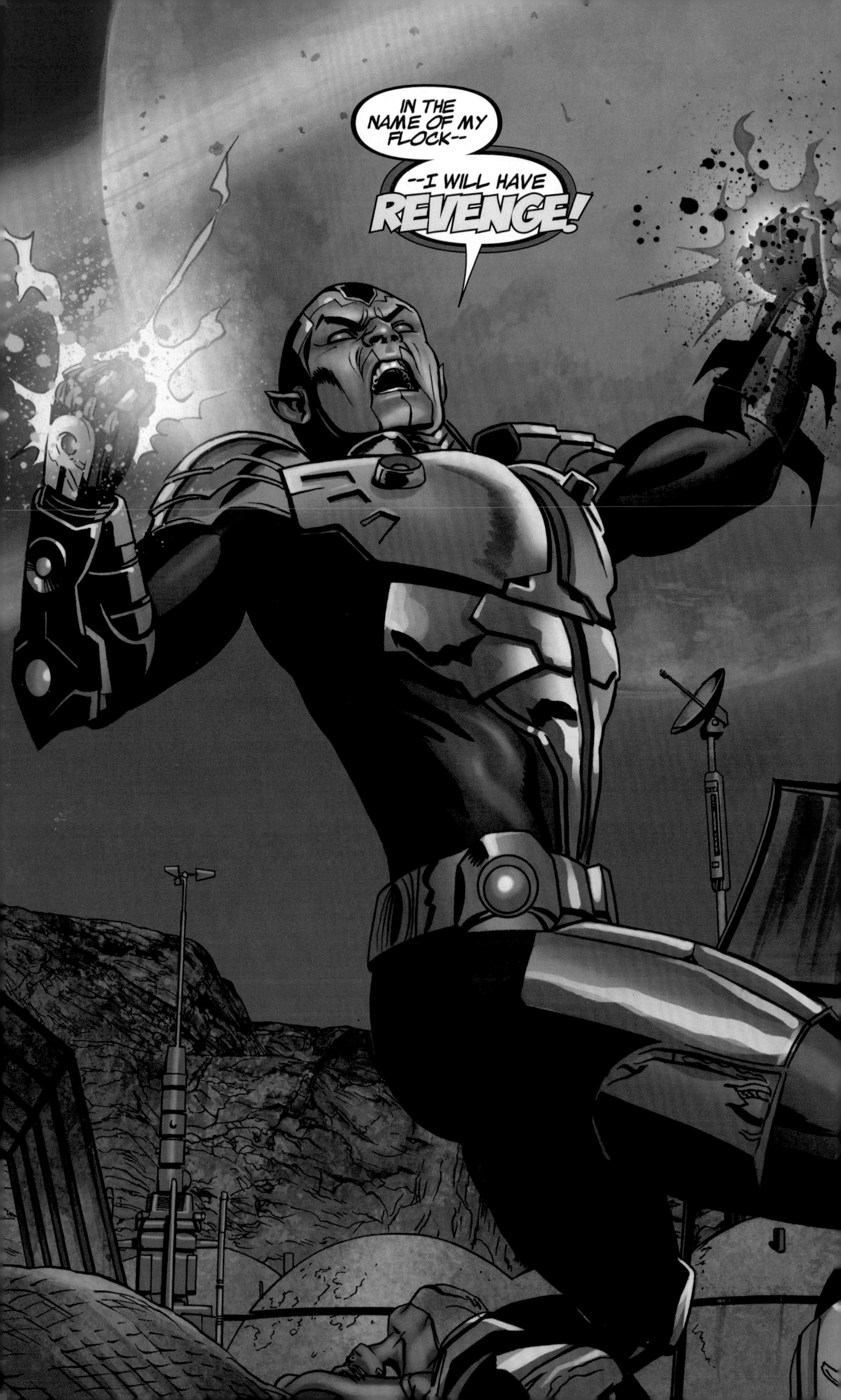
IN THE NAME OF MY FLOCK--
--I WILL HAVE REVENGE!

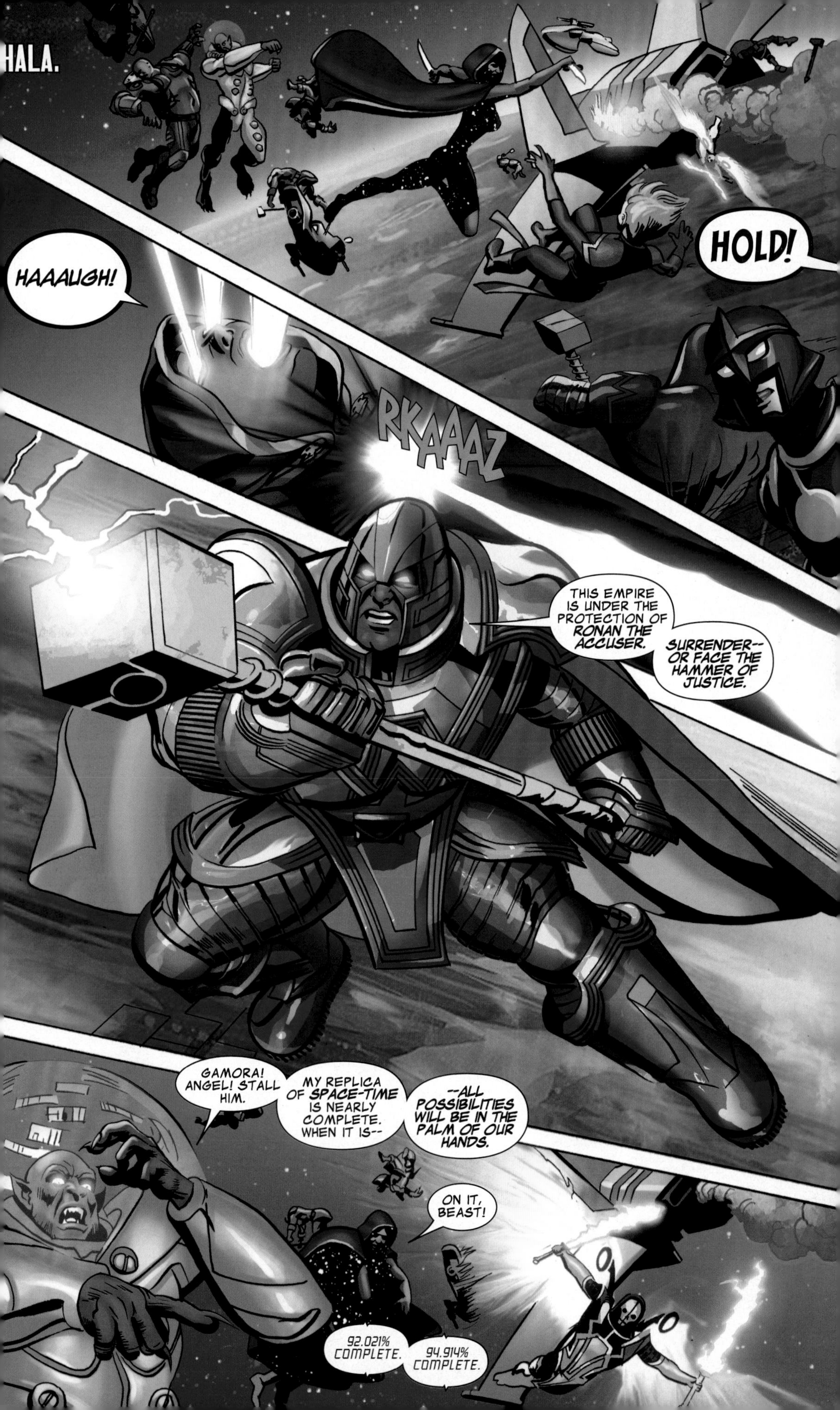
HALA.
HAAAUGH!
HOLD!
RKAAAZ
THIS EMPIRE IS UNDER THE PROTECTION OF RONAN THE ACCUSER.
SURRENDER-- OR FACE THE HAMMER OF JUSTICE.
GAMORA! ANGEL! STALL HIM.
MY REPLICA OF SPACE-TIME IS NEARLY COMPLETE. WHEN IT IS--
--ALL POSSIBILITIES WILL BE IN THE PALM OF OUR HANDS.
ON IT, BEAST!
92.021% COMPLETE.
94.914% COMPLETE.

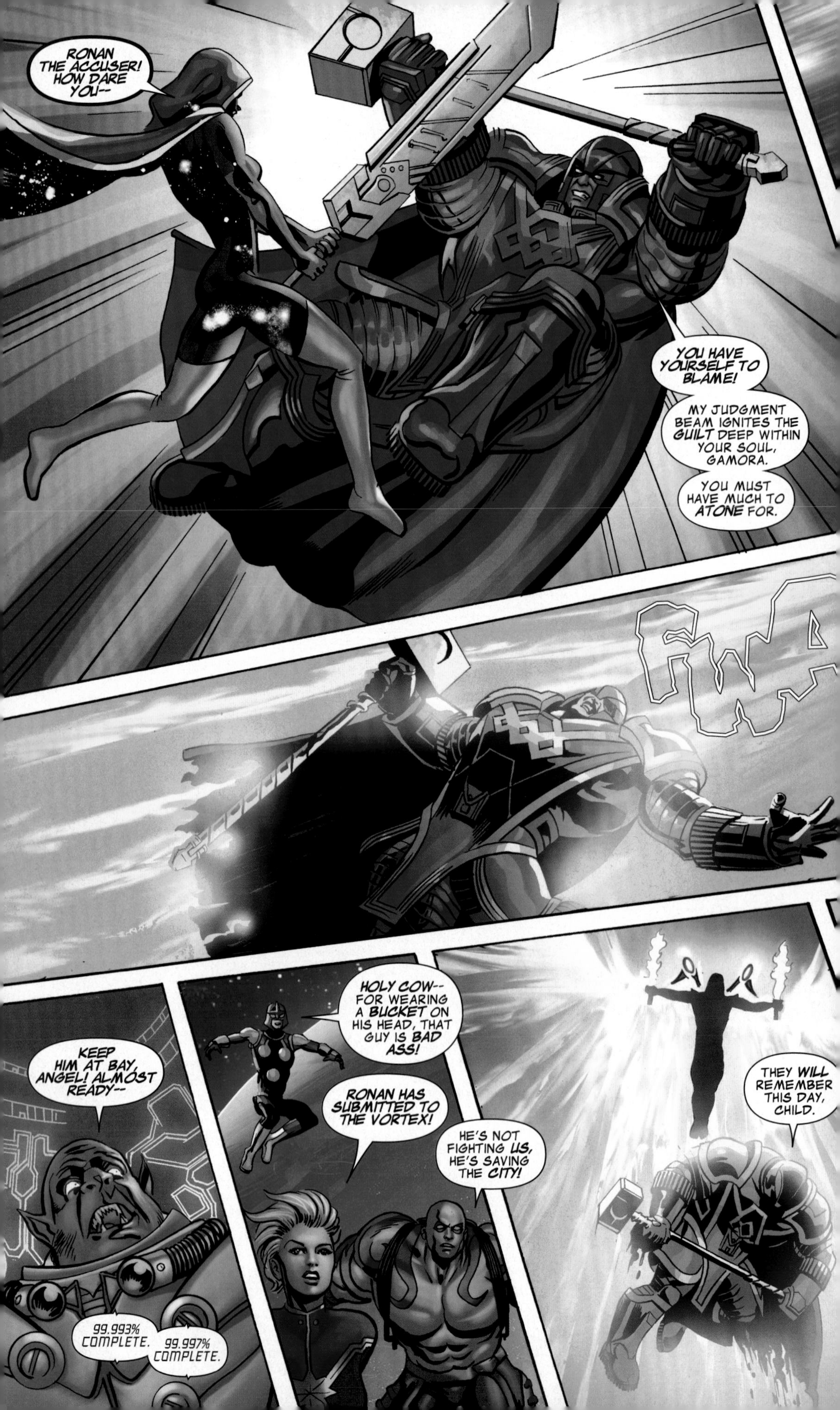
RONAN THE ACCUSER! HOW DARE YOU--
YOU HAVE YOURSELF TO BLAME!
MY JUDGMENT BEAM IGNITES THE GUILT DEEP WITHIN YOUR SOUL, GAMORA.
YOU MUST HAVE MUCH TO ATONE FOR.
FWA
KEEP HIM AT BAY, ANGEL! ALMOST READY--
99.993% COMPLETE.
99.997% COMPLETE.
HOLY COW--FOR WEARING A BUCKET ON HIS HEAD, THAT GUY IS BAD ASS!
RONAN HAS SUBMITTED TO THE VORTEX!
HE'S NOT FIGHTING US, HE'S SAVING THE CITY!
THEY WILL REMEMBER THIS DAY, CHILD.

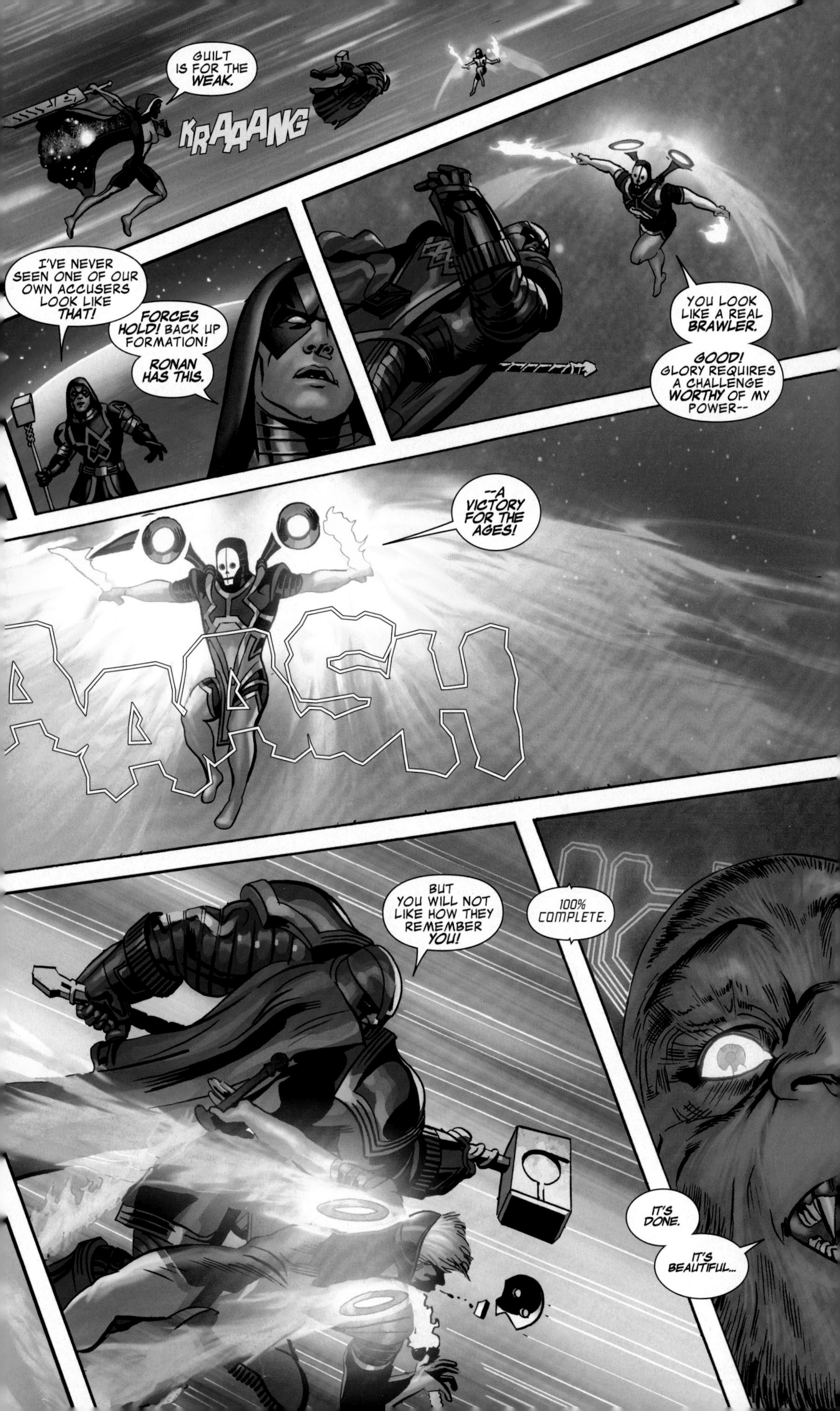

GUILT IS FOR THE WEAK.
KRAAANG
I'VE NEVER SEEN ONE OF OUR OWN ACCUSERS LOOK LIKE THAT!
FORCES HOLD! BACK UP FORMATION!
RONAN HAS THIS.
YOU LOOK LIKE A REAL BRAWLER.
GOOD! GLORY REQUIRES A CHALLENGE WORTHY OF MY POWER--
--A VICTORY FOR THE AGES!
BUT YOU WILL NOT LIKE HOW THEY REMEMBER YOU!
100% COMPLETE.
IT'S DONE.
IT'S BEAUTIFUL...

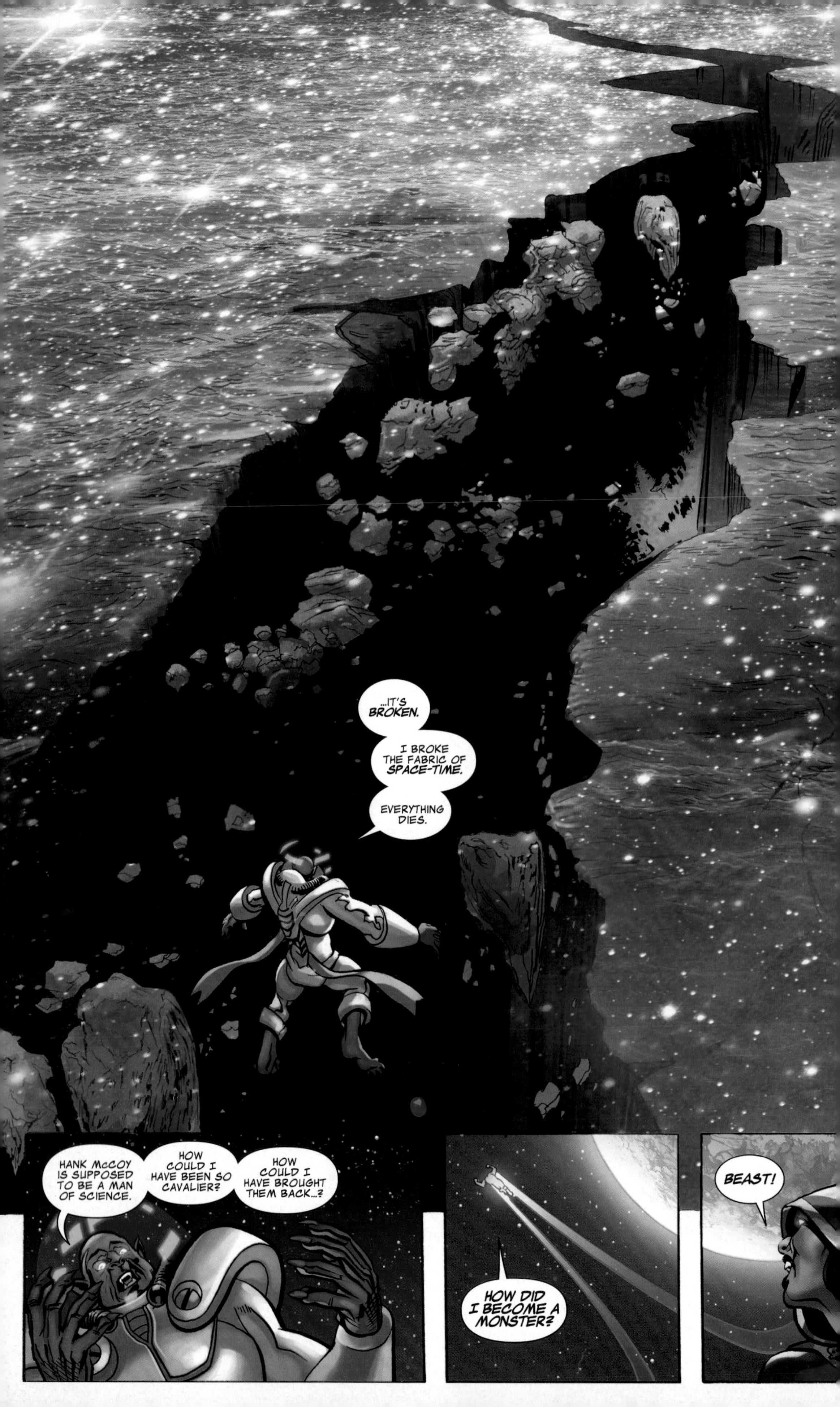

...IT'S BROKEN.
I BROKE THE FABRIC OF SPACE-TIME.
EVERYTHING DIES.
HANK McCOY IS SUPPOSED TO BE A MAN OF SCIENCE.
HOW COULD I HAVE BEEN SO CAVALIER?
HOW COULD I HAVE BROUGHT THEM BACK...?
HOW DID I BECOME A MONSTER?
BEAST!

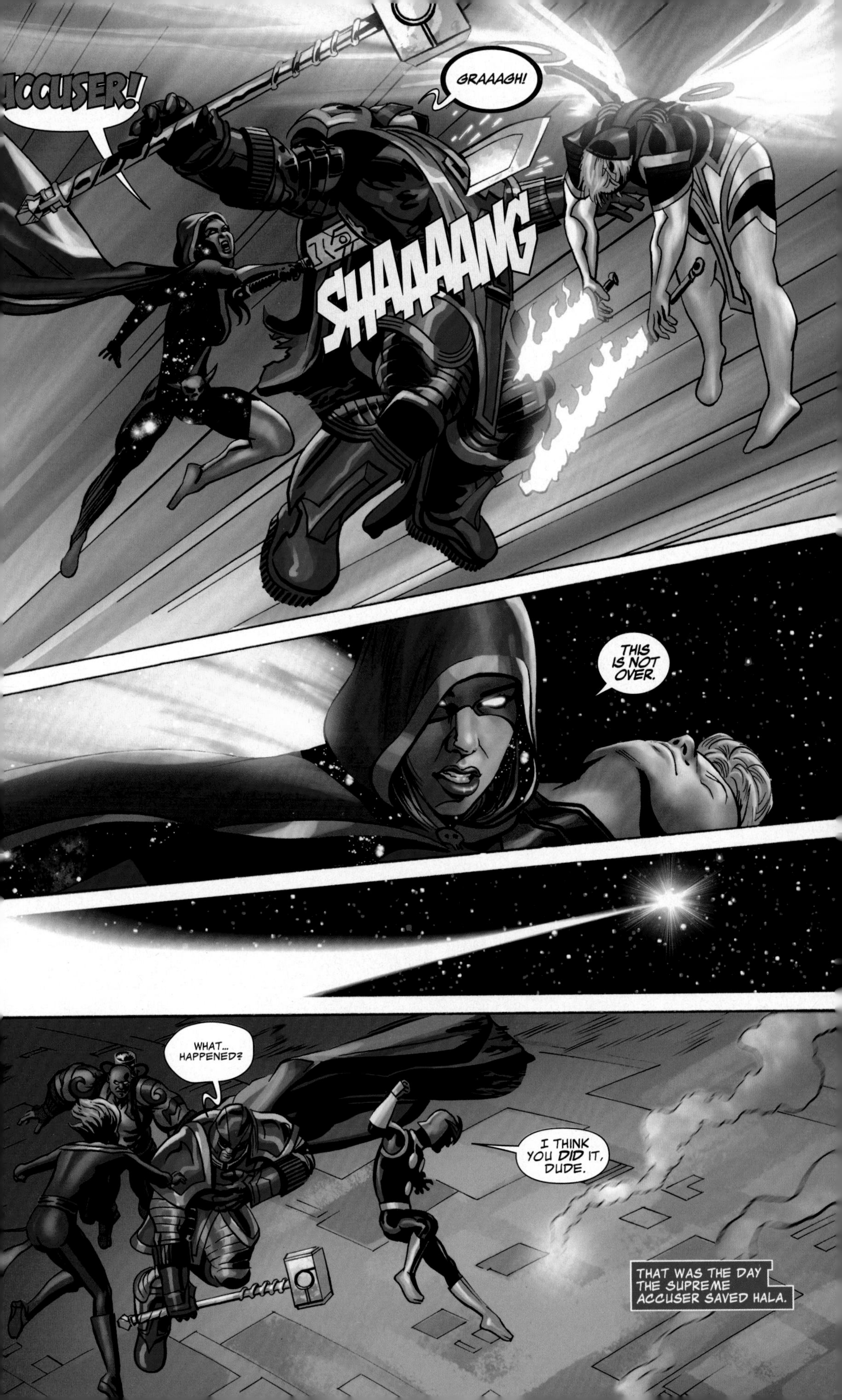
ACCUSER!
GRAAAGH!
SHAAAANG
THIS IS NOT OVER.
WHAT... HAPPENED?
I THINK YOU DID IT, DUDE.
THAT WAS THE DAY THE SUPREME ACCUSER SAVED HALA.

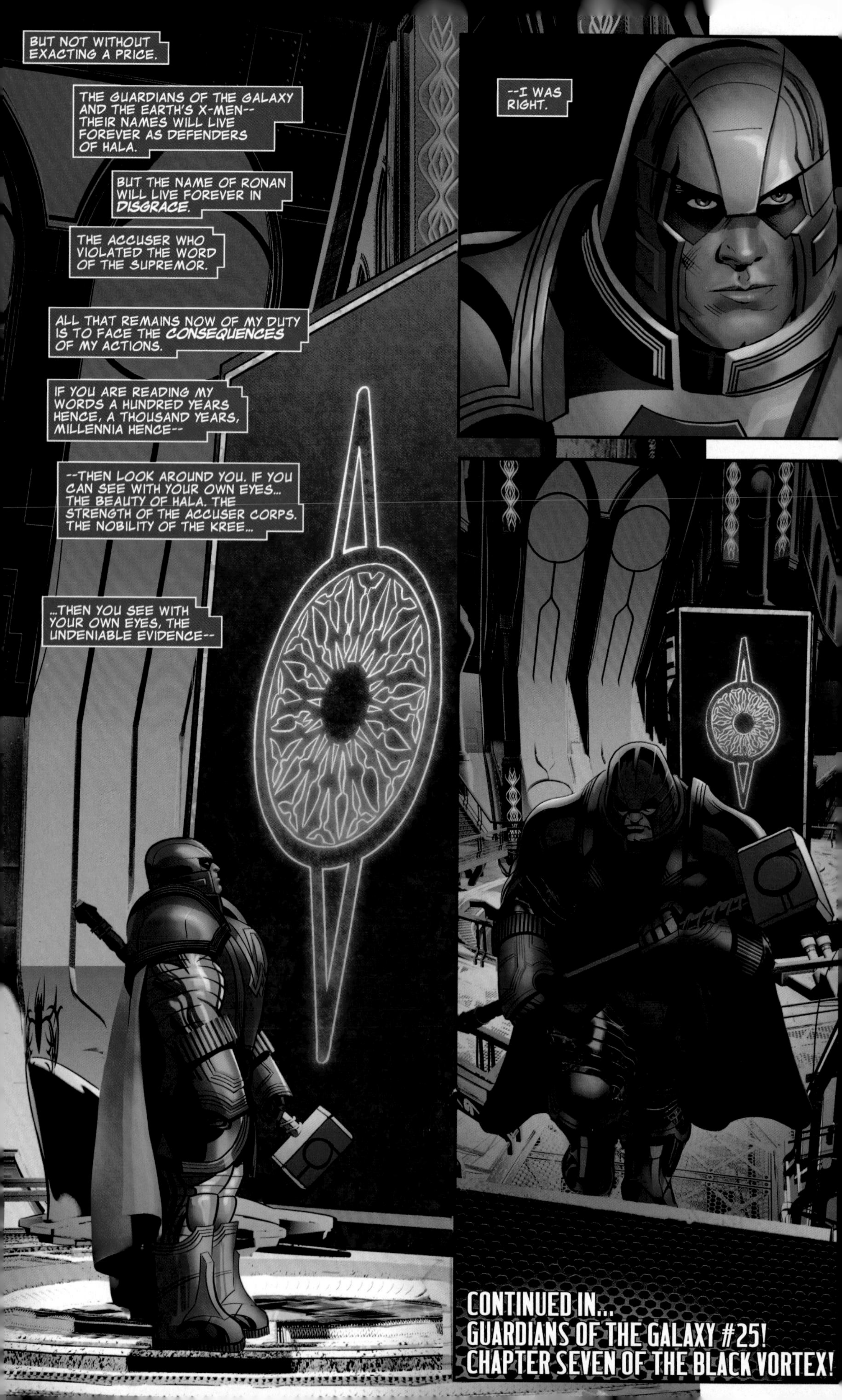
BUT NOT WITHOUT EXACTING A PRICE.
THE GUARDIANS OF THE GALAXY AND THE EARTH'S X-MEN-- THEIR NAMES WILL LIVE FOREVER AS DEFENDERS OF HALA.
BUT THE NAME OF RONAN WILL LIVE FOREVER IN DISGRACE.
THE ACCUSER WHO VIOLATED THE WORD OF THE SUPREMOR.
ALL THAT REMAINS NOW OF MY DUTY IS TO FACE THE CONSEQUENCES OF MY ACTIONS.
IF YOU ARE READING MY WORDS A HUNDRED YEARS HENCE, A THOUSAND YEARS, MILLENNIA HENCE--
--THEN LOOK AROUND YOU. IF YOU CAN SEE WITH YOUR OWN EYES... THE BEAUTY OF HALA. THE STRENGTH OF THE ACCUSER CORPS. THE NOBILITY OF THE KREE...
...THEN YOU SEE WITH YOUR OWN EYES, THE UNDENIABLE EVIDENCE--
--I WAS RIGHT.
CONTINUED IN...
GUARDIANS OF THE GALAXY #25!
CHAPTER SEVEN OF THE BLACK VORTEX!

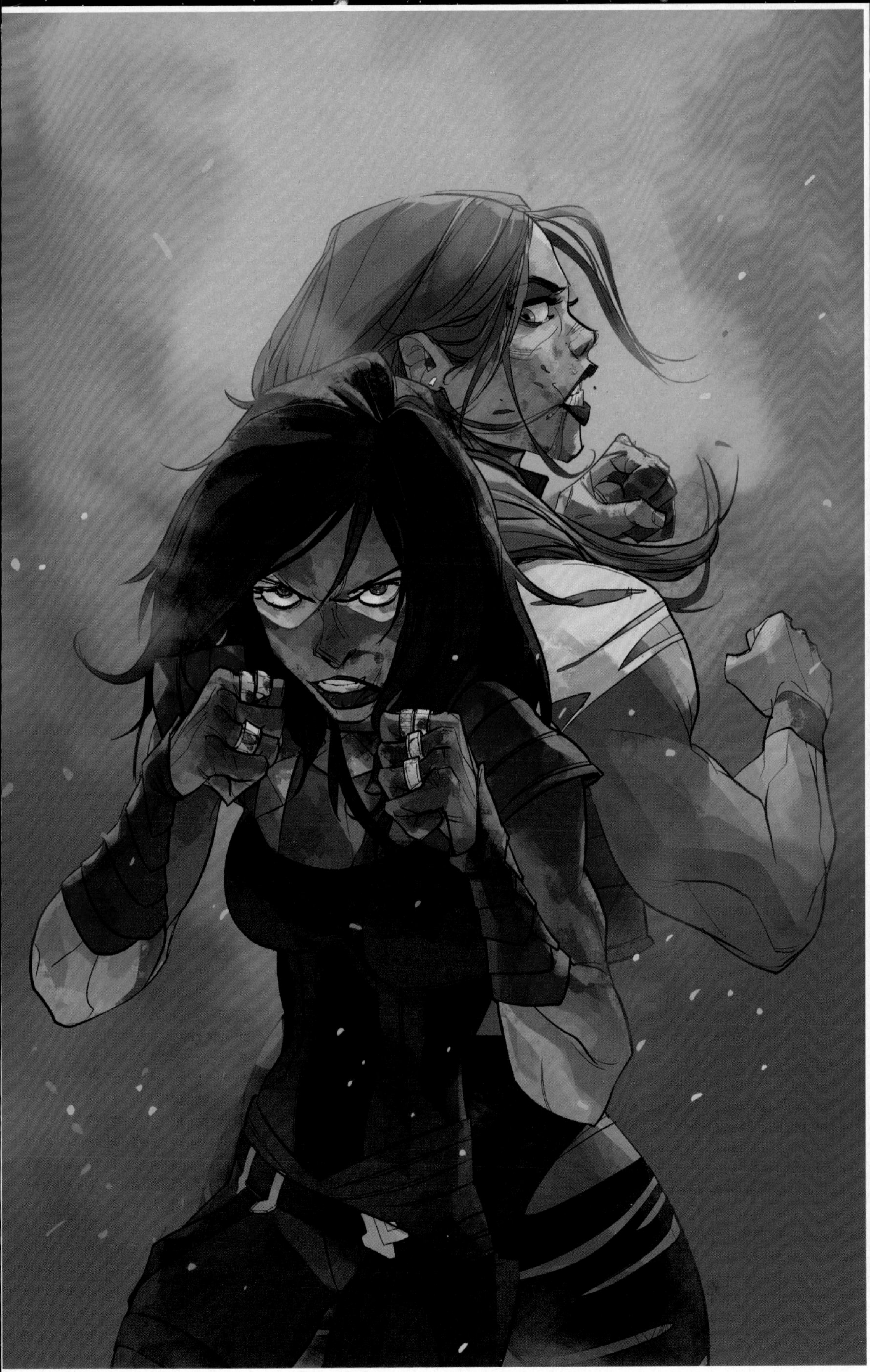

4

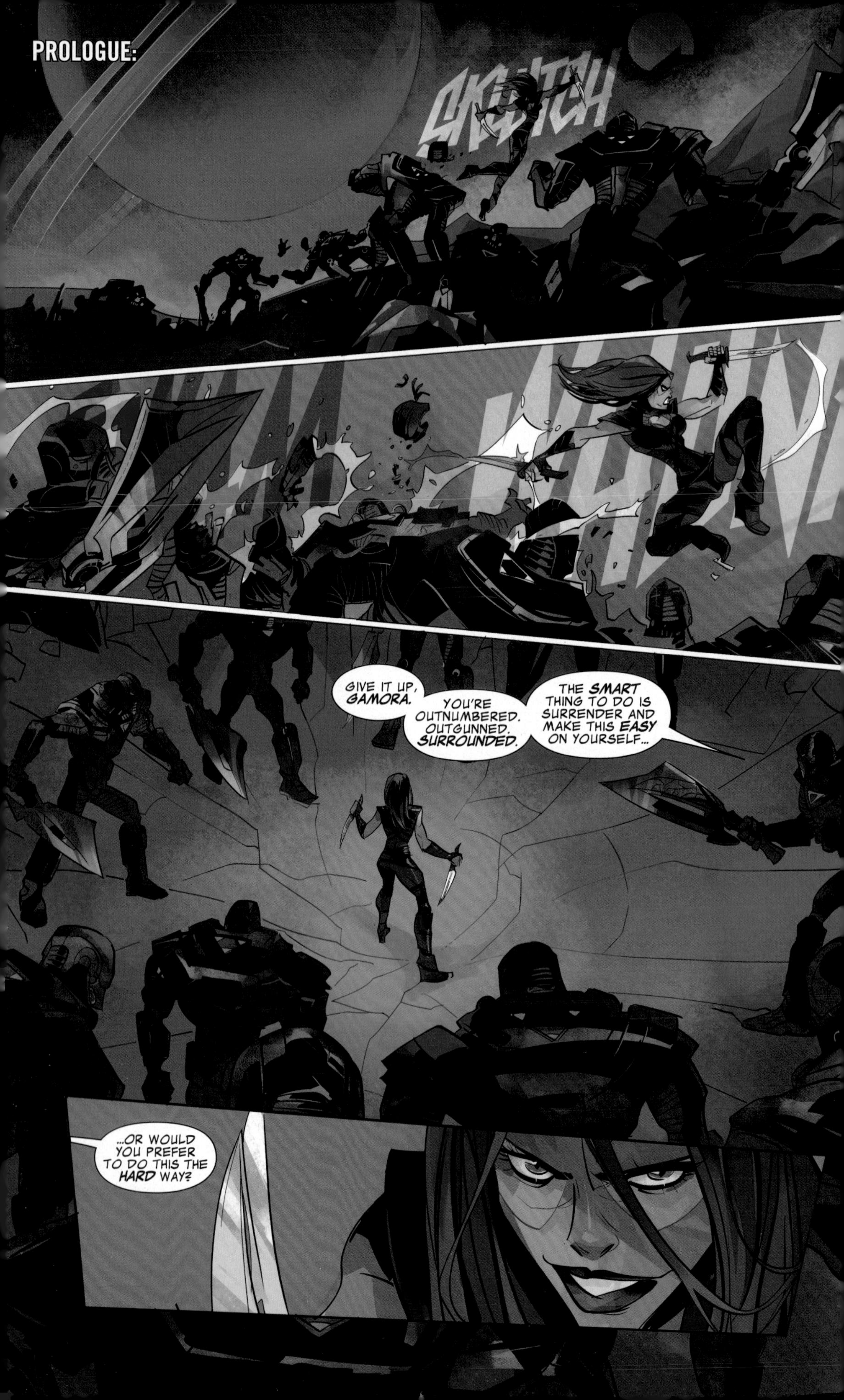
PROLOGUE:
SKLITCH
GIVE IT UP, GAMORA.
YOU'RE OUTNUMBERED. OUTGUNNED. SURROUNDED.
THE SMART THING TO DO IS SURRENDER AND MAKE THIS EASY ON YOURSELF...
...OR WOULD YOU PREFER TO DO THIS THE HARD WAY?

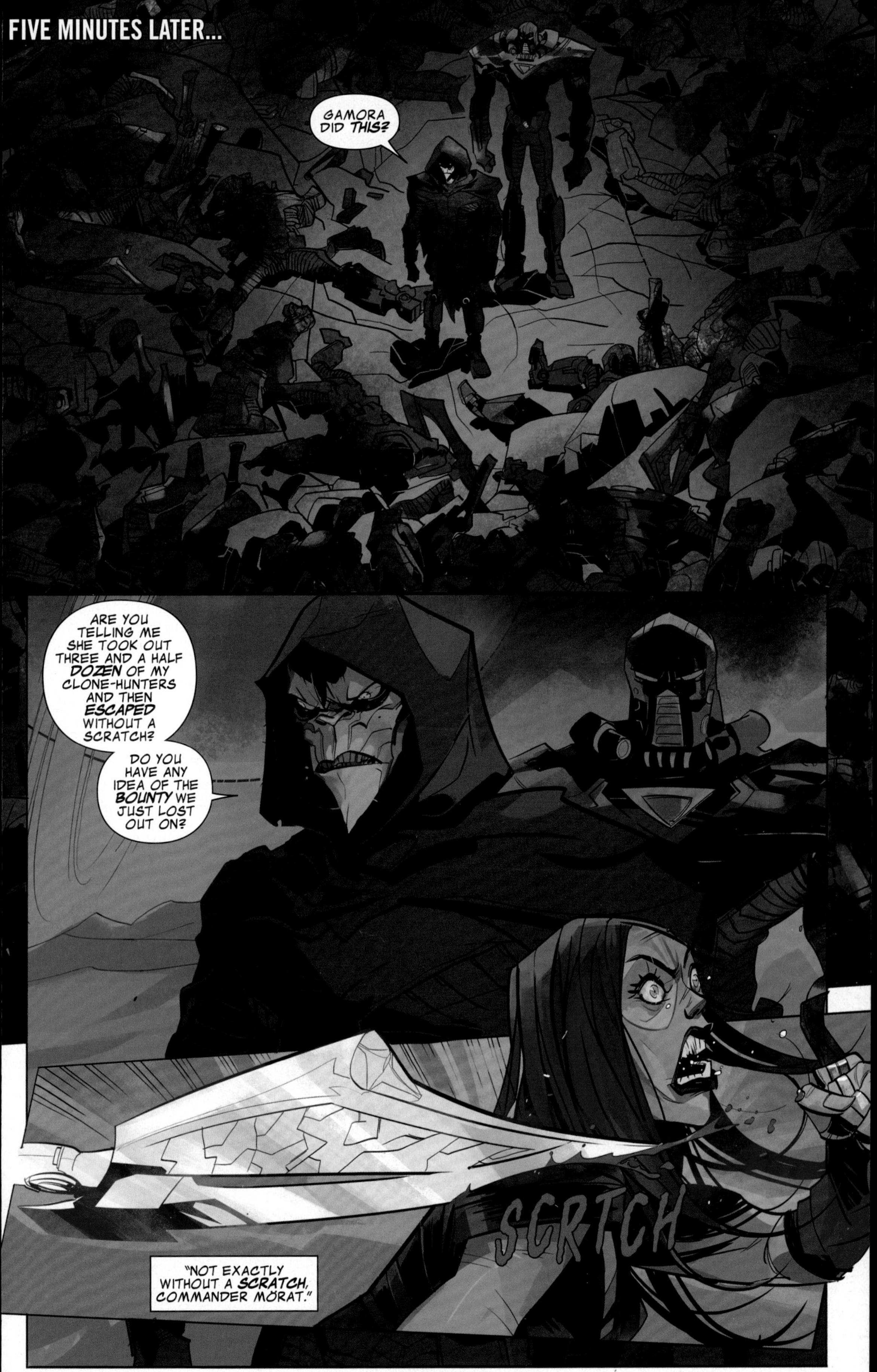
FIVE MINUTES LATER...
GAMORA DID THIS?
ARE YOU TELLING ME SHE TOOK OUT THREE AND A HALF DOZEN OF MY CLONE-HUNTERS AND THEN ESCAPED WITHOUT A SCRATCH?
DO YOU HAVE ANY IDEA OF THE BOUNTY WE JUST LOST OUT ON?
SCRTCH
"NOT EXACTLY WITHOUT A SCRATCH, COMMANDER MORAT."

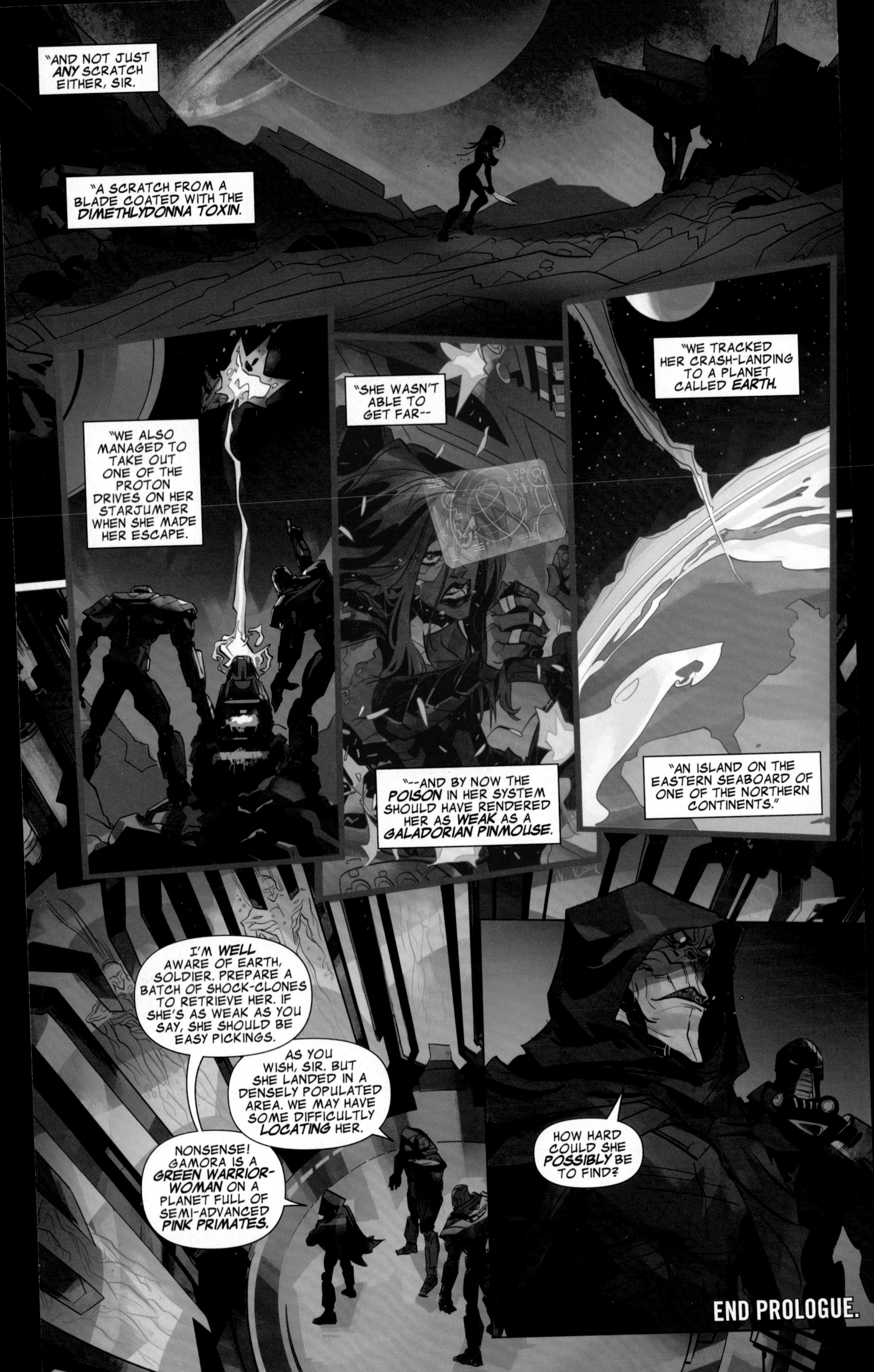
"AND NOT JUST ANY SCRATCH EITHER, SIR.
"A SCRATCH FROM A BLADE COATED WITH THE DIMETHLYDONNA TOXIN.
"WE ALSO MANAGED TO TAKE OUT ONE OF THE PROTON DRIVES ON HER STARJUMPER WHEN SHE MADE HER ESCAPE.
"SHE WASN'T ABLE TO GET FAR--
"--AND BY NOW THE POISON IN HER SYSTEM SHOULD HAVE RENDERED HER AS WEAK AS A GALADORIAN PINMOUSE.
"WE TRACKED HER CRASH-LANDING TO A PLANET CALLED EARTH.
"AN ISLAND ON THE EASTERN SEABOARD OF ONE OF THE NORTHERN CONTINENTS."
I'M WELL AWARE OF EARTH, SOLDIER. PREPARE A BATCH OF SHOCK-CLONES TO RETRIEVE HER. IF SHE'S AS WEAK AS YOU SAY, SHE SHOULD BE EASY PICKINGS.
AS YOU WISH, SIR. BUT SHE LANDED IN A DENSELY POPULATED AREA. WE MAY HAVE SOME DIFFICULTLY LOCATING HER.
NONSENSE! GAMORA IS A GREEN WARRIOR-WOMAN ON A PLANET FULL OF SEMI-ADVANCED PINK PRIMATES.
HOW HARD COULD SHE POSSIBLY BE TO FIND?
END PROLOGUE.

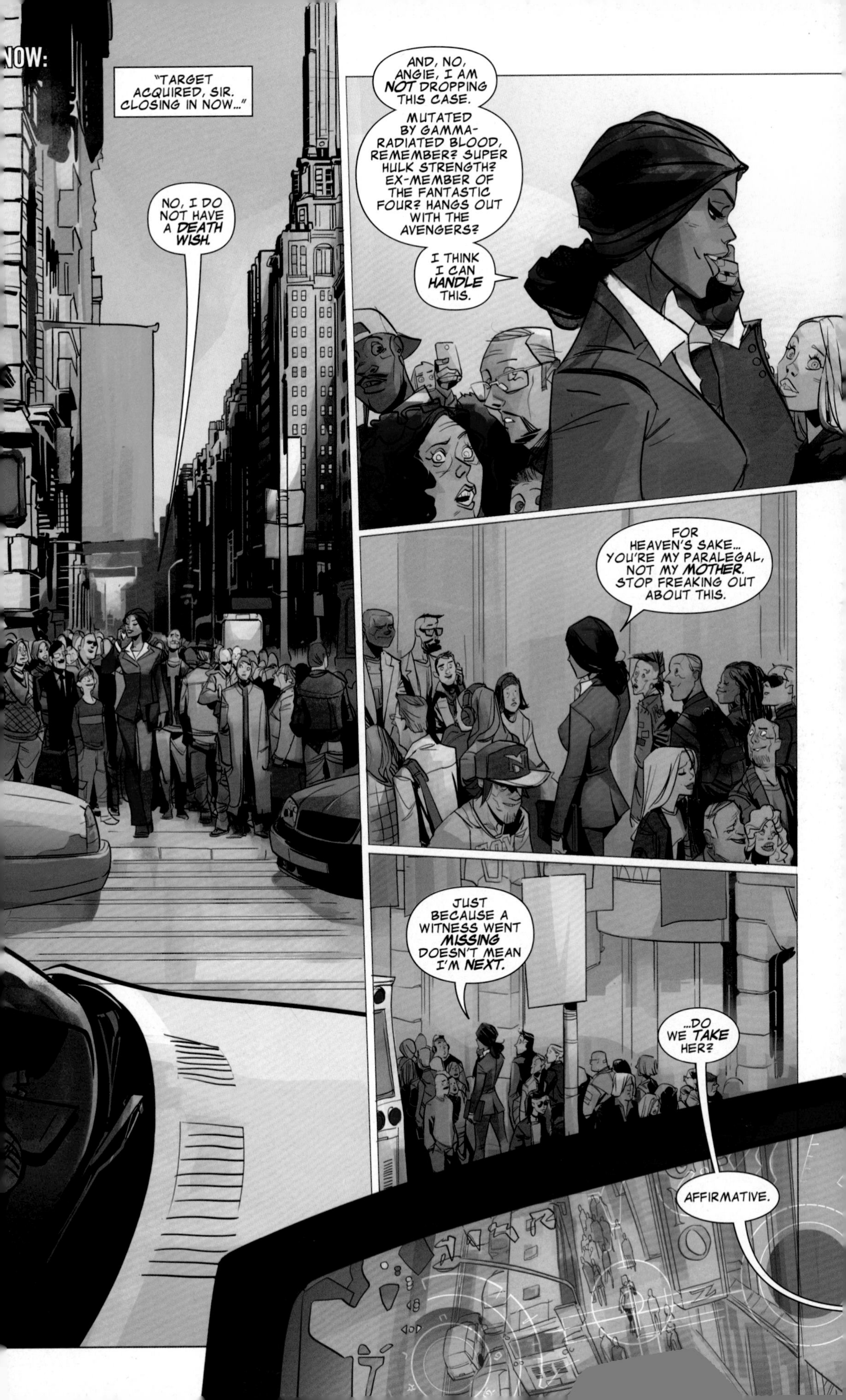
NOW:
"TARGET ACQUIRED, SIR. CLOSING IN NOW..."
NO, I DO NOT HAVE A DEATH WISH.
AND, NO, ANGIE, I AM NOT DROPPING THIS CASE.
MUTATED BY GAMMA-RADIATED BLOOD, REMEMBER? SUPER HULK STRENGTH? EX-MEMBER OF THE FANTASTIC FOUR? HANGS OUT WITH THE AVENGERS?
I THINK I CAN HANDLE THIS.
FOR HEAVEN'S SAKE... YOU'RE MY PARALEGAL, NOT MY MOTHER. STOP FREAKING OUT ABOUT THIS.
JUST BECAUSE A WITNESS WENT MISSING DOESN'T MEAN I'M NEXT.
...DO WE TAKE HER?
AFFIRMATIVE.

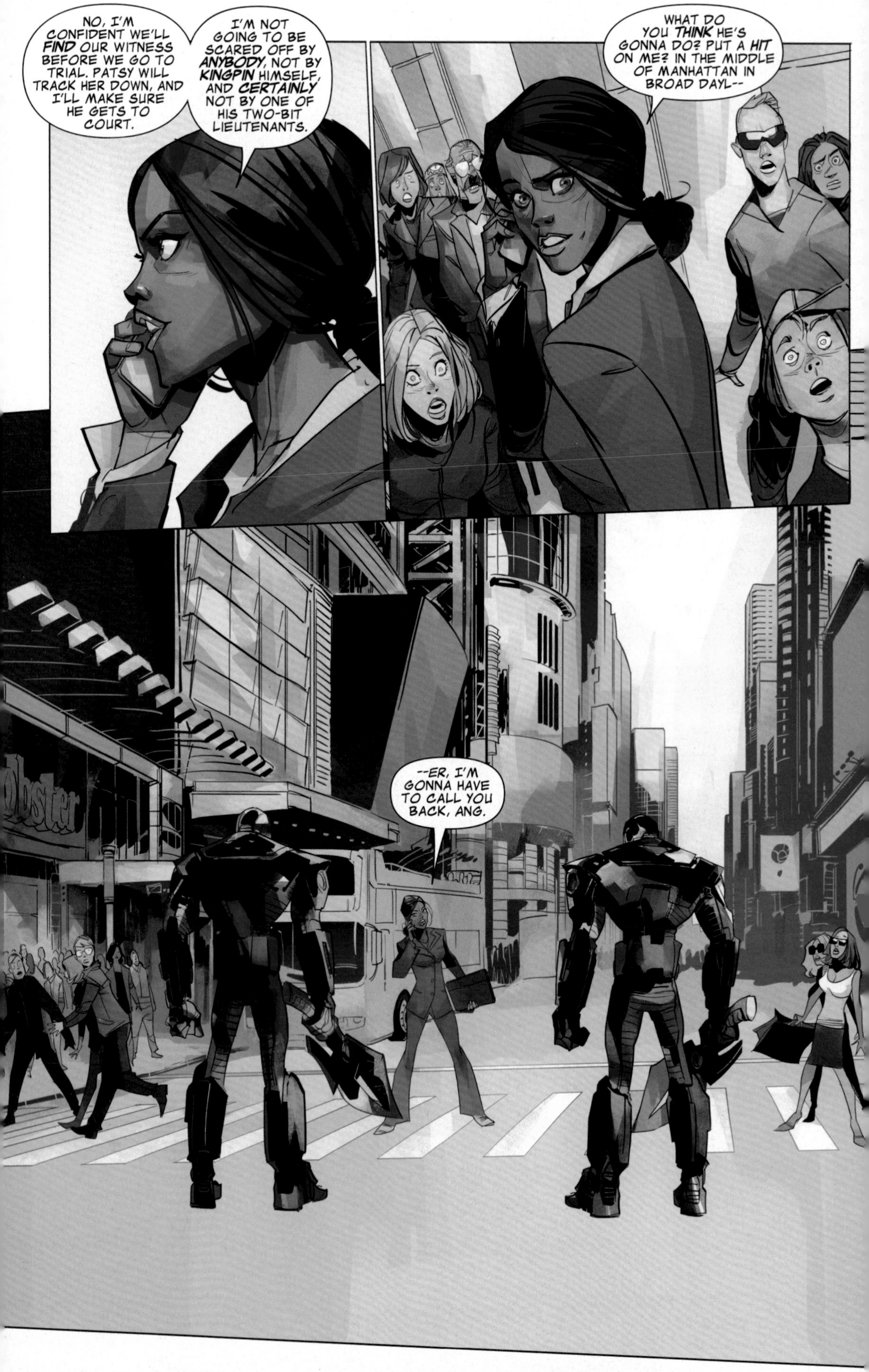

NO, I'M CONFIDENT WE'LL FIND OUR WITNESS BEFORE WE GO TO TRIAL. PATSY WILL TRACK HER DOWN, AND I'LL MAKE SURE HE GETS TO COURT.
I'M NOT GOING TO BE SCARED OFF BY ANYBODY, NOT BY KINGPIN HIMSELF, AND CERTAINLY NOT BY ONE OF HIS TWO-BIT LIEUTENANTS.
WHAT DO YOU THINK HE'S GONNA DO? PUT A HIT ON ME? IN THE MIDDLE OF MANHATTAN IN BROAD DAYL--
--ER, I'M GONNA HAVE TO CALL YOU BACK, ANG.

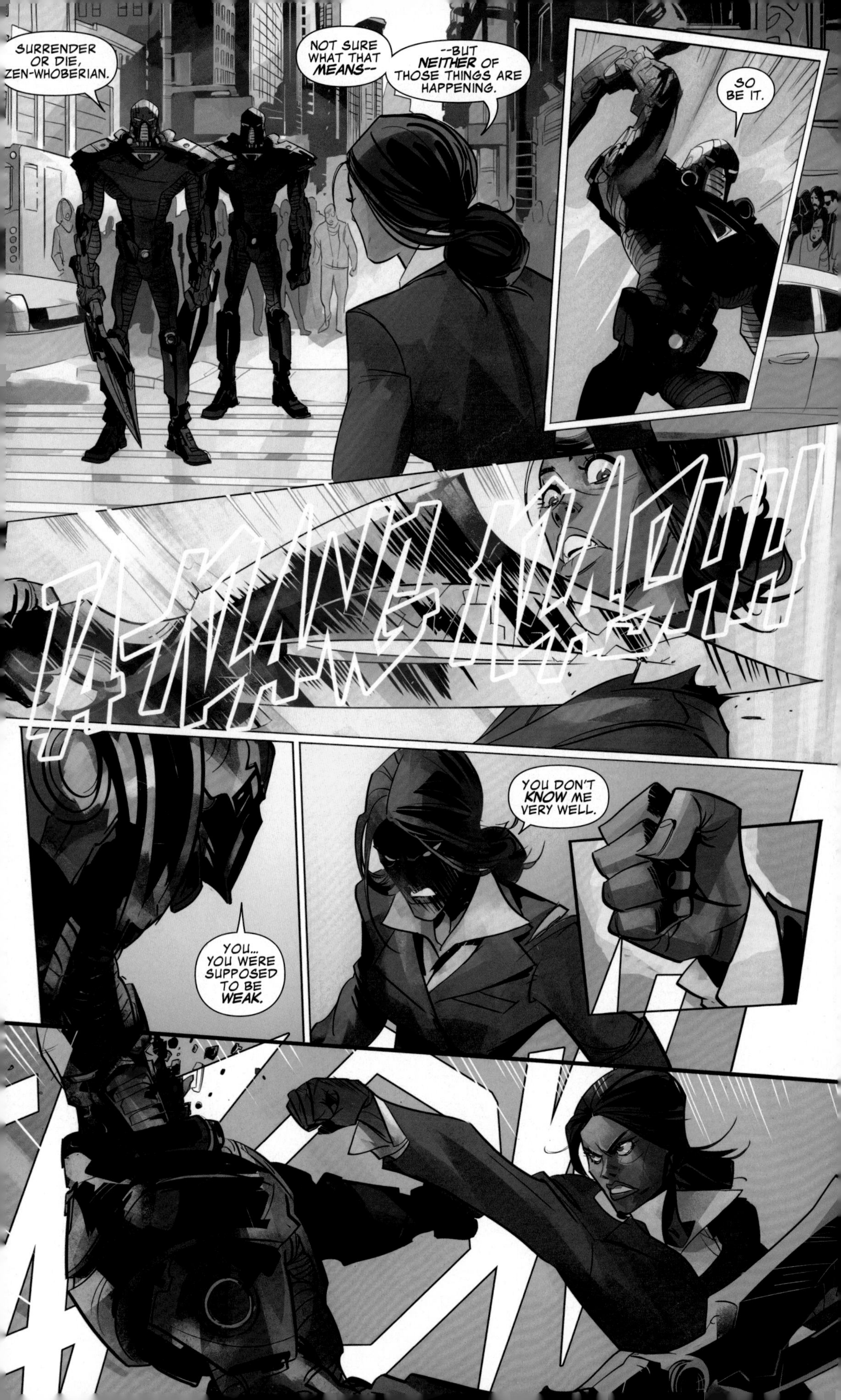
SURRENDER OR DIE, ZEN-WHOBERIAN.
NOT SURE WHAT THAT MEANS--
--BUT NEITHER OF THOSE THINGS ARE HAPPENING.
SO BE IT.
YOU DON'T KNOW ME VERY WELL.
YOU... YOU WERE SUPPOSED TO BE WEAK.

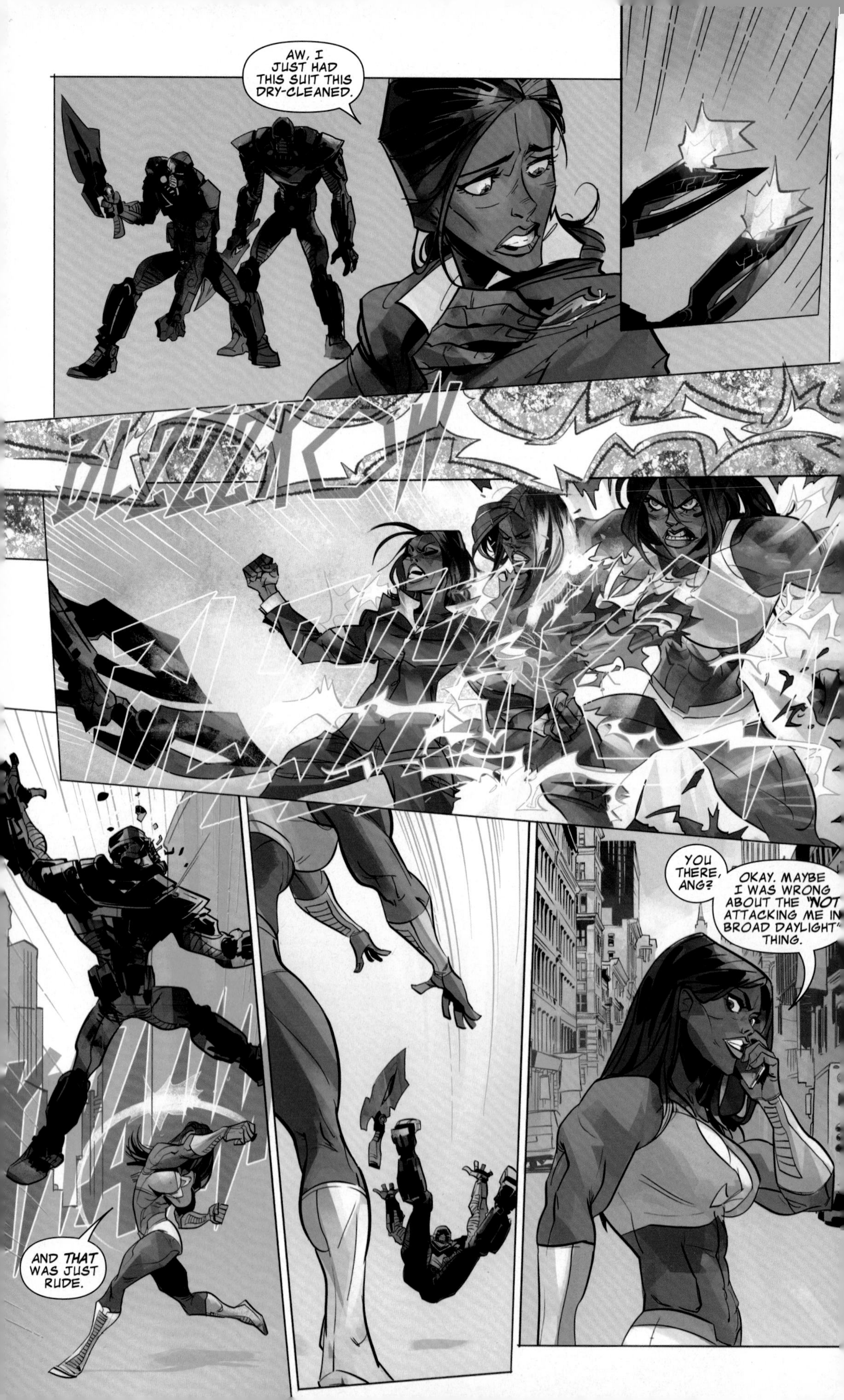
AW, I JUST HAD THIS SUIT THIS DRY-CLEANED.
AND THAT WAS JUST RUDE.
YOU THERE, ANG?
OKAY. MAYBE I WAS WRONG ABOUT THE "NOT ATTACKING ME IN BROAD DAYLIGHT" THING.

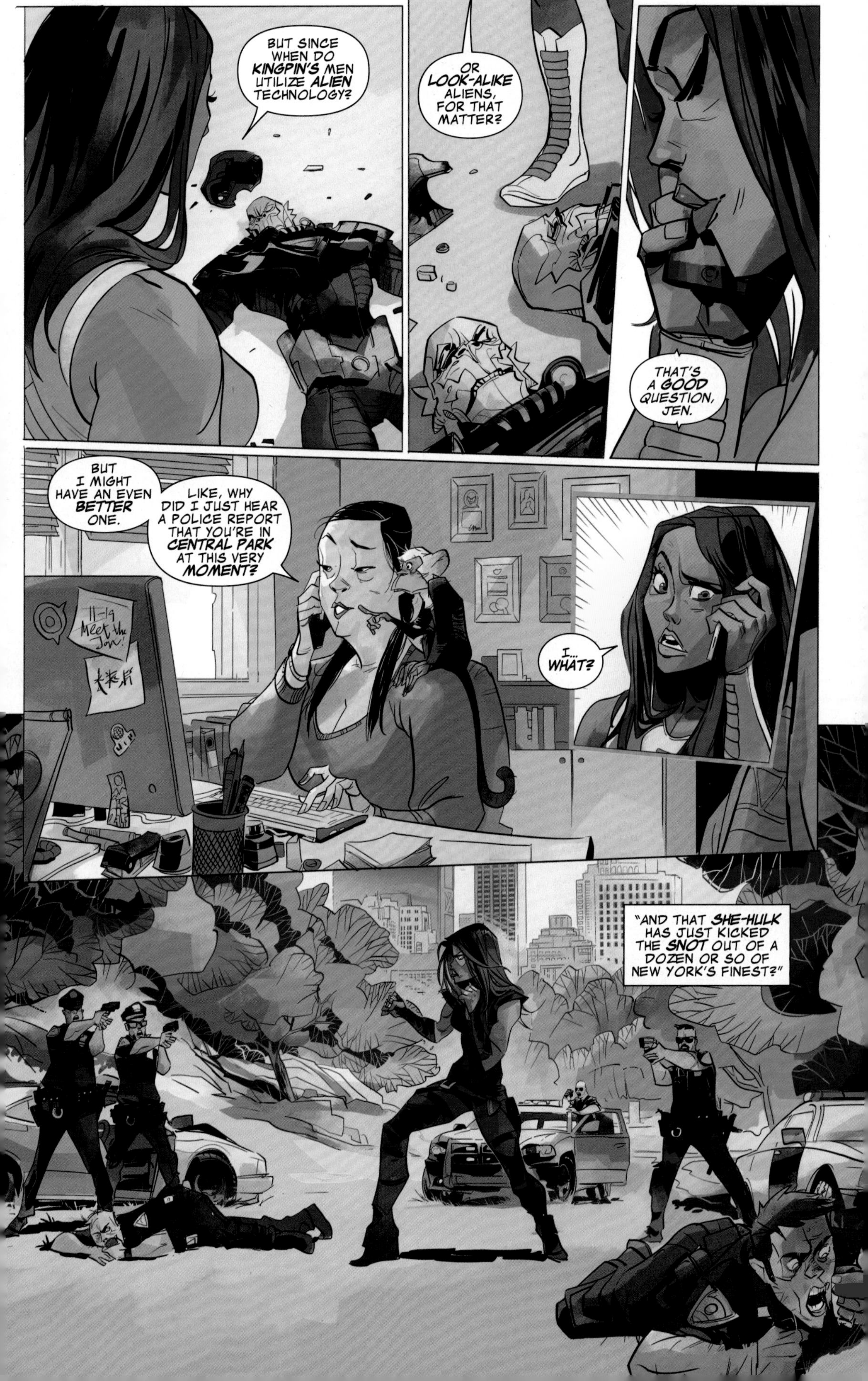
BUT SINCE WHEN DO KINGPIN'S MEN UTILIZE ALIEN TECHNOLOGY?
OR LOOK-ALIKE ALIENS, FOR THAT MATTER?
THAT'S A GOOD QUESTION, JEN.
BUT I MIGHT HAVE AN EVEN BETTER ONE.
LIKE, WHY DID I JUST HEAR A POLICE REPORT THAT YOU'RE IN CENTRAL PARK AT THIS VERY MOMENT?
11-19 Meet the Jon!
I... WHAT?
"AND THAT SHE-HULK HAS JUST KICKED THE SNOT OUT OF A DOZEN OR SO OF NEW YORK'S FINEST?"

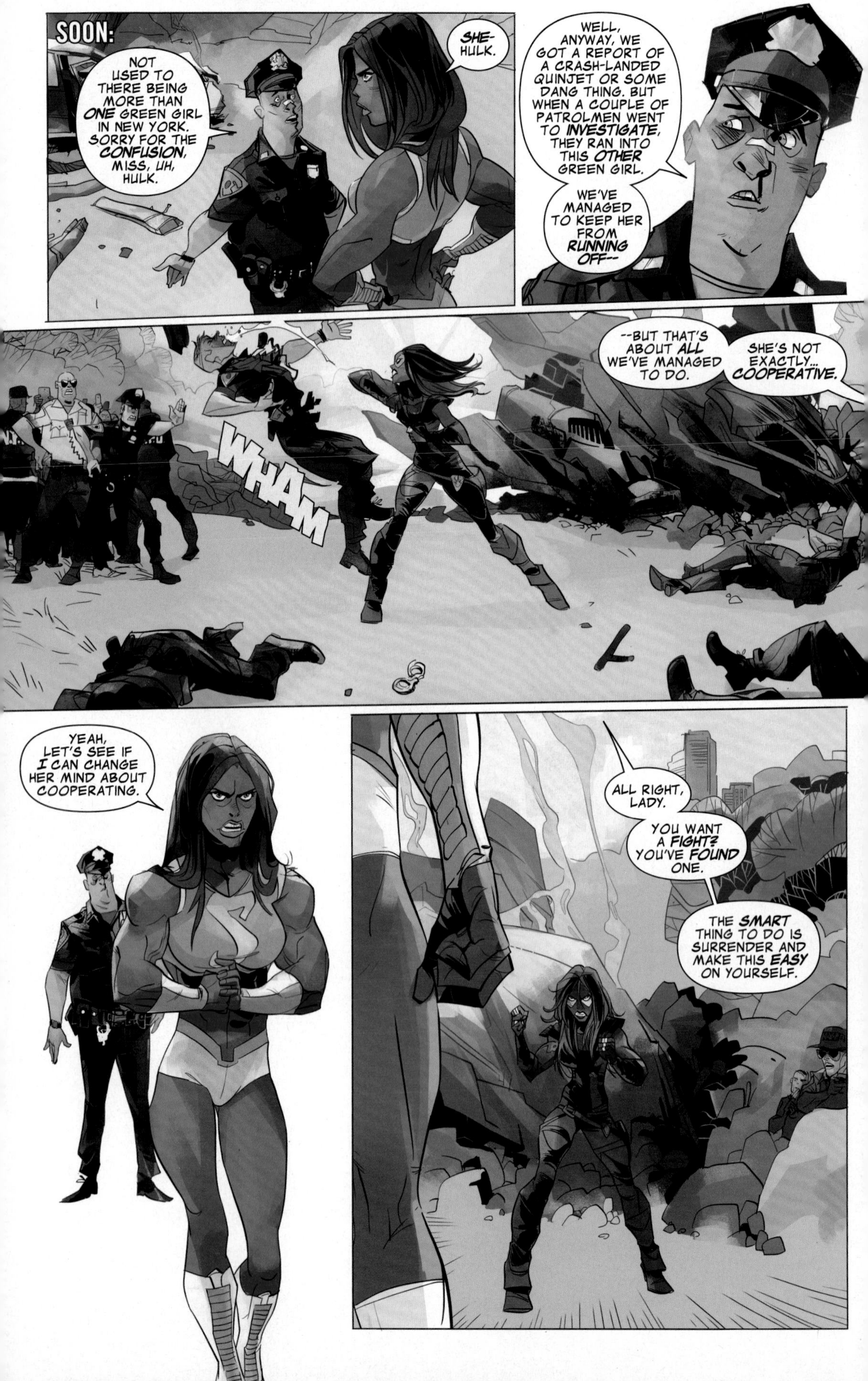
SOON:
NOT USED TO THERE BEING MORE THAN ONE GREEN GIRL IN NEW YORK. SORRY FOR THE CONFUSION, MISS, UH, HULK.
SHE-HULK.
WELL, ANYWAY, WE GOT A REPORT OF A CRASH-LANDED QUINJET OR SOME DANG THING. BUT WHEN A COUPLE OF PATROLMEN WENT TO INVESTIGATE, THEY RAN INTO THIS OTHER GREEN GIRL.
WE'VE MANAGED TO KEEP HER FROM RUNNING OFF--
--BUT THAT'S ABOUT ALL WE'VE MANAGED TO DO.
SHE'S NOT EXACTLY... COOPERATIVE.
WHAM
YEAH, LET'S SEE IF I CAN CHANGE HER MIND ABOUT COOPERATING.
ALL RIGHT, LADY.
YOU WANT A FIGHT? YOU'VE FOUND ONE.
THE SMART THING TO DO IS SURRENDER AND MAKE THIS EASY ON YOURSELF.

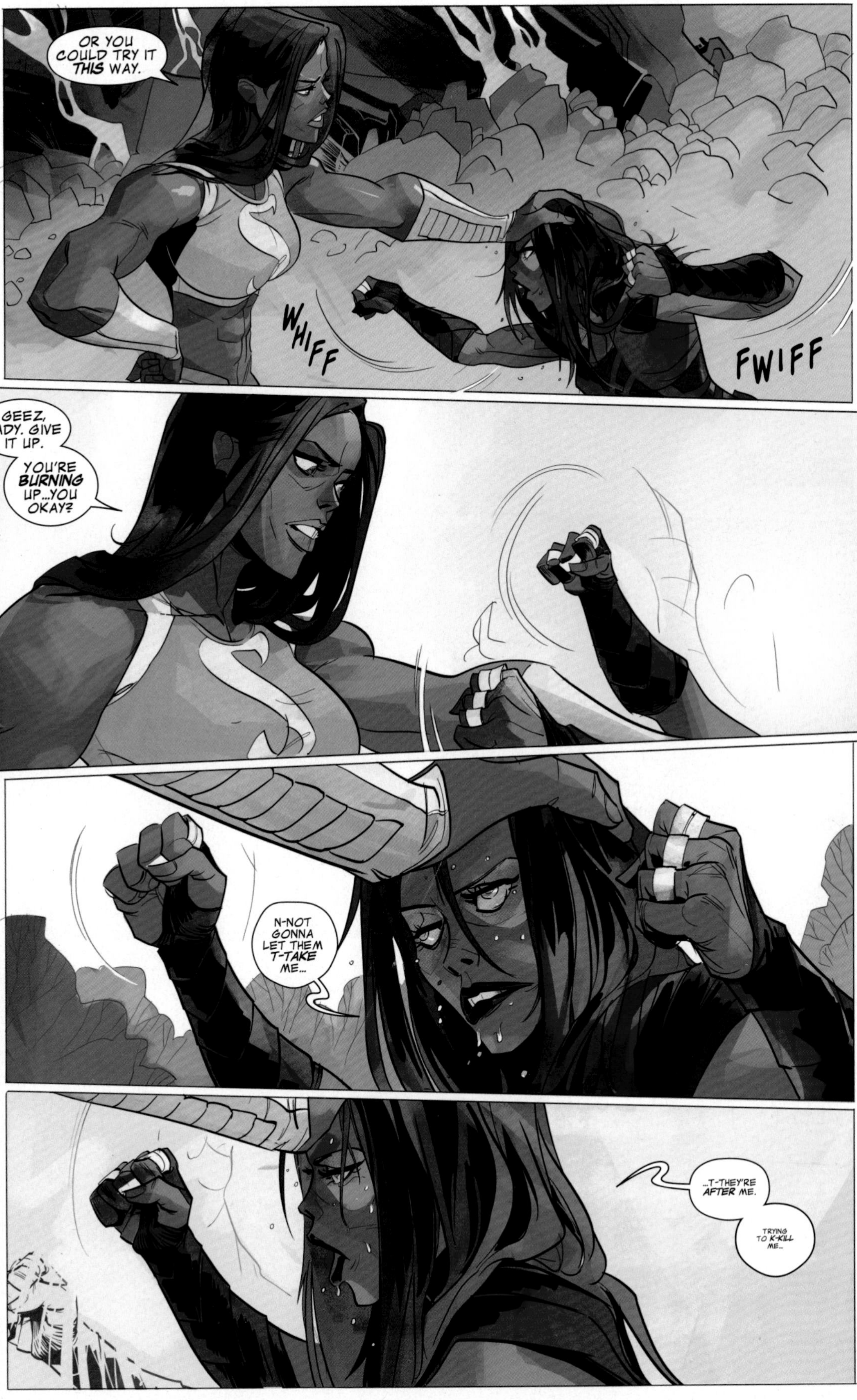
OR YOU COULD TRY IT THIS WAY.
WHIFF
FWIFF
GEEZ, ADY. GIVE IT UP.
YOU'RE BURNING UP...YOU OKAY?
N-NOT GONNA LET THEM T-TAKE ME...
...T-THEY'RE AFTER ME.
TRYING TO K-KILL ME...

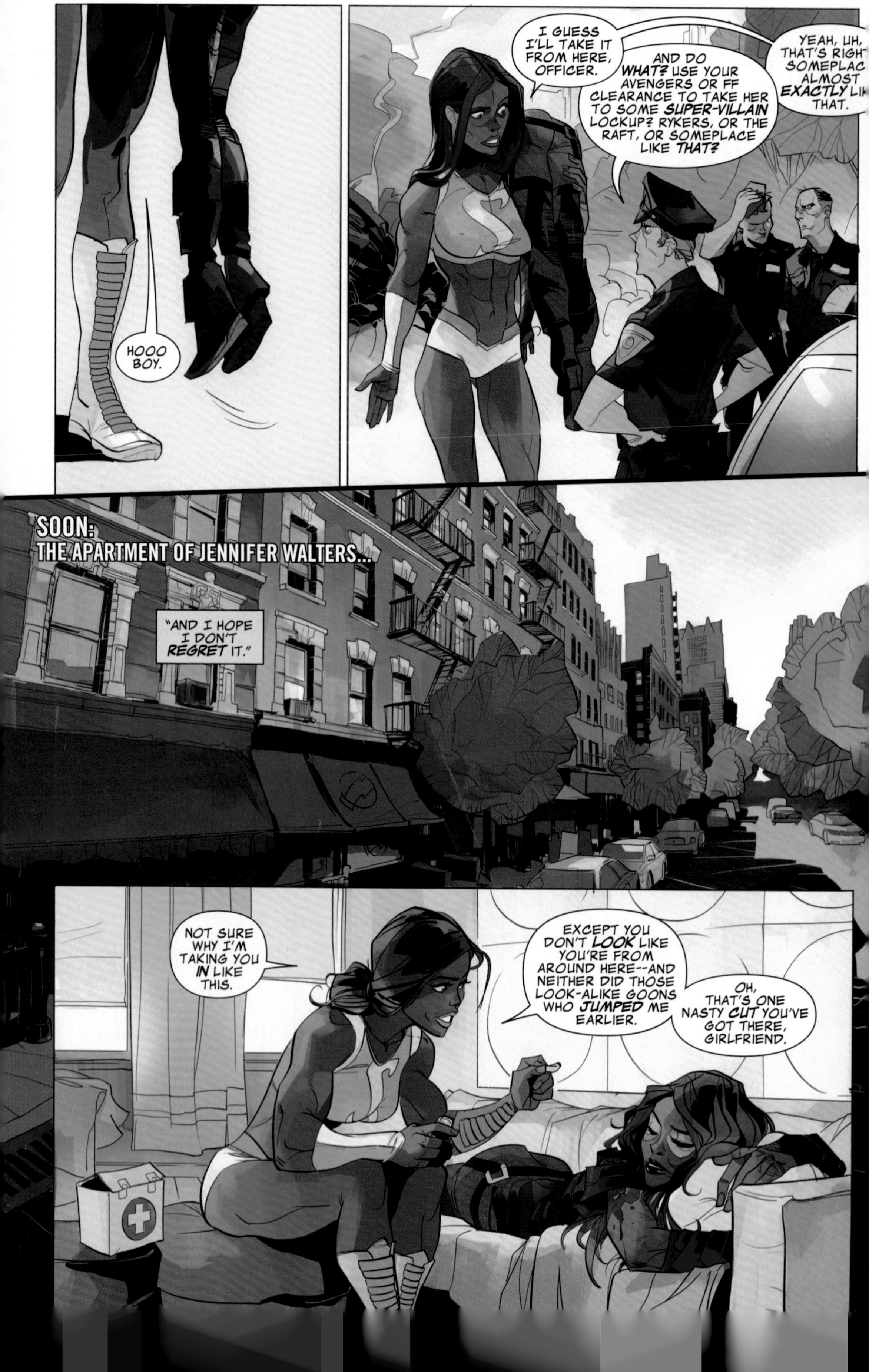
HOOO BOY.
I GUESS I'LL TAKE IT FROM HERE, OFFICER.
AND DO WHAT? USE YOUR AVENGERS OR FF CLEARANCE TO TAKE HER TO SOME SUPER-VILLAIN LOCKUP? RYKERS, OR THE RAFT, OR SOMEPLACE LIKE THAT?
YEAH, UH, THAT'S RIGHT SOMEPLAC ALMOST EXACTLY LI THAT.
SOON: THE APARTMENT OF JENNIFER WALTERS...
"AND I HOPE I DON'T REGRET IT."
NOT SURE WHY I'M TAKING YOU IN LIKE THIS.
EXCEPT YOU DON'T LOOK LIKE YOU'RE FROM AROUND HERE--AND NEITHER DID THOSE LOOK-ALIKE GOONS WHO JUMPED ME EARLIER.
OH, THAT'S ONE NASTY CUT YOU'VE GOT THERE, GIRLFRIEND.

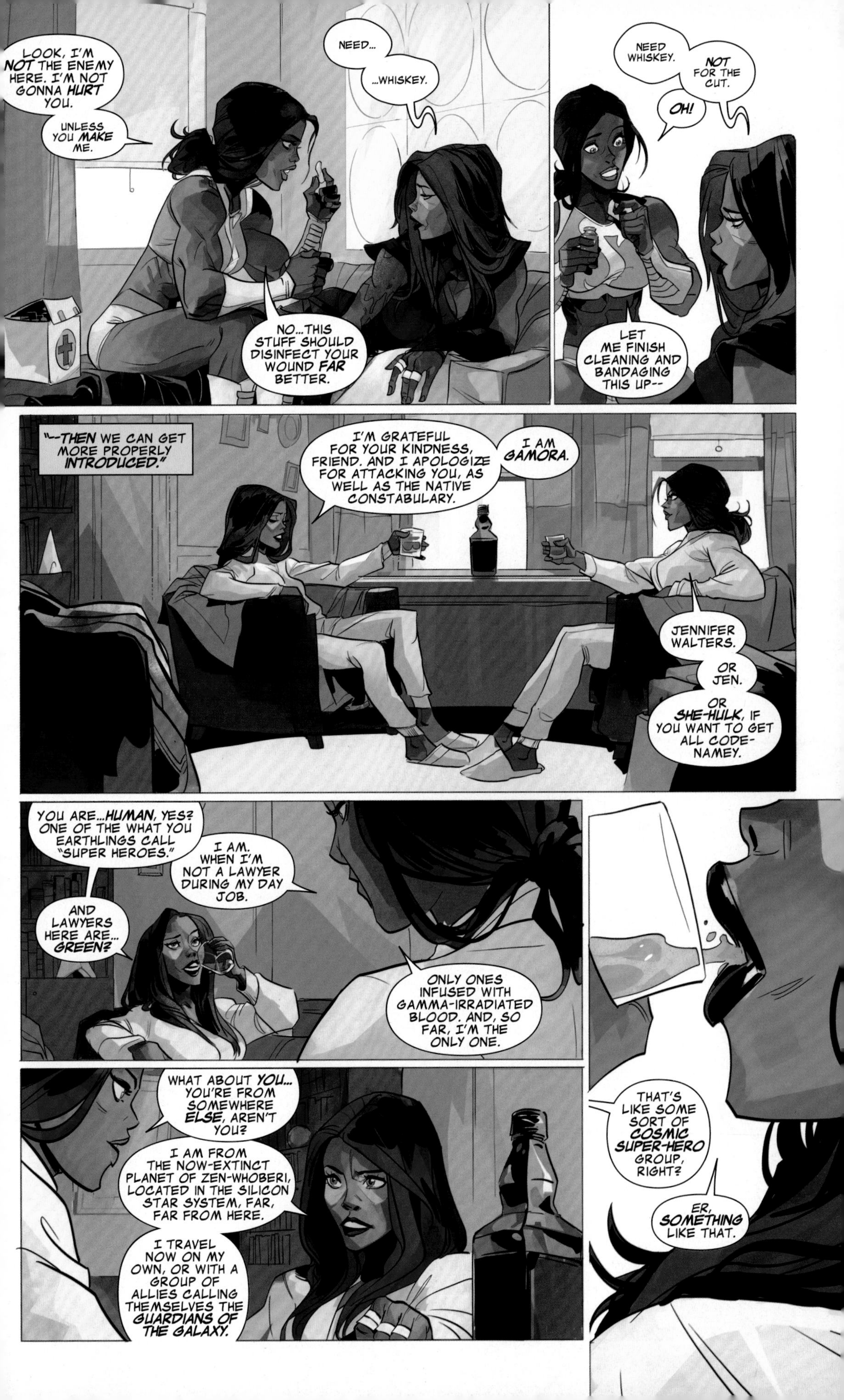

LOOK, I'M NOT THE ENEMY HERE. I'M NOT GONNA HURT YOU.
UNLESS YOU MAKE ME.
NEED...
...WHISKEY.
NO...THIS STUFF SHOULD DISINFECT YOUR WOUND FAR BETTER.
NEED WHISKEY.
NOT FOR THE CUT.
OH!
LET ME FINISH CLEANING AND BANDAGING THIS UP--
"--THEN WE CAN GET MORE PROPERLY INTRODUCED."
I'M GRATEFUL FOR YOUR KINDNESS, FRIEND. AND I APOLOGIZE FOR ATTACKING YOU, AS WELL AS THE NATIVE CONSTABULARY.
I AM GAMORA.
JENNIFER WALTERS.
OR JEN.
OR SHE-HULK, IF YOU WANT TO GET ALL CODE-NAMEY.
YOU ARE...HUMAN, YES? ONE OF THE WHAT YOU EARTHLINGS CALL "SUPER HEROES."
I AM. WHEN I'M NOT A LAWYER DURING MY DAY JOB.
AND LAWYERS HERE ARE... GREEN?
ONLY ONES INFUSED WITH GAMMA-IRRADIATED BLOOD. AND, SO FAR, I'M THE ONLY ONE.
WHAT ABOUT YOU... YOU'RE FROM SOMEWHERE ELSE, AREN'T YOU?
I AM FROM THE NOW-EXTINCT PLANET OF ZEN-WHOBERI, LOCATED IN THE SILICON STAR SYSTEM, FAR, FAR FROM HERE.
I TRAVEL NOW ON MY OWN, OR WITH A GROUP OF ALLIES CALLING THEMSELVES THE GUARDIANS OF THE GALAXY.
THAT'S LIKE SOME SORT OF COSMIC SUPER-HERO GROUP, RIGHT?
ER, SOMETHING LIKE THAT.

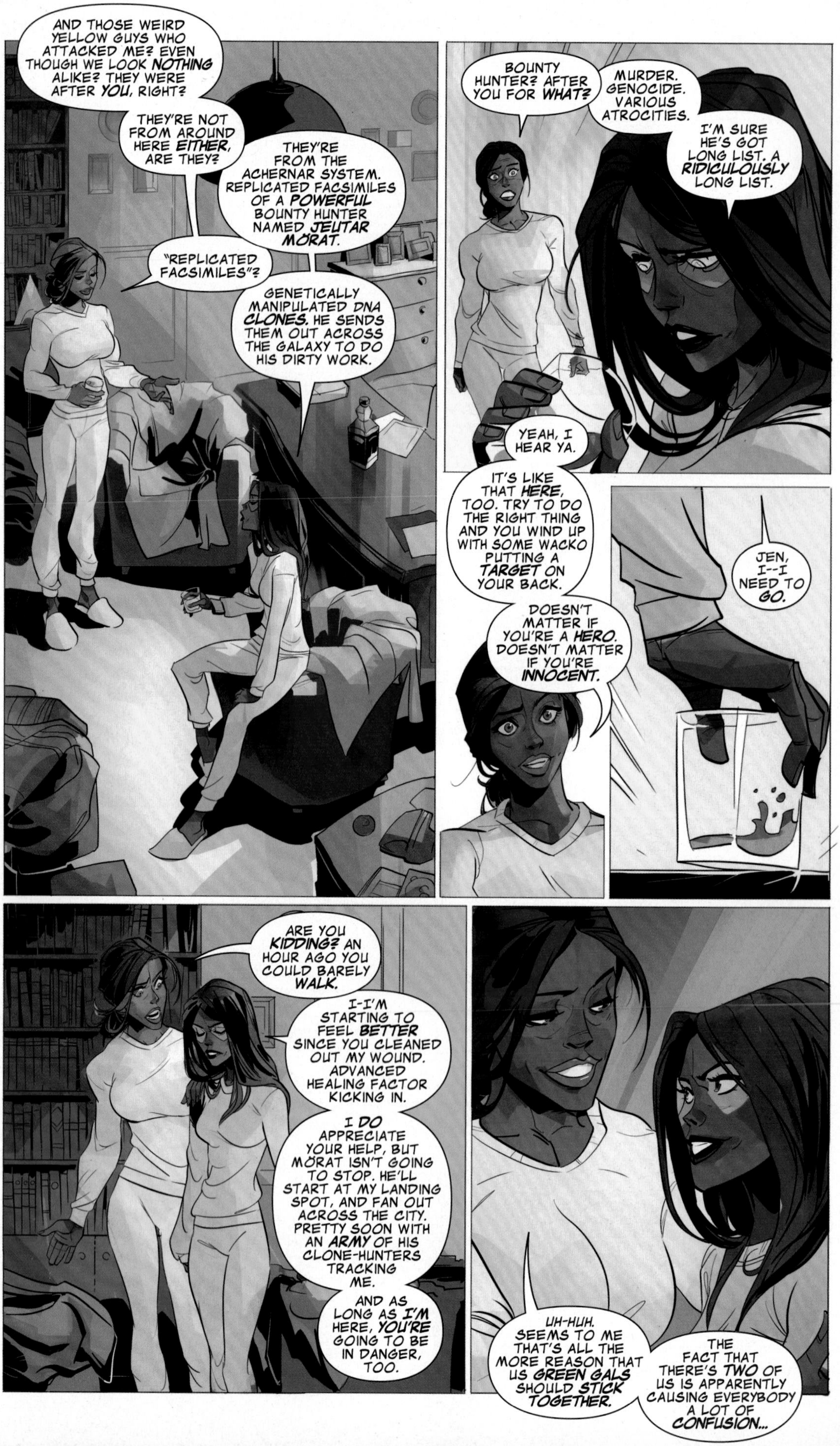
AND THOSE WEIRD YELLOW GUYS WHO ATTACKED ME? EVEN THOUGH WE LOOK NOTHING ALIKE? THEY WERE AFTER YOU, RIGHT?
THEY'RE NOT FROM AROUND HERE EITHER, ARE THEY?
THEY'RE FROM THE ACHERNAR SYSTEM. REPLICATED FACSIMILES OF A POWERFUL BOUNTY HUNTER NAMED JEUTAR MÖRAT.
"REPLICATED FACSIMILES"?
GENETICALLY MANIPULATED DNA CLONES. HE SENDS THEM OUT ACROSS THE GALAXY TO DO HIS DIRTY WORK.
BOUNTY HUNTER? AFTER YOU FOR WHAT?
MURDER. GENOCIDE. VARIOUS ATROCITIES.
I'M SURE HE'S GOT LONG LIST. A RIDICULOUSLY LONG LIST.
YEAH, I HEAR YA.
IT'S LIKE THAT HERE, TOO. TRY TO DO THE RIGHT THING AND YOU WIND UP WITH SOME WACKO PUTTING A TARGET ON YOUR BACK.
DOESN'T MATTER IF YOU'RE A HERO. DOESN'T MATTER IF YOU'RE INNOCENT.
JEN, I--I NEED TO GO.
ARE YOU KIDDING? AN HOUR AGO YOU COULD BARELY WALK.
I-I'M STARTING TO FEEL BETTER SINCE YOU CLEANED OUT MY WOUND. ADVANCED HEALING FACTOR KICKING IN.
I DO APPRECIATE YOUR HELP, BUT MÖRAT ISN'T GOING TO STOP. HE'LL START AT MY LANDING SPOT, AND FAN OUT ACROSS THE CITY. PRETTY SOON WITH AN ARMY OF HIS CLONE-HUNTERS TRACKING ME.
AND AS LONG AS I'M HERE, YOU'RE GOING TO BE IN DANGER, TOO.
UH-HUH. SEEMS TO ME THAT'S ALL THE MORE REASON THAT US GREEN GALS SHOULD STICK TOGETHER.
THE FACT THAT THERE'S TWO OF US IS APPARENTLY CAUSING EVERYBODY A LOT OF CONFUSION...

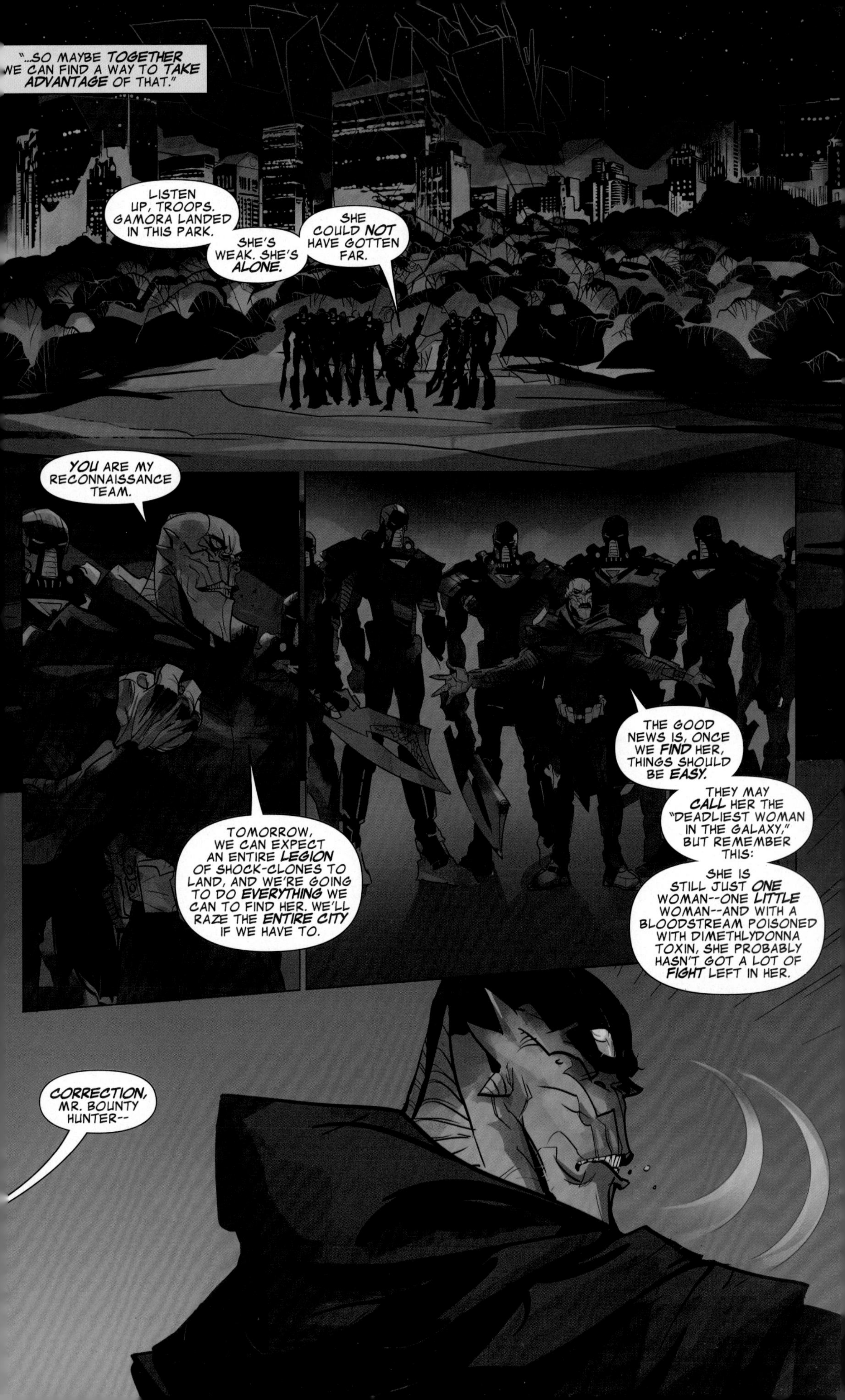
"...SO MAYBE TOGETHER WE CAN FIND A WAY TO TAKE ADVANTAGE OF THAT."
LISTEN UP, TROOPS. GAMORA LANDED IN THIS PARK.
SHE'S WEAK. SHE'S ALONE.
SHE COULD NOT HAVE GOTTEN FAR.
YOU ARE MY RECONNAISSANCE TEAM.
TOMORROW, WE CAN EXPECT AN ENTIRE LEGION OF SHOCK-CLONES TO LAND, AND WE'RE GOING TO DO EVERYTHING WE CAN TO FIND HER. WE'LL RAZE THE ENTIRE CITY IF WE HAVE TO.
THE GOOD NEWS IS, ONCE WE FIND HER, THINGS SHOULD BE EASY.
THEY MAY CALL HER THE "DEADLIEST WOMAN IN THE GALAXY," BUT REMEMBER THIS:
SHE IS STILL JUST ONE WOMAN--ONE LITTLE WOMAN--AND WITH A BLOODSTREAM POISONED WITH DIMETHLYDONNA TOXIN, SHE PROBABLY HASN'T GOT A LOT OF FIGHT LEFT IN HER.
CORRECTION, MR. BOUNTY HUNTER--

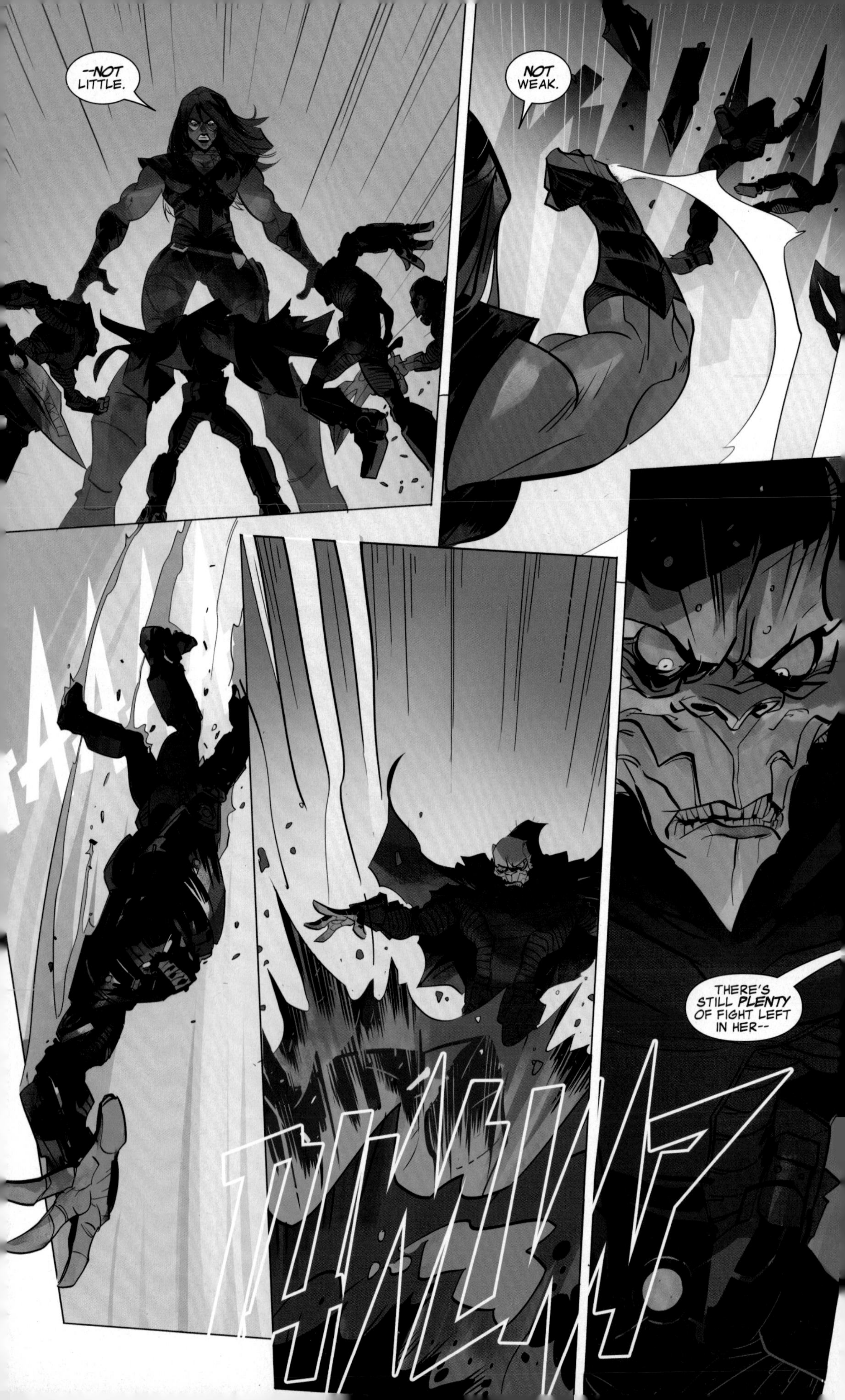
--NOT LITTLE.
NOT WEAK.
THERE'S STILL PLENTY OF FIGHT LEFT IN HER--
THWUNT

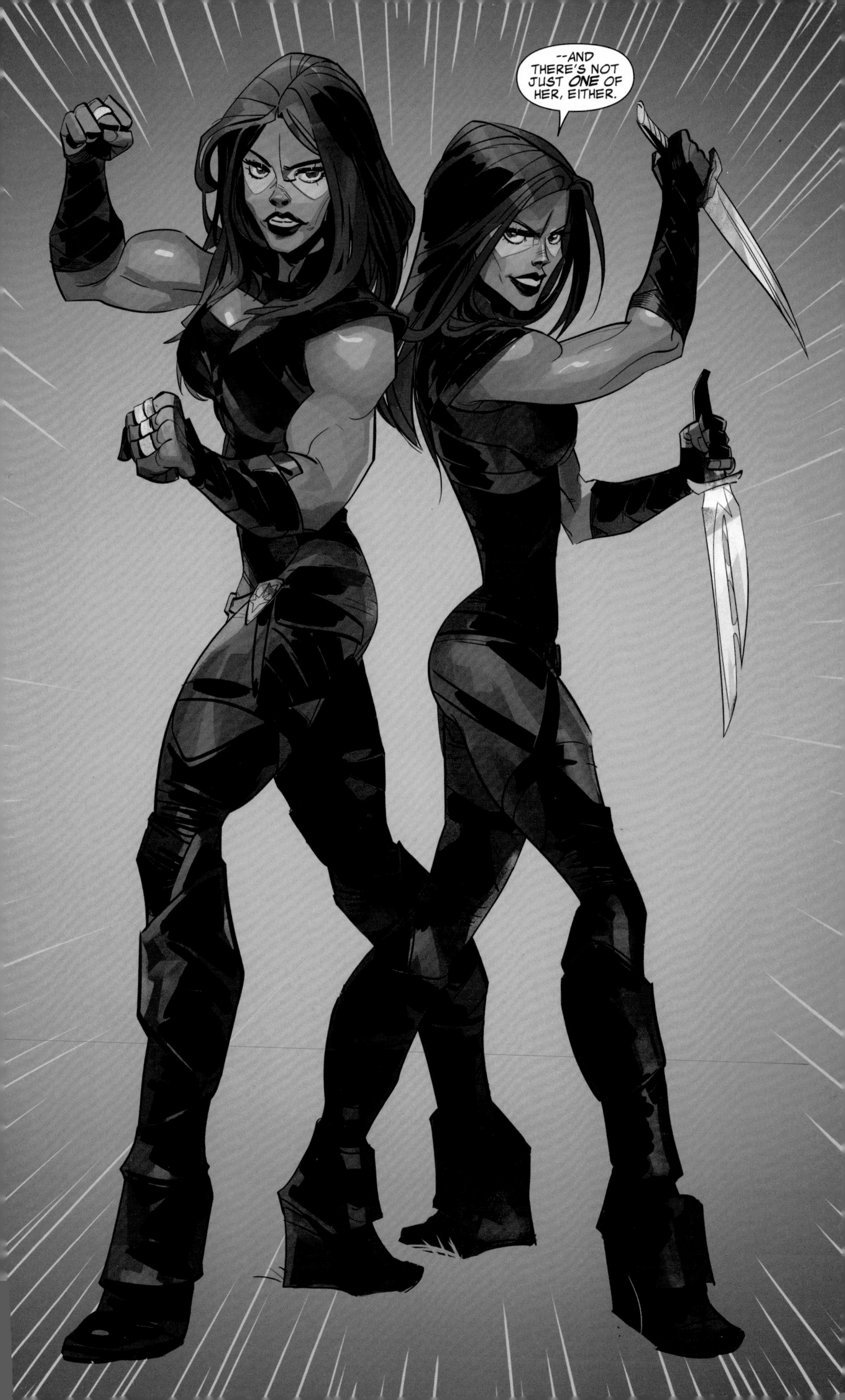
--AND THERE'S NOT JUST ONE OF HER, EITHER.

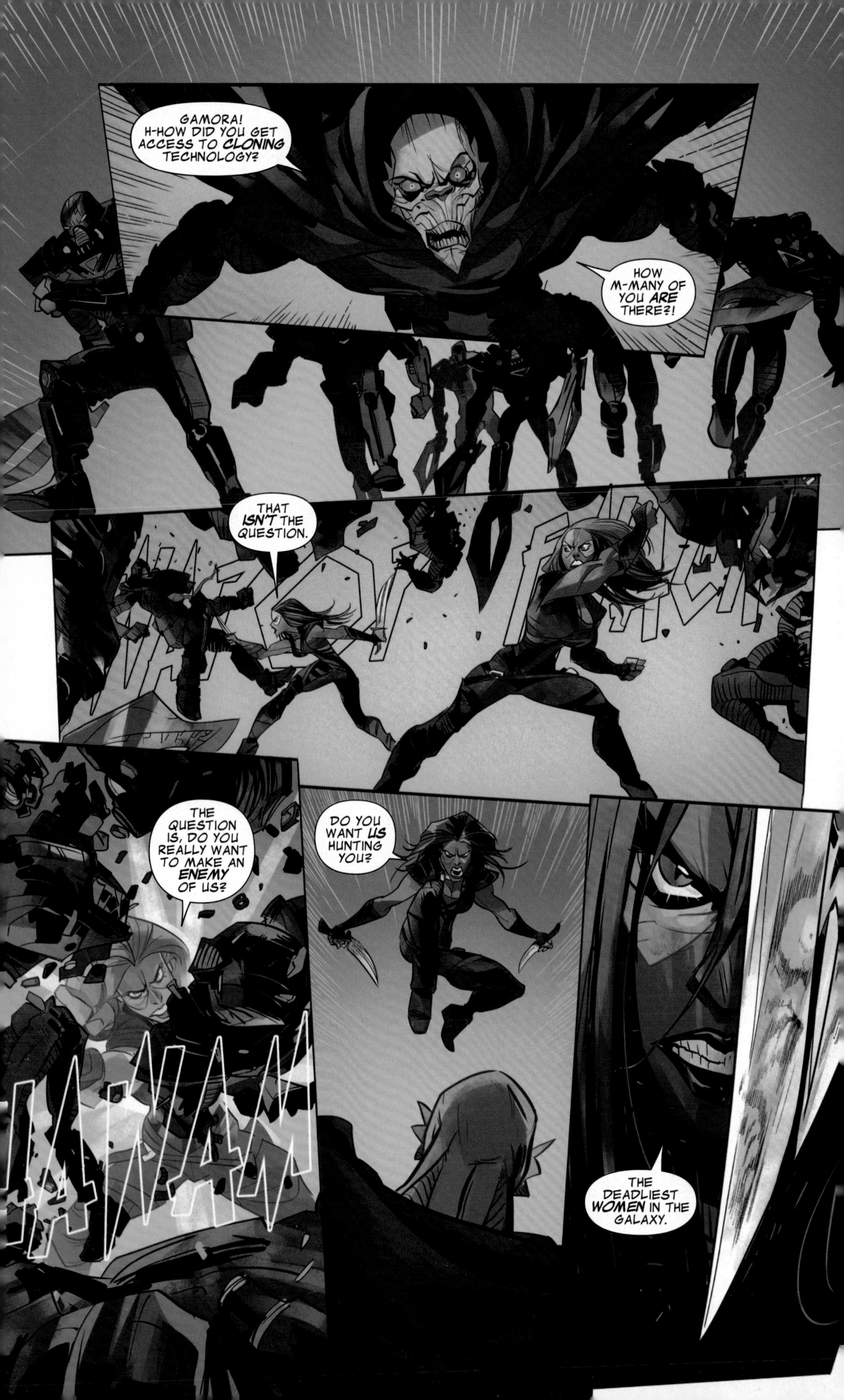
GAMORA! H-HOW DID YOU GET ACCESS TO CLONING TECHNOLOGY?
HOW M-MANY OF YOU ARE THERE?!
THAT ISN'T THE QUESTION.
THE QUESTION IS, DO YOU REALLY WANT TO MAKE AN ENEMY OF US?
DO YOU WANT US HUNTING YOU?
THE DEADLIEST WOMEN IN THE GALAXY.

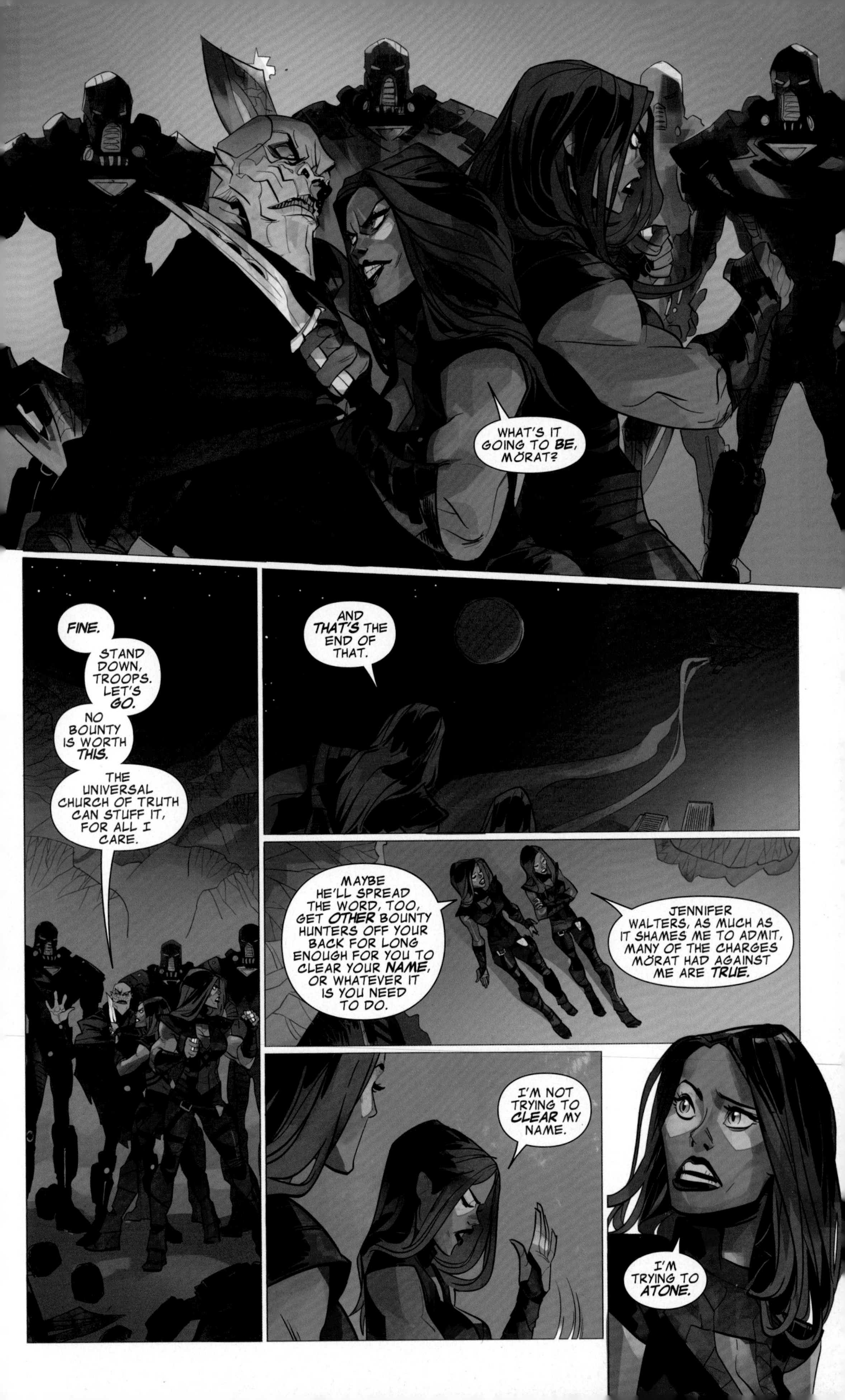
WHAT'S IT GOING TO BE, MÖRAT?
FINE.
STAND DOWN, TROOPS. LET'S GO.
NO BOUNTY IS WORTH THIS.
THE UNIVERSAL CHURCH OF TRUTH CAN STUFF IT, FOR ALL I CARE.
AND THAT'S THE END OF THAT.
MAYBE HE'LL SPREAD THE WORD, TOO, GET OTHER BOUNTY HUNTERS OFF YOUR BACK FOR LONG ENOUGH FOR YOU TO CLEAR YOUR NAME, OR WHATEVER IT IS YOU NEED TO DO.
JENNIFER WALTERS, AS MUCH AS IT SHAMES ME TO ADMIT, MANY OF THE CHARGES MÖRAT HAD AGAINST ME ARE TRUE.
I'M NOT TRYING TO CLEAR MY NAME.
I'M TRYING TO ATONE.

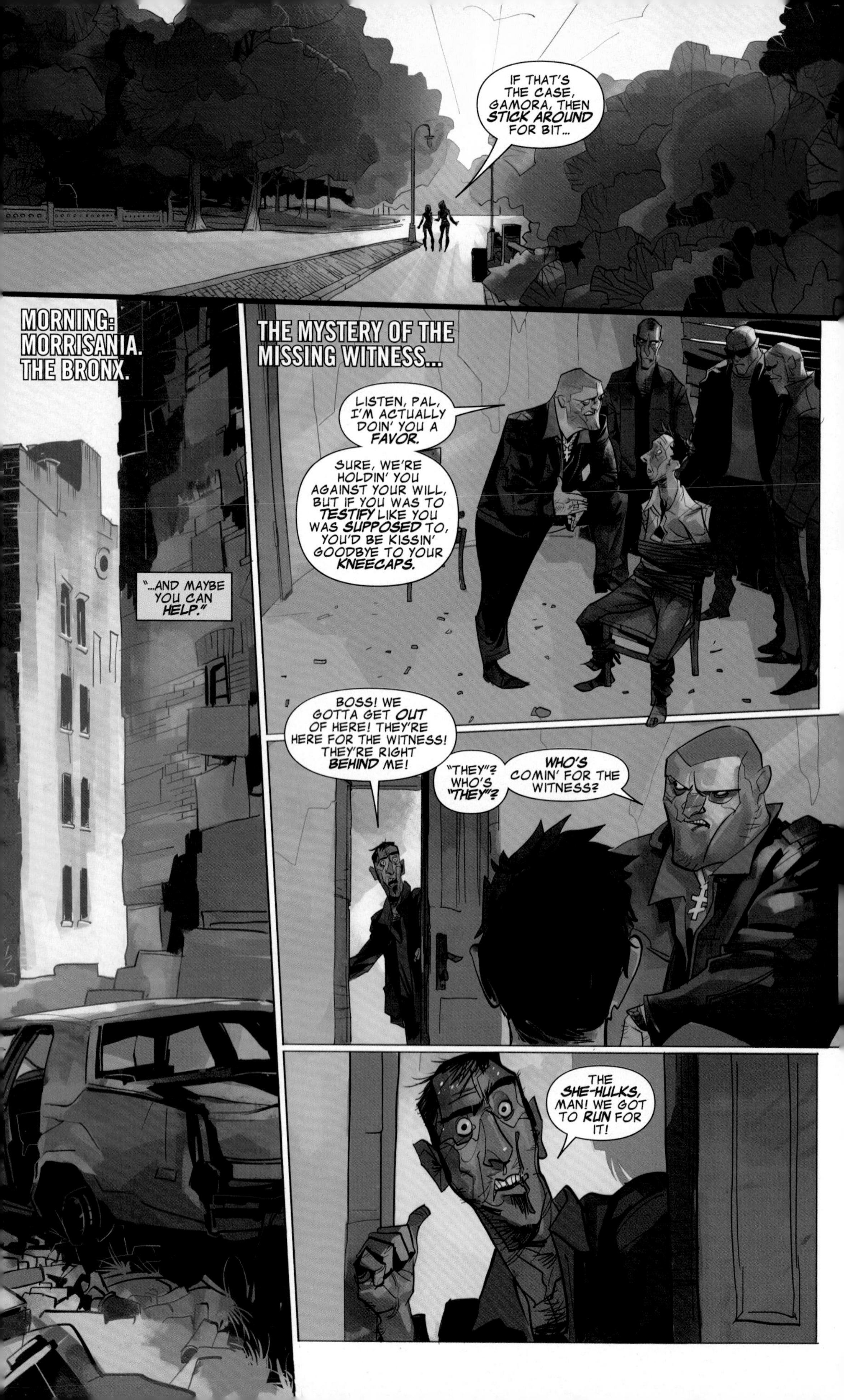
IF THAT'S THE CASE, GAMORA, THEN STICK AROUND FOR BIT...
MORNING: MORRISANIA. THE BRONX.
THE MYSTERY OF THE MISSING WITNESS...
"...AND MAYBE YOU CAN HELP."
LISTEN, PAL, I'M ACTUALLY DOIN' YOU A FAVOR.
SURE, WE'RE HOLDIN' YOU AGAINST YOUR WILL, BUT IF YOU WAS TO TESTIFY LIKE YOU WAS SUPPOSED TO, YOU'D BE KISSIN' GOODBYE TO YOUR KNEECAPS.
BOSS! WE GOTTA GET OUT OF HERE! THEY'RE HERE FOR THE WITNESS! THEY'RE RIGHT BEHIND ME!
"THEY"? WHO'S "THEY"?
WHO'S COMIN' FOR THE WITNESS?
THE SHE-HULKS, MAN! WE GOT TO RUN FOR IT!

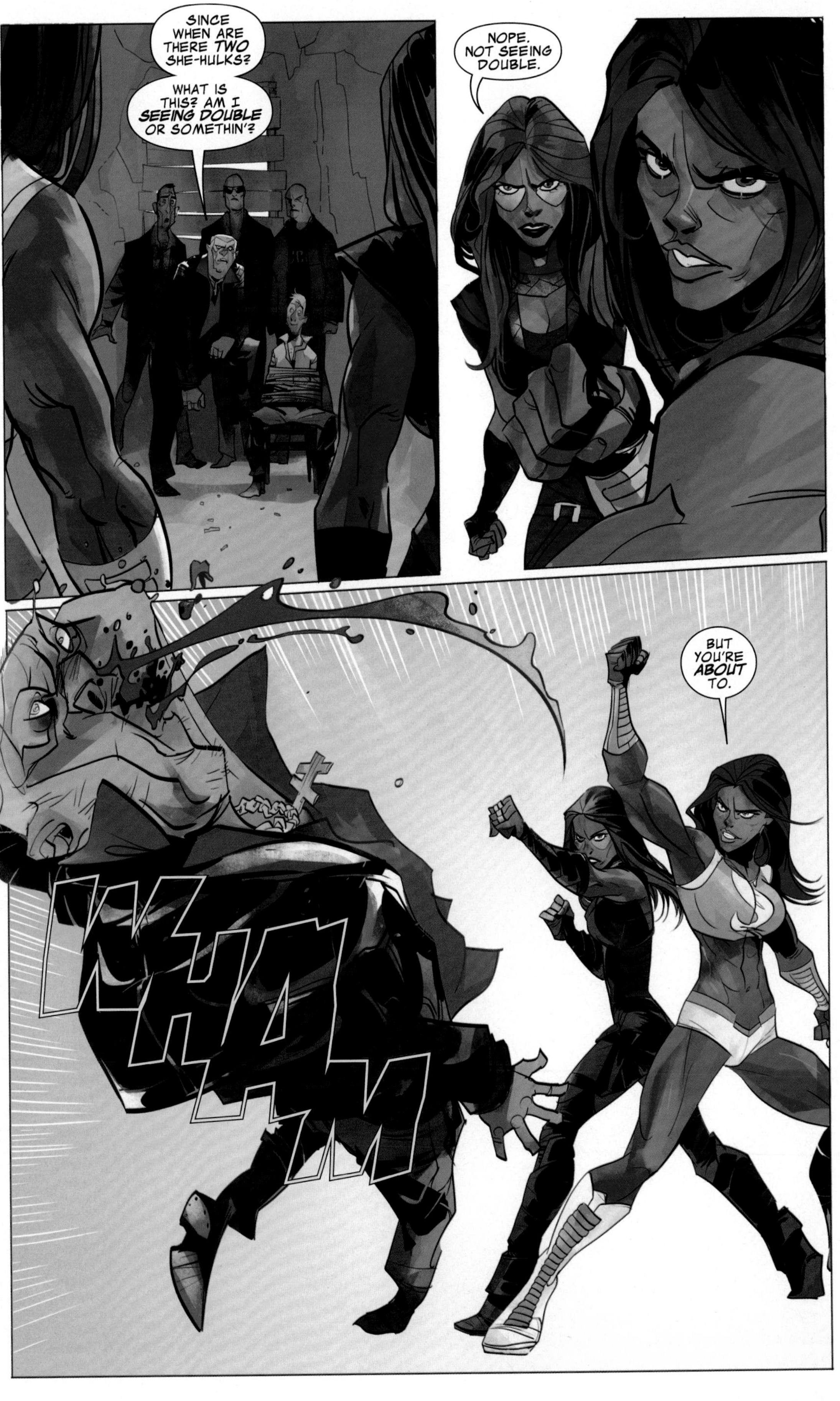
SINCE WHEN ARE THERE TWO SHE-HULKS?
WHAT IS THIS? AM I SEEING DOUBLE OR SOMETHIN'?
NOPE. NOT SEEING DOUBLE.
BUT YOU'RE ABOUT TO.
WHAM

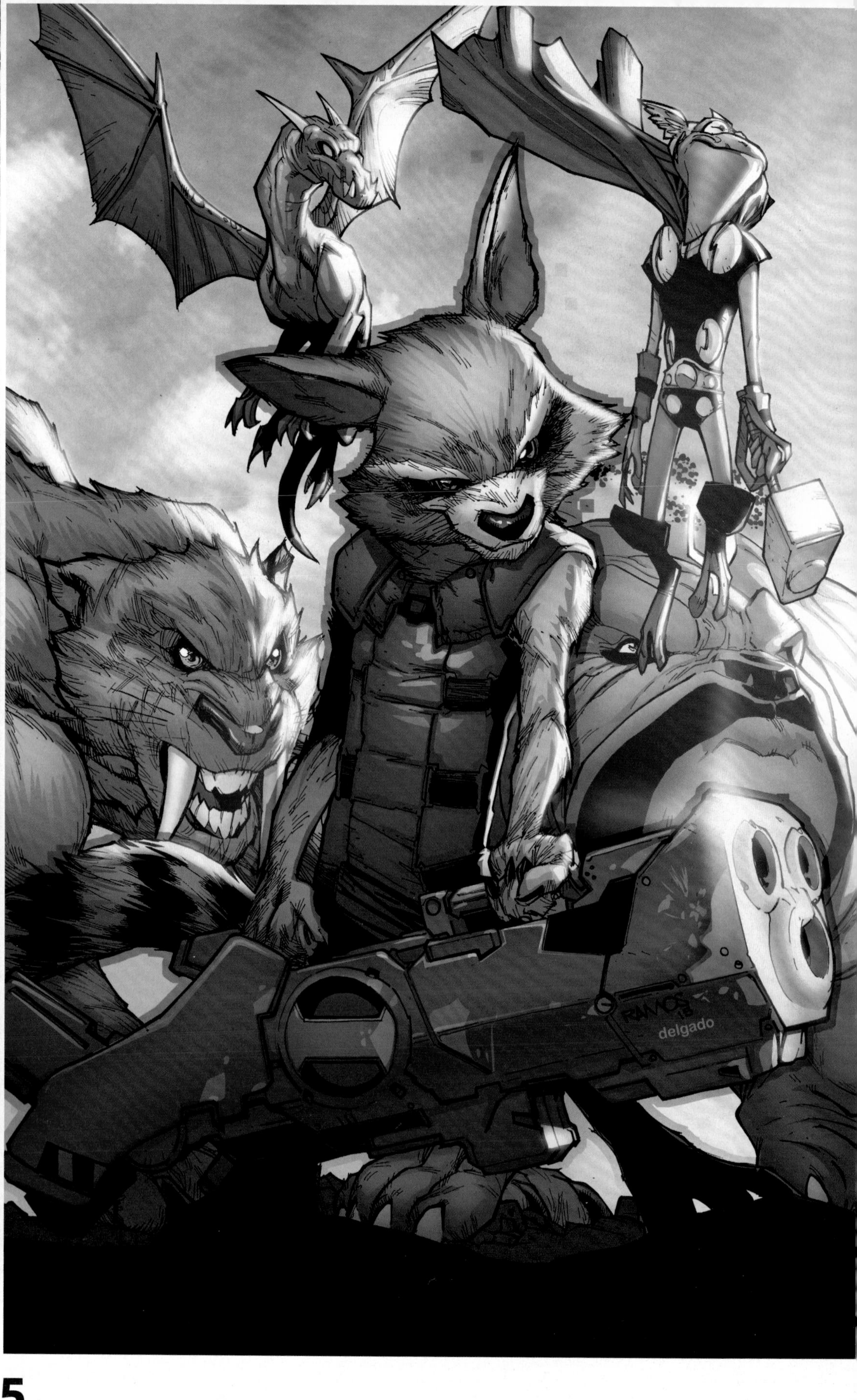
RAMOS 15
delgado

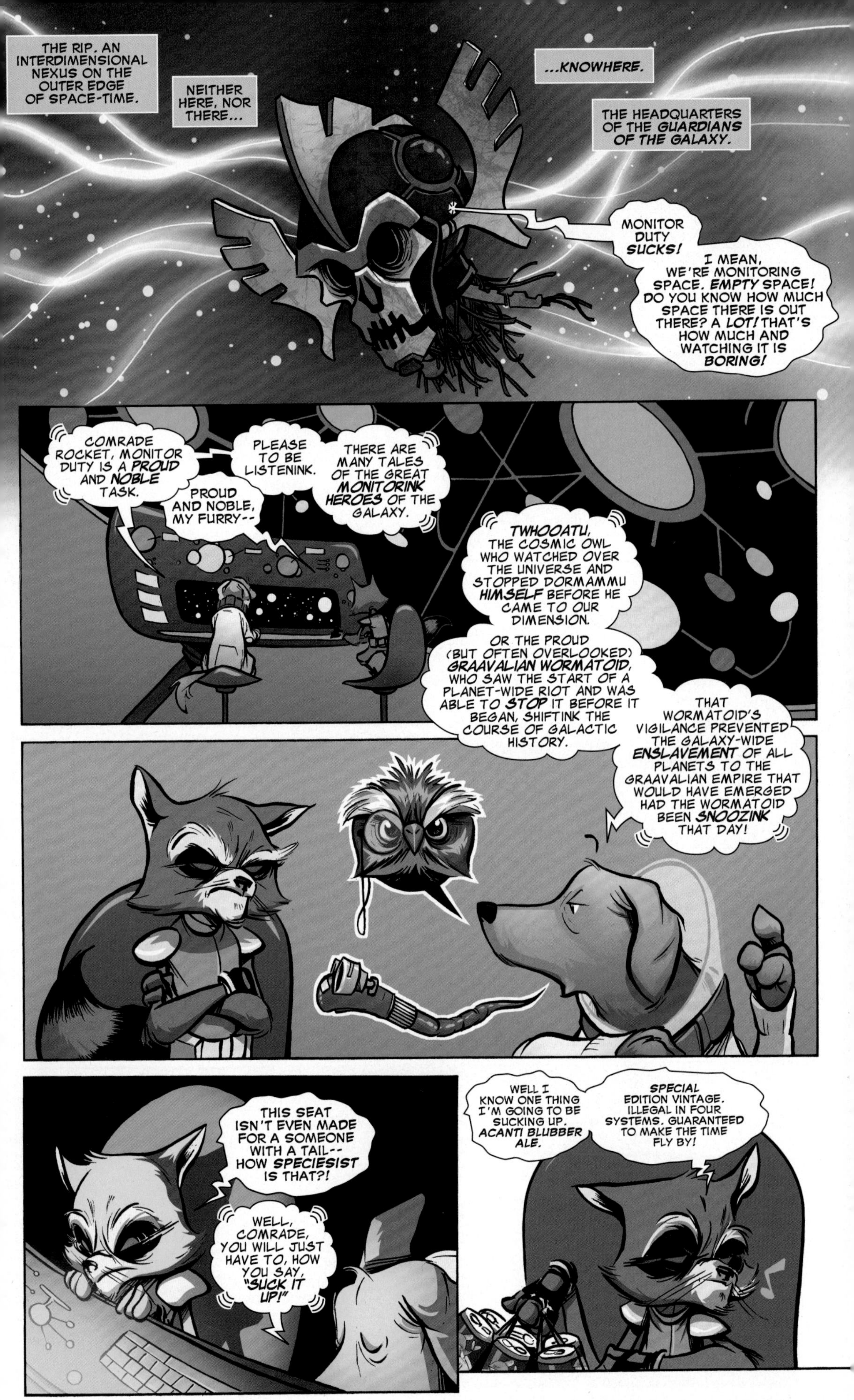
THE RIP. AN INTERDIMENSIONAL NEXUS ON THE OUTER EDGE OF SPACE-TIME.
NEITHER HERE, NOR THERE...
...KNOWHERE.
THE HEADQUARTERS OF THE GUARDIANS OF THE GALAXY.
MONITOR DUTY SUCKS!
I MEAN, WE'RE MONITORING SPACE. EMPTY SPACE! DO YOU KNOW HOW MUCH SPACE THERE IS OUT THERE? A LOT! THAT'S HOW MUCH AND WATCHING IT IS BORING!
COMRADE ROCKET, MONITOR DUTY IS A PROUD AND NOBLE TASK.
PROUD AND NOBLE, MY FURRY--
PLEASE TO BE LISTENINK.
THERE ARE MANY TALES OF THE GREAT MONITORINK HEROES OF THE GALAXY.
TWHOOATU, THE COSMIC OWL WHO WATCHED OVER THE UNIVERSE AND STOPPED DORMAMMU HIMSELF BEFORE HE CAME TO OUR DIMENSION.
OR THE PROUD (BUT OFTEN OVERLOOKED) GRAAVALIAN WORMATOID, WHO SAW THE START OF A PLANET-WIDE RIOT AND WAS ABLE TO STOP IT BEFORE IT BEGAN, SHIFTINK THE COURSE OF GALACTIC HISTORY.
THAT WORMATOID'S VIGILANCE PREVENTED THE GALAXY-WIDE ENSLAVEMENT OF ALL PLANETS TO THE GRAAVALIAN EMPIRE THAT WOULD HAVE EMERGED HAD THE WORMATOID BEEN SNOOZINK THAT DAY!
THIS SEAT ISN'T EVEN MADE FOR A SOMEONE WITH A TAIL-- HOW SPECIESIST IS THAT?!
WELL, COMRADE, YOU WILL JUST HAVE TO, HOW YOU SAY, "SUCK IT UP!"
WELL I KNOW ONE THING I'M GOING TO BE SUCKING UP. ACANTI BLUBBER ALE.
SPECIAL EDITION VINTAGE. ILLEGAL IN FOUR SYSTEMS. GUARANTEED TO MAKE THE TIME FLY BY!

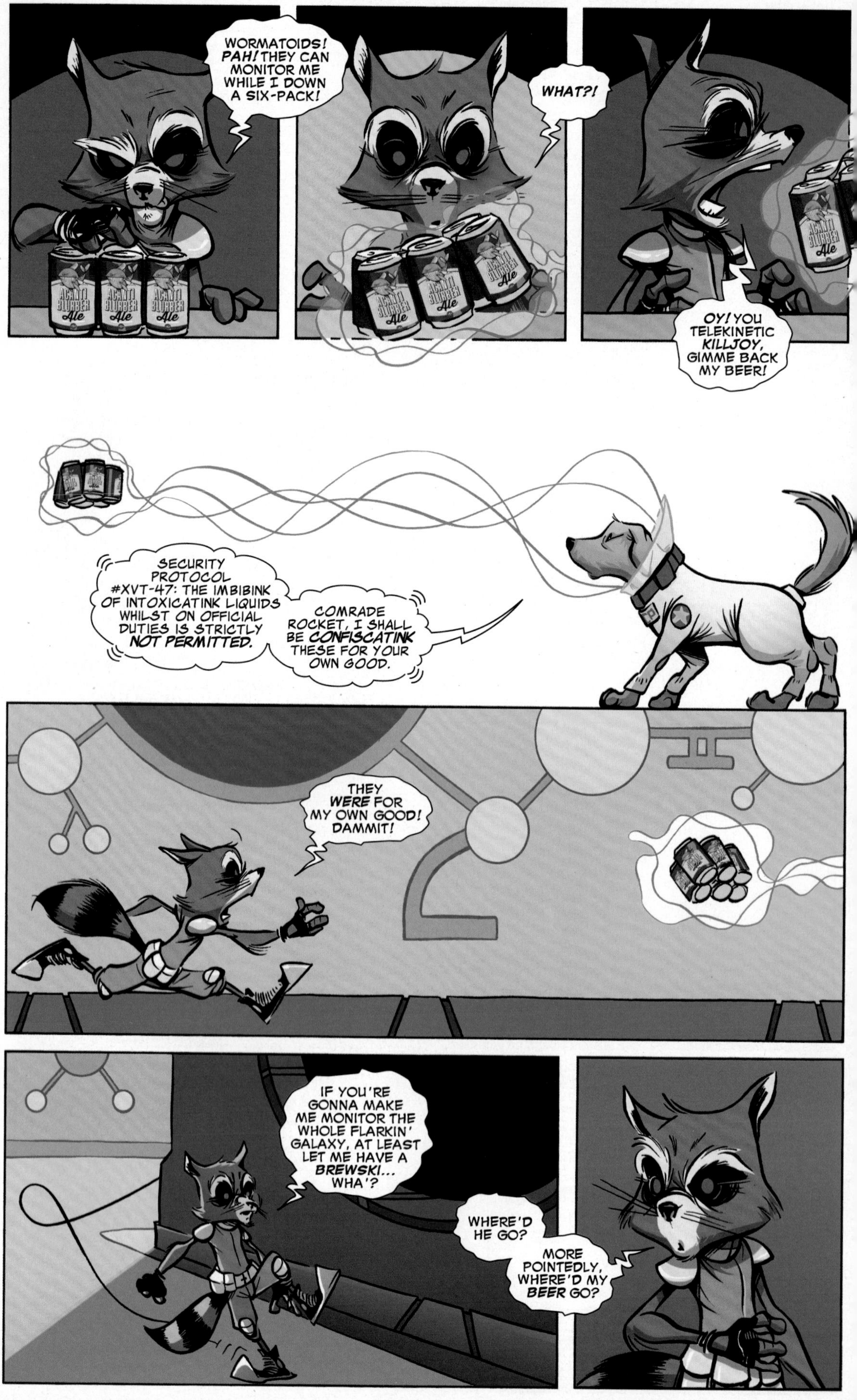

WORMATOIDS! PAH! THEY CAN MONITOR ME WHILE I DOWN A SIX-PACK!
WHAT?!
OY! YOU TELEKINETIC KILLJOY, GIMME BACK MY BEER!
SECURITY PROTOCOL #XVT-47: THE IMBIBINK OF INTOXICATINK LIQUIDS WHILST ON OFFICIAL DUTIES IS STRICTLY NOT PERMITTED.
COMRADE ROCKET, I SHALL BE CONFISCATINK THESE FOR YOUR OWN GOOD.
THEY WERE FOR MY OWN GOOD! DAMMIT!
IF YOU'RE GONNA MAKE ME MONITOR THE WHOLE FLARKIN' GALAXY, AT LEAST LET ME HAVE A BREWSKI... WHA'?
WHERE'D HE GO?
MORE POINTEDLY, WHERE'D MY BEER GO?

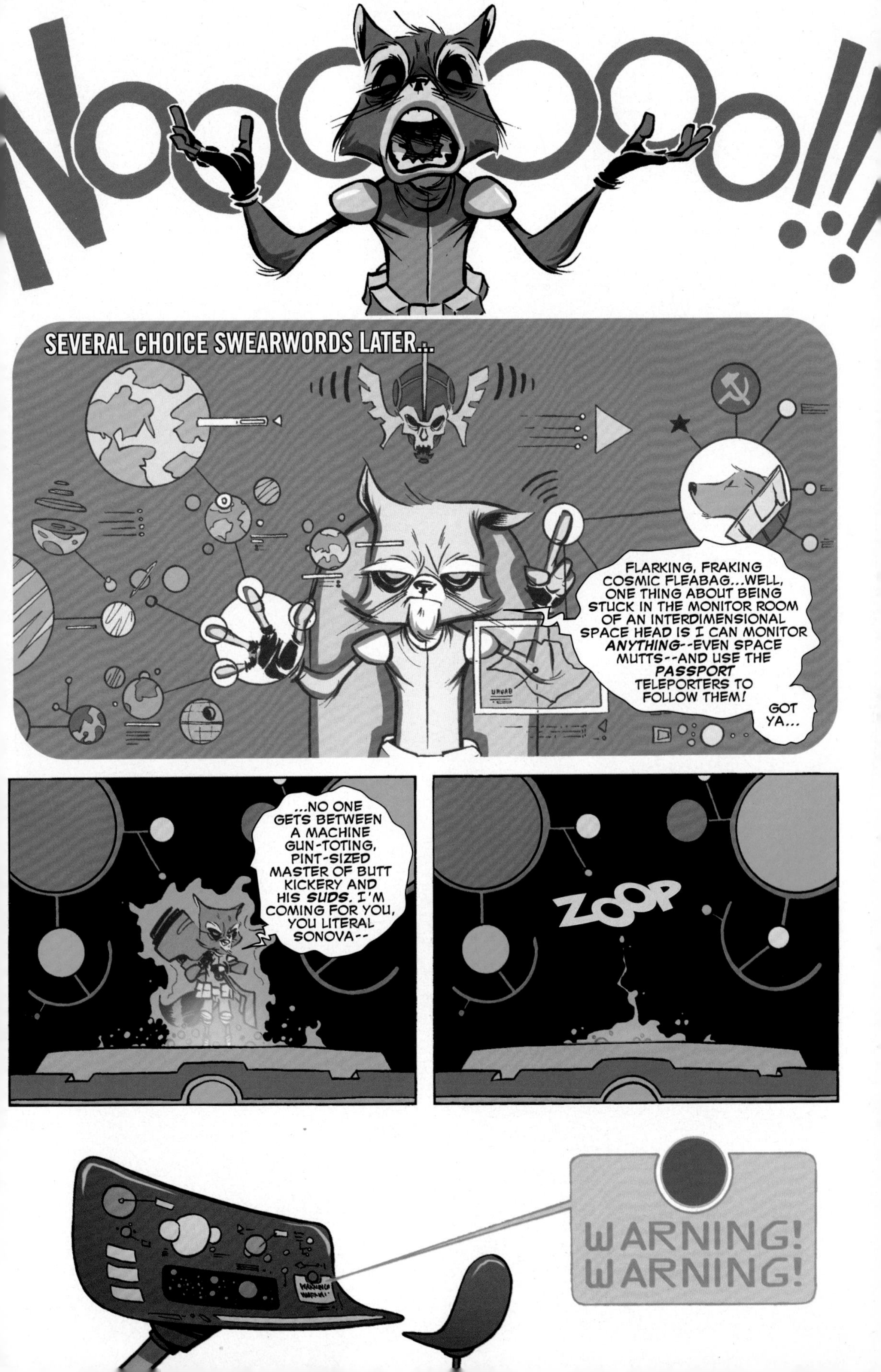
NOOOOOOO!!!
SEVERAL CHOICE SWEARWORDS LATER...
FLARKING, FRAKING COSMIC FLEABAG...WELL, ONE THING ABOUT BEING STUCK IN THE MONITOR ROOM OF AN INTERDIMENSIONAL SPACE HEAD IS I CAN MONITOR ANYTHING--EVEN SPACE MUTTS--AND USE THE PASSPORT TELEPORTERS TO FOLLOW THEM!
GOT YA...
...NO ONE GETS BETWEEN A MACHINE GUN-TOTING, PINT-SIZED MASTER OF BUTT KICKERY AND HIS SUDS. I'M COMING FOR YOU, YOU LITERAL SONOVA--
ZOOP
WARNING! WARNING!

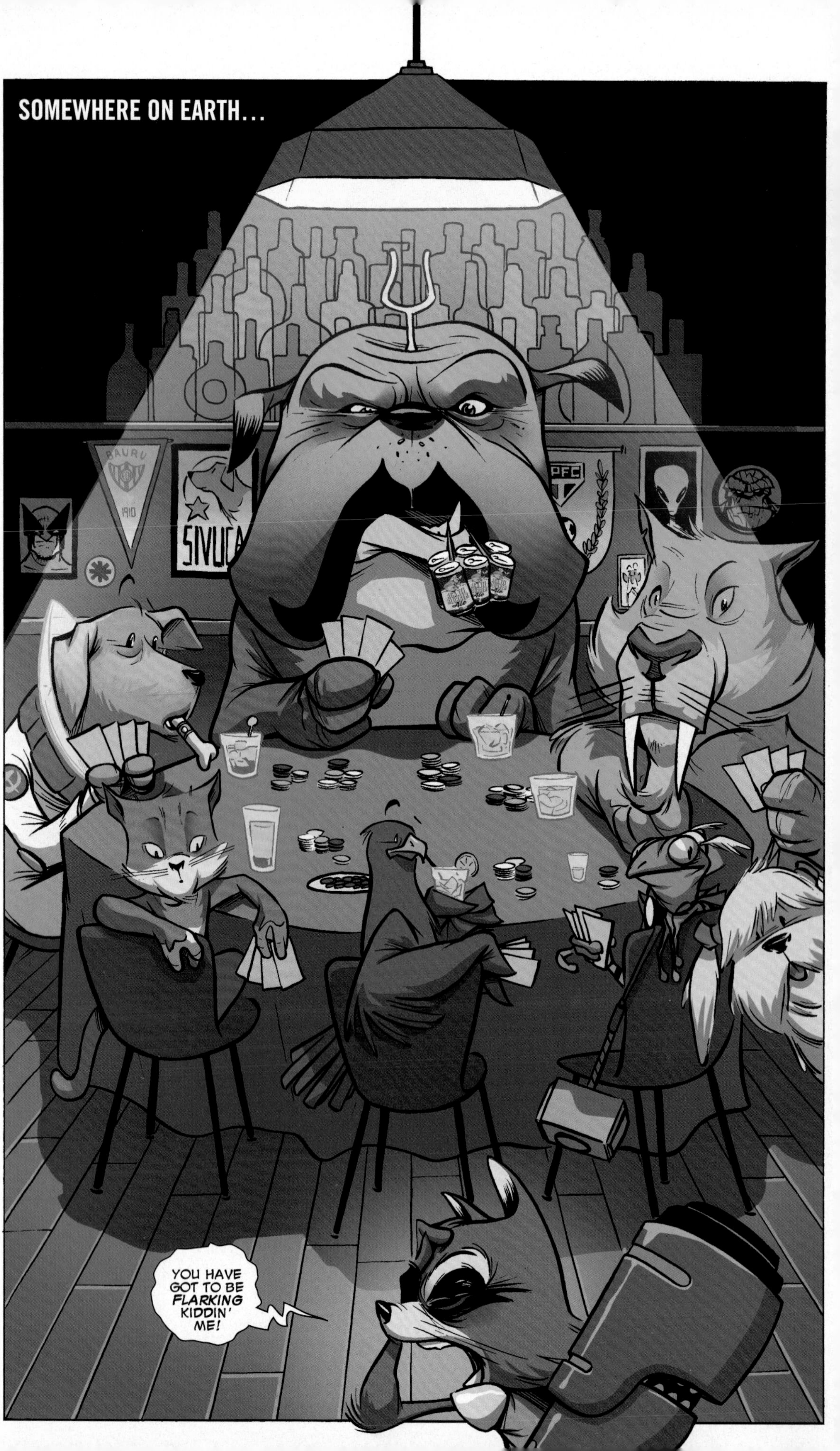
SOMEWHERE ON EARTH...
BAURU
1910
SIVUCA
SPFC
YOU HAVE GOT TO BE FLARKING KIDDIN' ME!

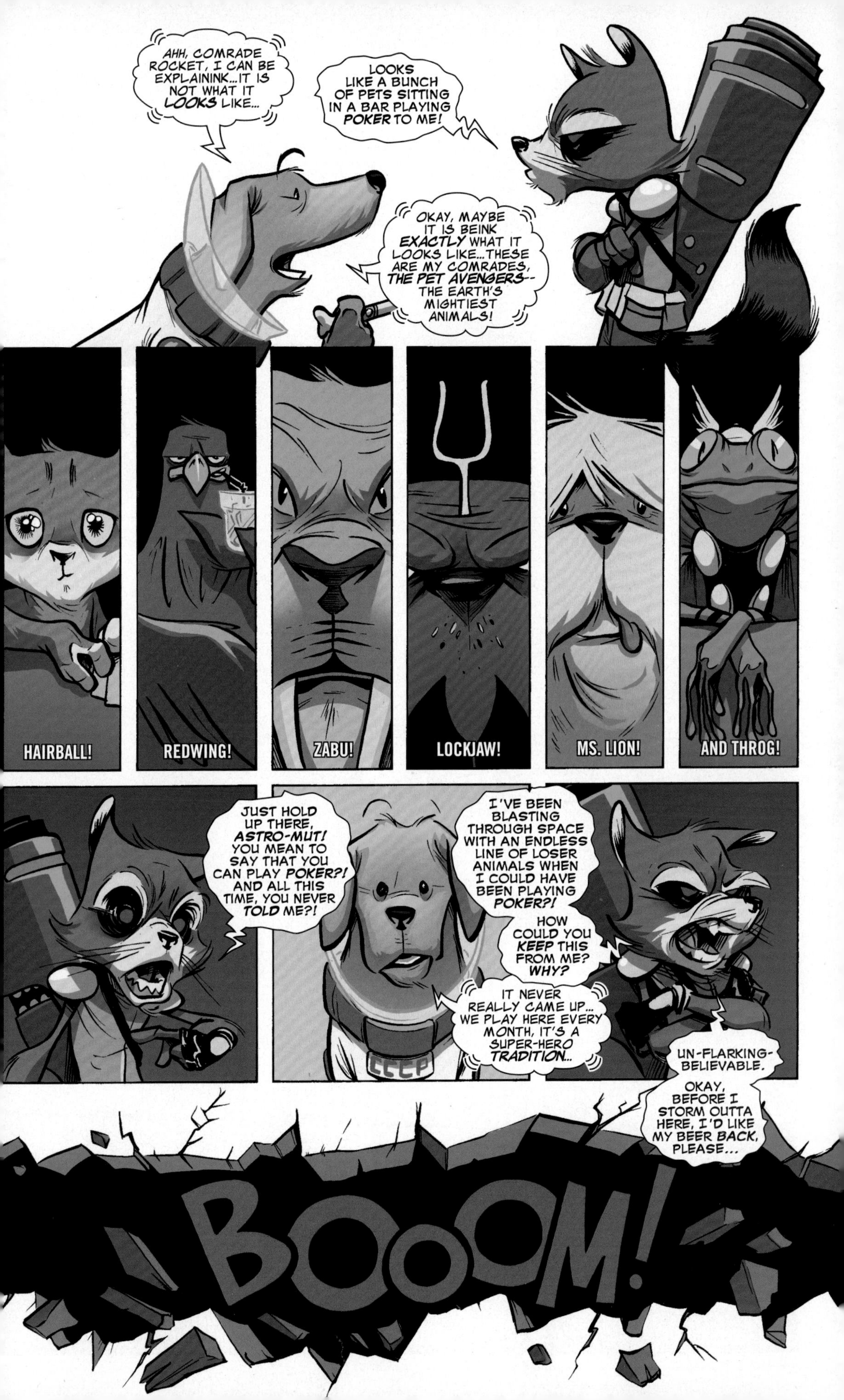
AHH, COMRADE ROCKET, I CAN BE EXPLAININK...IT IS NOT WHAT IT LOOKS LIKE...
LOOKS LIKE A BUNCH OF PETS SITTING IN A BAR PLAYING POKER TO ME!
OKAY, MAYBE IT IS BEINK EXACTLY WHAT IT LOOKS LIKE...THESE ARE MY COMRADES, THE PET AVENGERS-- THE EARTH'S MIGHTIEST ANIMALS!
HAIRBALL!
REDWING!
ZABU!
LOCKJAW!
MS. LION!
AND THROG!
JUST HOLD UP THERE, ASTRO-MUT! YOU MEAN TO SAY THAT YOU CAN PLAY POKER?! AND ALL THIS TIME, YOU NEVER TOLD ME?!
I'VE BEEN BLASTING THROUGH SPACE WITH AN ENDLESS LINE OF LOSER ANIMALS WHEN I COULD HAVE BEEN PLAYING POKER?!
HOW COULD YOU KEEP THIS FROM ME? WHY?
IT NEVER REALLY CAME UP... WE PLAY HERE EVERY MONTH, IT'S A SUPER-HERO TRADITION...
CCCP
UN-FLARKING-BELIEVABLE.
OKAY, BEFORE I STORM OUTTA HERE, I'D LIKE MY BEER BACK, PLEASE...
BOOOM!

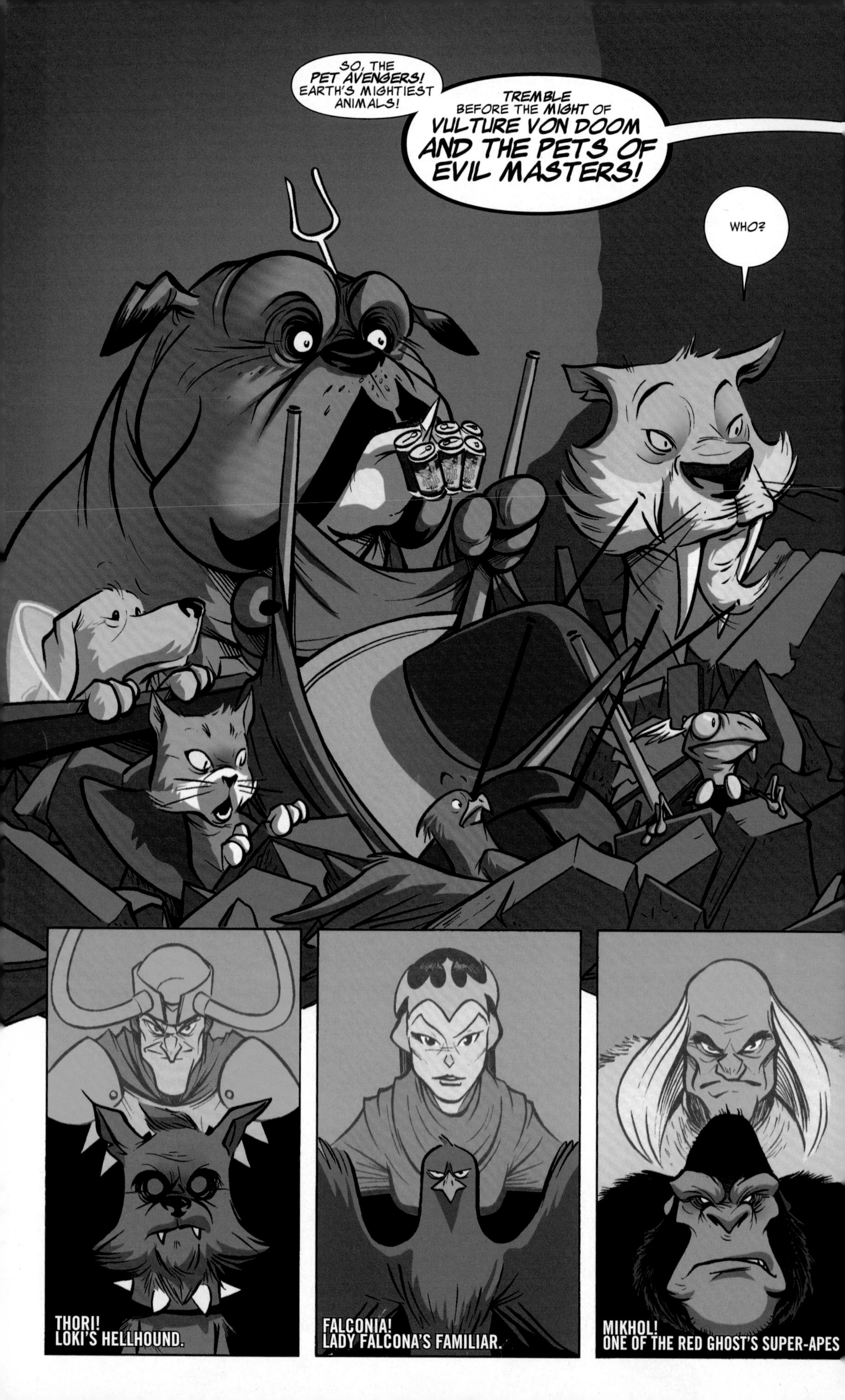
SO, THE PET AVENGERS! EARTH'S MIGHTIEST ANIMALS!
TREMBLE BEFORE THE MIGHT OF VULTURE VON DOOM AND THE PETS OF EVIL MASTERS!
WHO?
THORI! LOKI'S HELLHOUND.
FALCONIA! LADY FALCONA'S FAMILIAR.
MIKHOL! ONE OF THE RED GHOST'S SUPER-APES

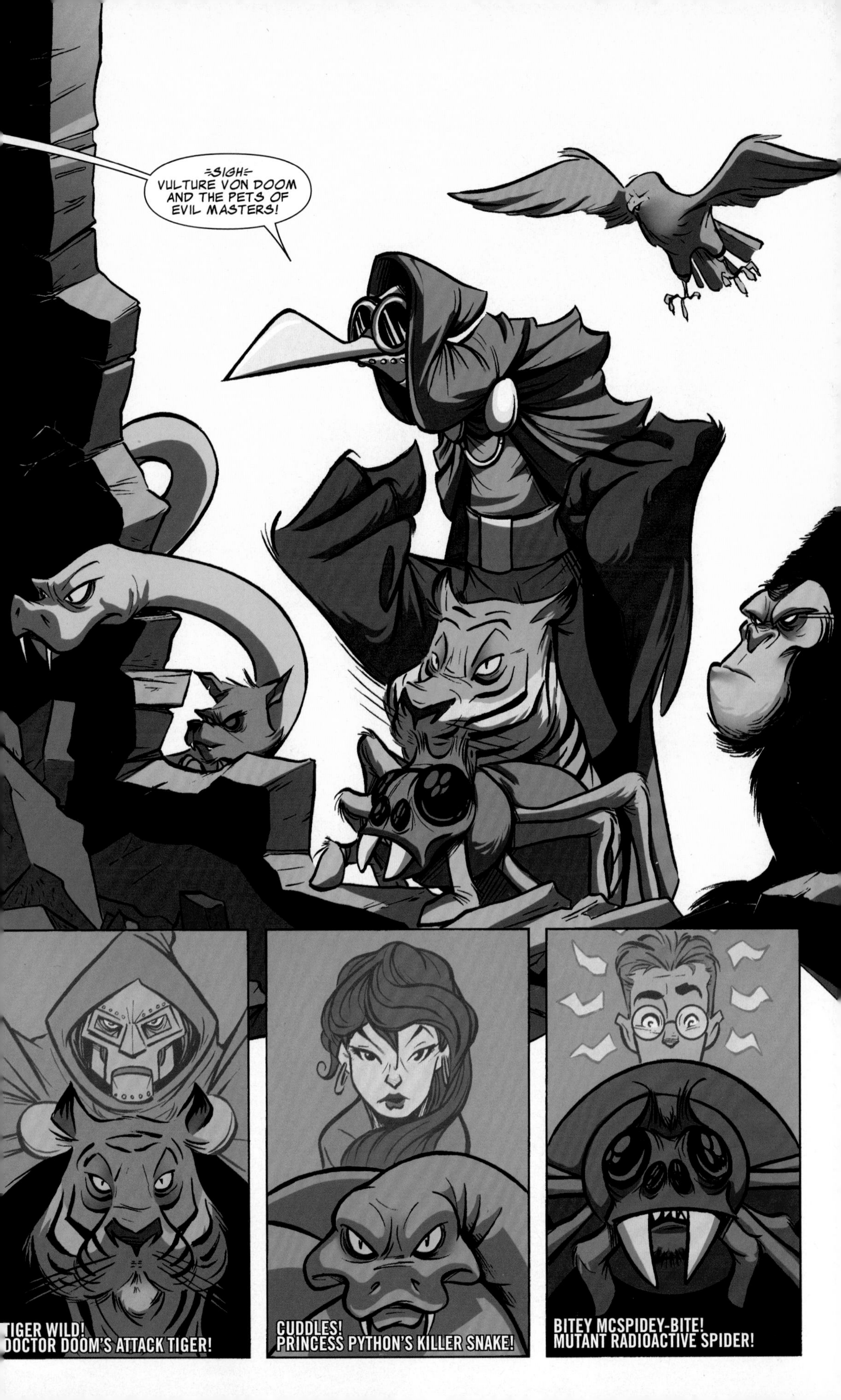

=SIGH=
VULTURE VON DOOM
AND THE PETS OF
EVIL MASTERS!
TIGER WILD!
DOCTOR DOOM'S ATTACK TIGER!
CUDDLES!
PRINCESS PYTHON'S KILLER SNAKE!
BITEY MCSPIDEY-BITE!
MUTANT RADIOACTIVE SPIDER!

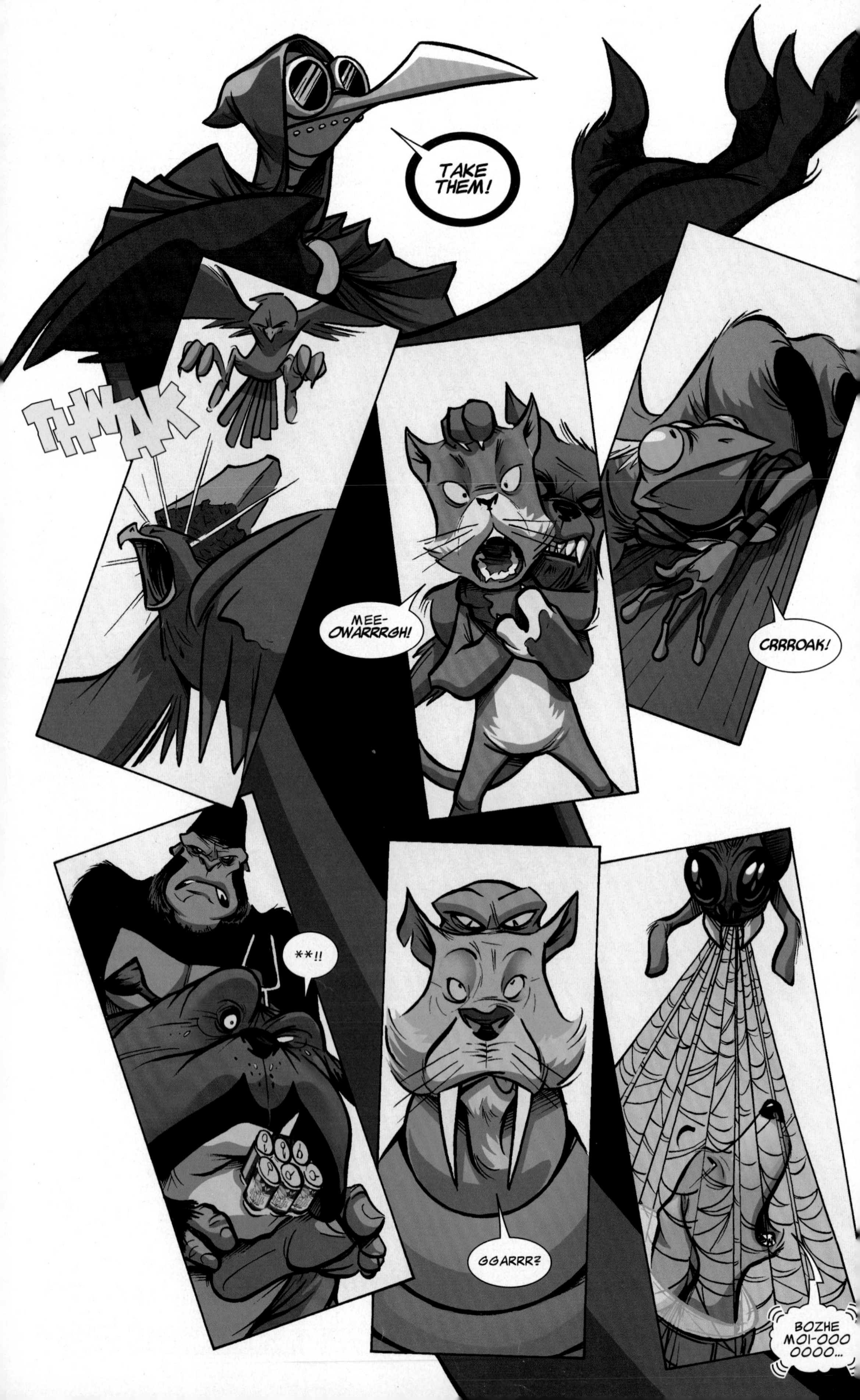
TAKE THEM!
THWAK
MEE-OWARRRGH!
CRRROAK!
**!!
GGARRR?
BOZHE MOI-OOO OOOO...

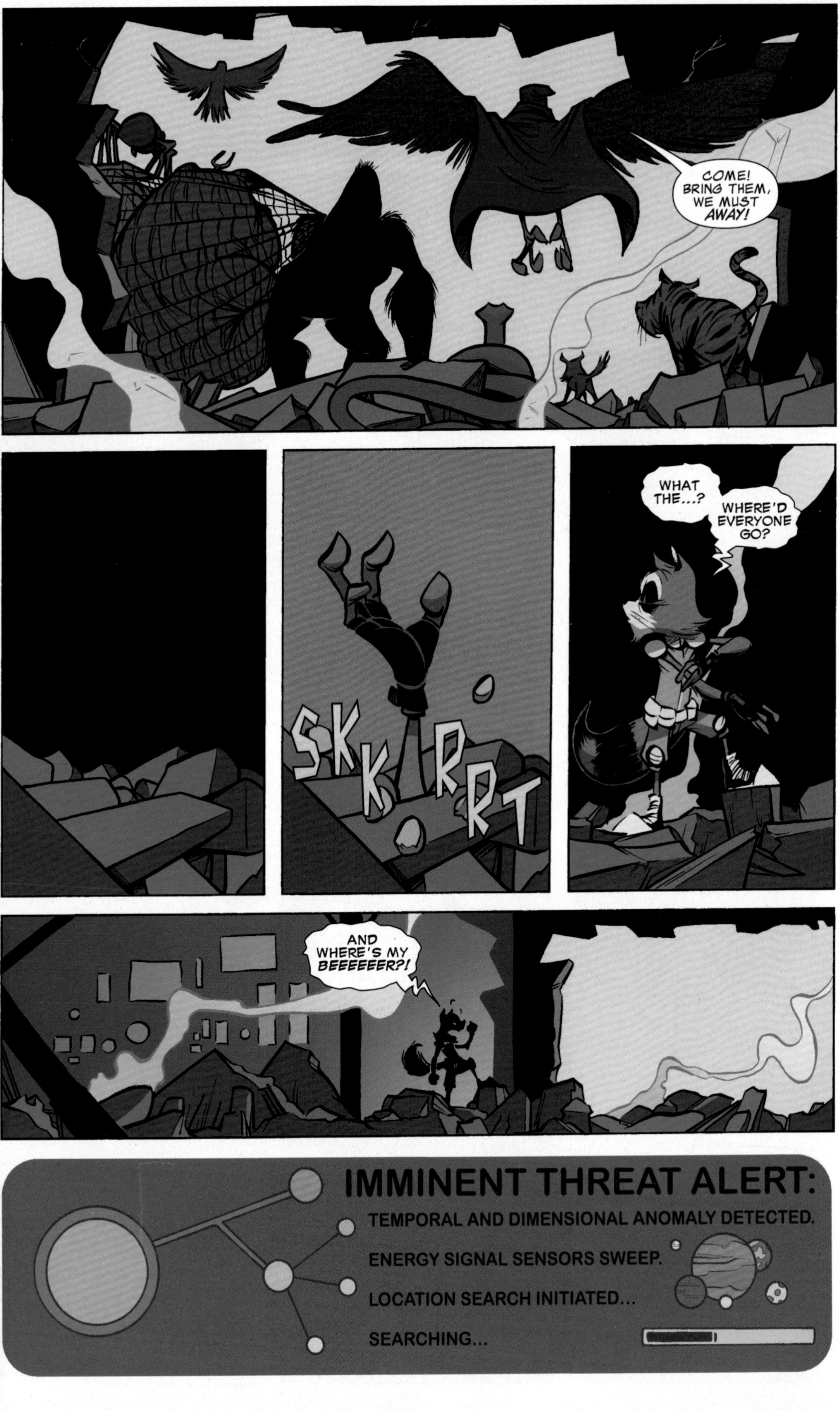
COME! BRING THEM, WE MUST *AWAY!*
SKKRRT
WHAT THE...?
WHERE'D EVERYONE GO?
AND WHERE'S MY *BEEEEEER?!*
IMMINENT THREAT ALERT:
TEMPORAL AND DIMENSIONAL ANOMALY DETECTED.
ENERGY SIGNAL SENSORS SWEEP.
LOCATION SEARCH INITIATED...
SEARCHING...

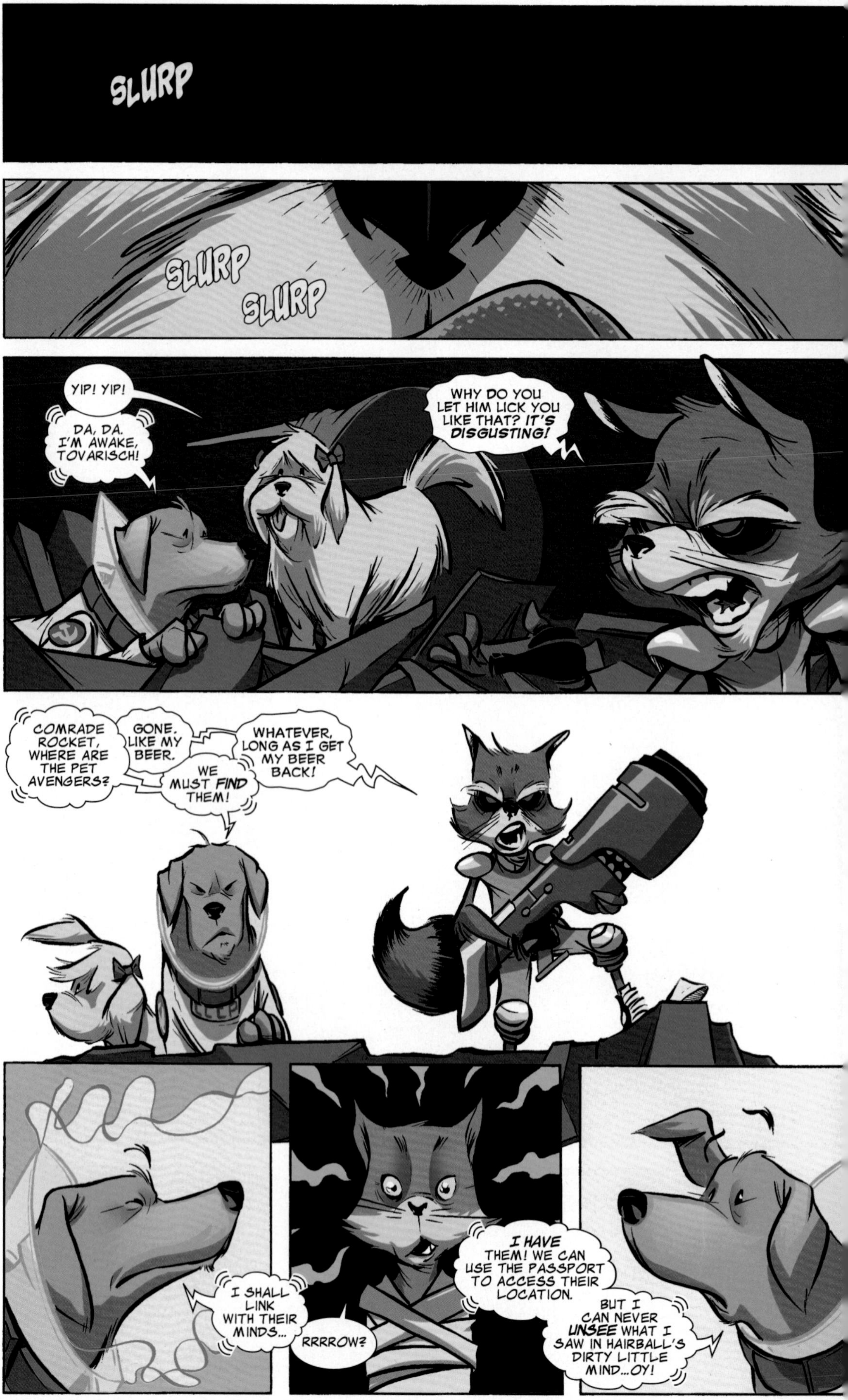
SLURP
SLURP
SLURP
YIP! YIP!
DA, DA. I'M AWAKE, TOVARISCH!
WHY DO YOU LET HIM LICK YOU LIKE THAT? IT'S DISGUSTING!
COMRADE ROCKET, WHERE ARE THE PET AVENGERS?
GONE. LIKE MY BEER.
WE MUST FIND THEM!
WHATEVER, LONG AS I GET MY BEER BACK!
I SHALL LINK WITH THEIR MINDS...
RRRROW?
I HAVE THEM! WE CAN USE THE PASSPORT TO ACCESS THEIR LOCATION.
BUT I CAN NEVER UNSEE WHAT I SAW IN HAIRBALL'S DIRTY LITTLE MIND...OY!

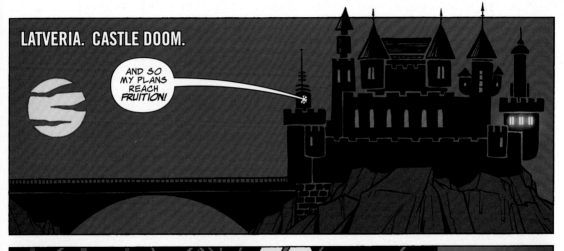

LATVERIA. CASTLE DOOM.

AND SO MY PLANS REACH *FRUITION!*

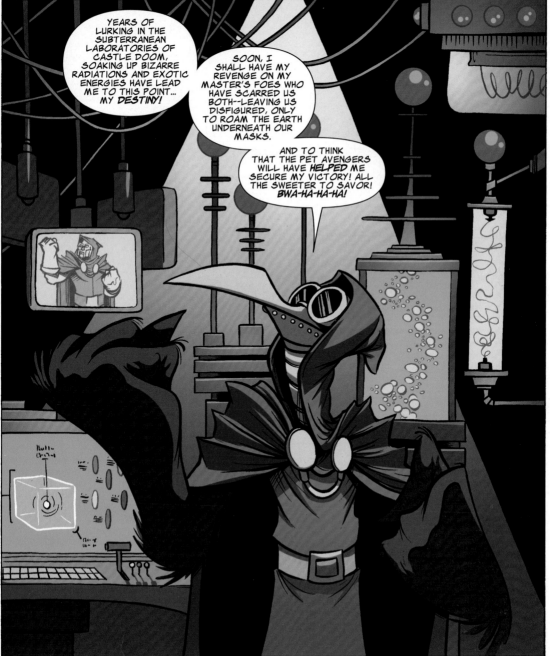

YEARS OF LURKING IN THE SUBTERRANEAN LABORATORIES OF CASTLE DOOM, SOAKING UP BIZARRE RADIATIONS AND EXOTIC ENERGIES HAVE LEAD ME TO THIS POINT... MY *DESTINY!*

SOON, I SHALL HAVE MY REVENGE ON MY MASTER'S FOES WHO HAVE SCARRED US BOTH--LEAVING US DISFIGURED, ONLY TO ROAM THE EARTH UNDERNEATH OUR MASKS.

AND TO THINK THAT THE PET AVENGERS WILL HAVE *HELPED* ME SECURE MY VICTORY! ALL THE SWEETER TO SAVOR! *BWA-HA-HA-HA!*

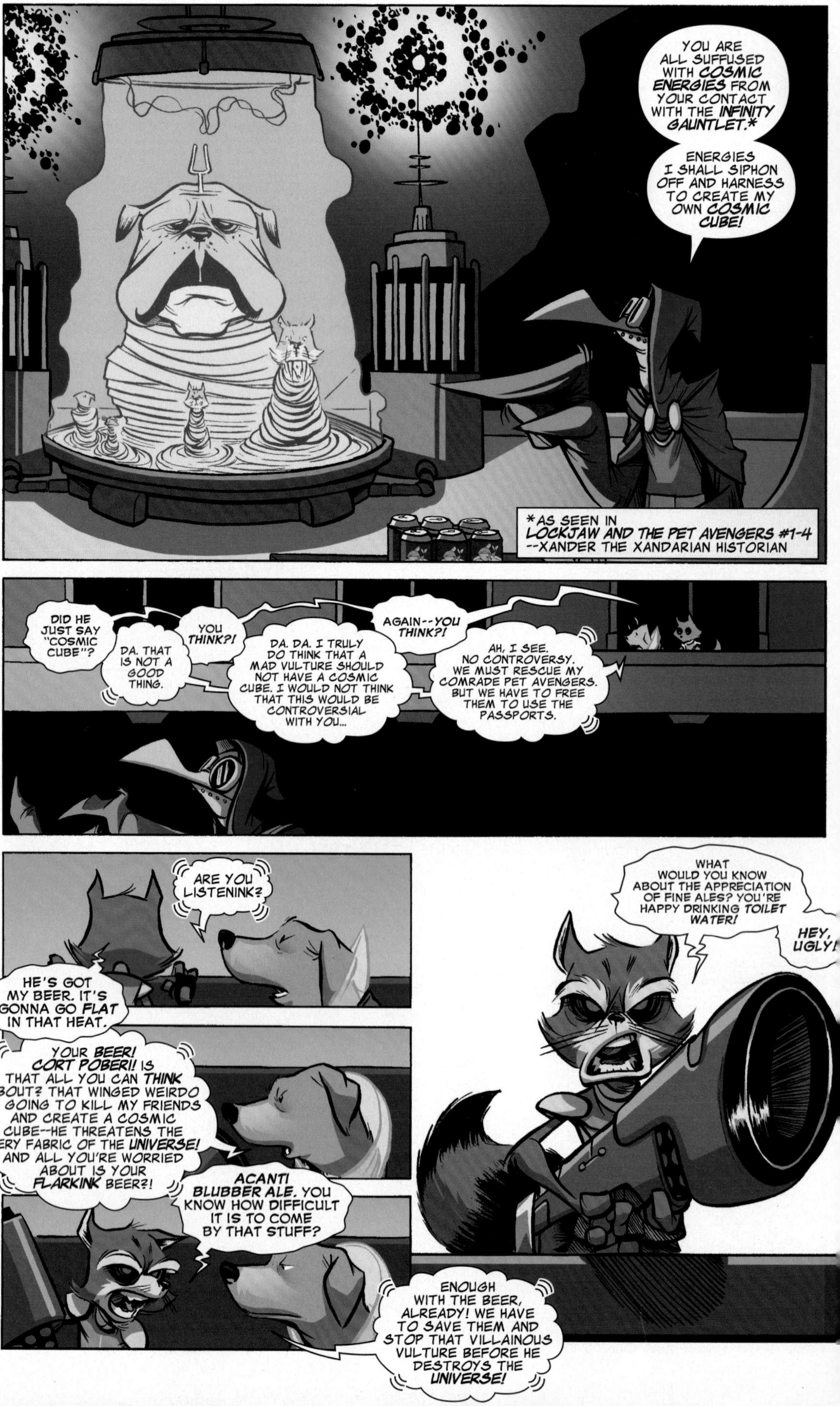
YOU ARE ALL SUFFUSED WITH COSMIC ENERGIES FROM YOUR CONTACT WITH THE INFINITY GAUNTLET.*
ENERGIES I SHALL SIPHON OFF AND HARNESS TO CREATE MY OWN COSMIC CUBE!
*AS SEEN IN LOCKJAW AND THE PET AVENGERS #1-4 --XANDER THE XANDARIAN HISTORIAN
DID HE JUST SAY "COSMIC CUBE"?
DA. THAT IS NOT A GOOD THING.
YOU THINK?!
DA. DA. I TRULY DO THINK THAT A MAD VULTURE SHOULD NOT HAVE A COSMIC CUBE. I WOULD NOT THINK THAT THIS WOULD BE CONTROVERSIAL WITH YOU...
AGAIN--YOU THINK?!
AH, I SEE. NO CONTROVERSY. WE MUST RESCUE MY COMRADE PET AVENGERS. BUT WE HAVE TO FREE THEM TO USE THE PASSPORTS.
ARE YOU LISTENINK?
HE'S GOT MY BEER. IT'S GONNA GO FLAT IN THAT HEAT.
YOUR BEER! CORT POBER!! IS THAT ALL YOU CAN THINK ABOUT? THAT WINGED WEIRDO IS GOING TO KILL MY FRIENDS AND CREATE A COSMIC CUBE--HE THREATENS THE VERY FABRIC OF THE UNIVERSE! AND ALL YOU'RE WORRIED ABOUT IS YOUR FLARKINK BEER?!
ACANTI BLUBBER ALE. YOU KNOW HOW DIFFICULT IT IS TO COME BY THAT STUFF?
ENOUGH WITH THE BEER, ALREADY! WE HAVE TO SAVE THEM AND STOP THAT VILLAINOUS VULTURE BEFORE HE DESTROYS THE UNIVERSE!
WHAT WOULD YOU KNOW ABOUT THE APPRECIATION OF FINE ALES? YOU'RE HAPPY DRINKING TOILET WATER!
HEY, UGLY!

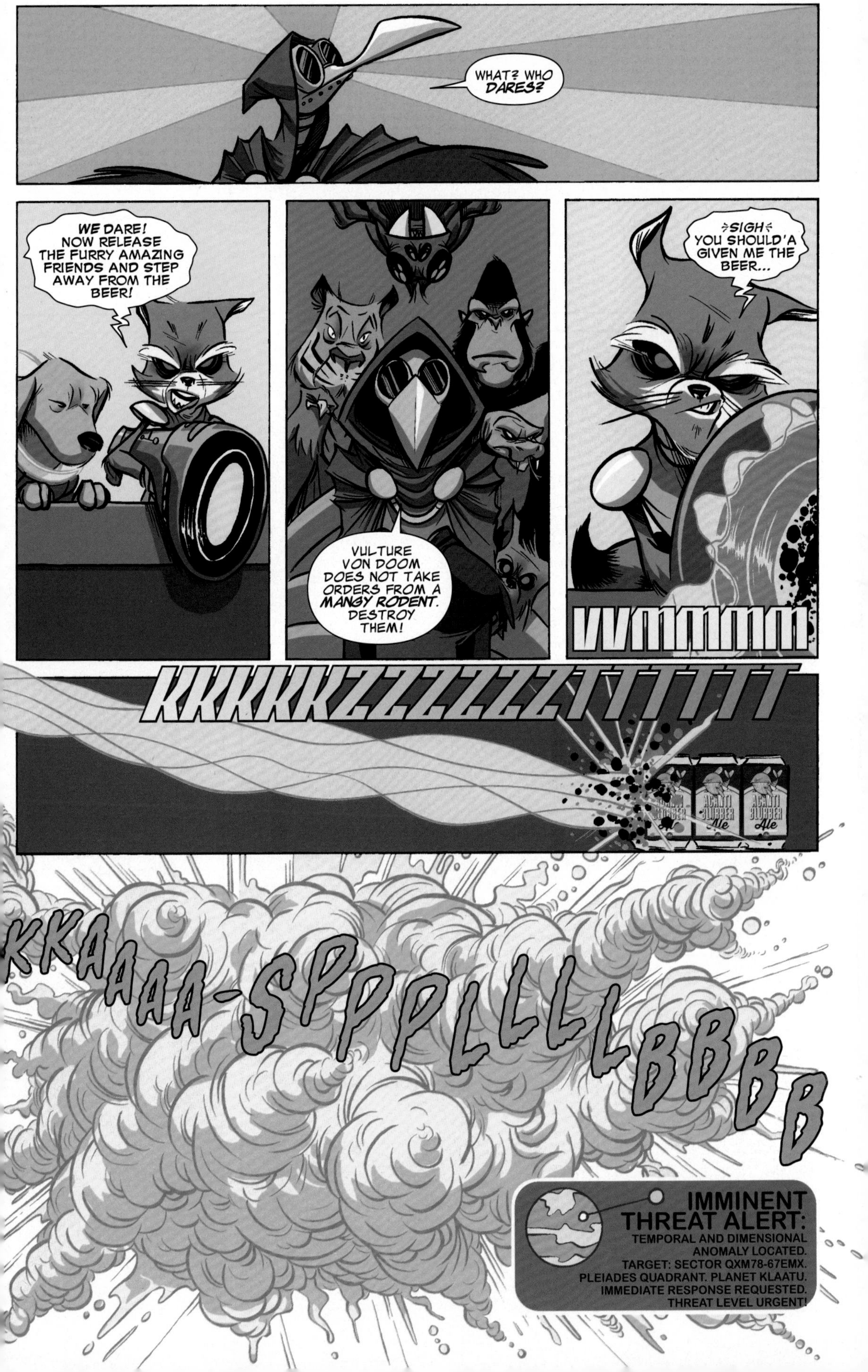
WHAT? WHO DARES?
WE DARE! NOW RELEASE THE FURRY AMAZING FRIENDS AND STEP AWAY FROM THE BEER!
VULTURE VON DOOM DOES NOT TAKE ORDERS FROM A MANGY RODENT. DESTROY THEM!
SIGH YOU SHOULD'A GIVEN ME THE BEER...
VVMMMMM
KKKKKZZZZZZZTTTTTT
ACANTI BLUBBER Ale
KKAAAAA-SPPPLLLLLBBBBB
IMMINENT THREAT ALERT:
TEMPORAL AND DIMENSIONAL ANOMALY LOCATED.
TARGET: SECTOR QXM78-67EMX.
PLEIADES QUADRANT. PLANET KLAATU.
IMMEDIATE RESPONSE REQUESTED.
THREAT LEVEL URGENT!

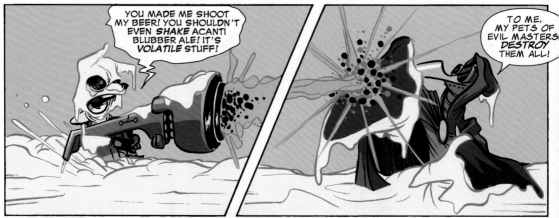

YOU MADE ME SHOOT MY BEER! YOU SHOULDN'T EVEN *SHAKE* ACANTI BLUBBER ALE! IT'S *VOLATILE* STUFF!

TO ME, MY PETS OF EVIL MASTERS *DESTROY* THEM ALL!

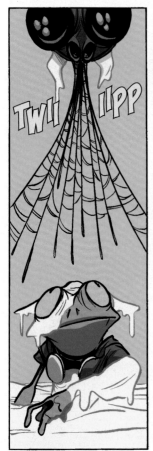

TWIIIPP

KA-ZZZ ZZ ACK

YELP!

THUUB

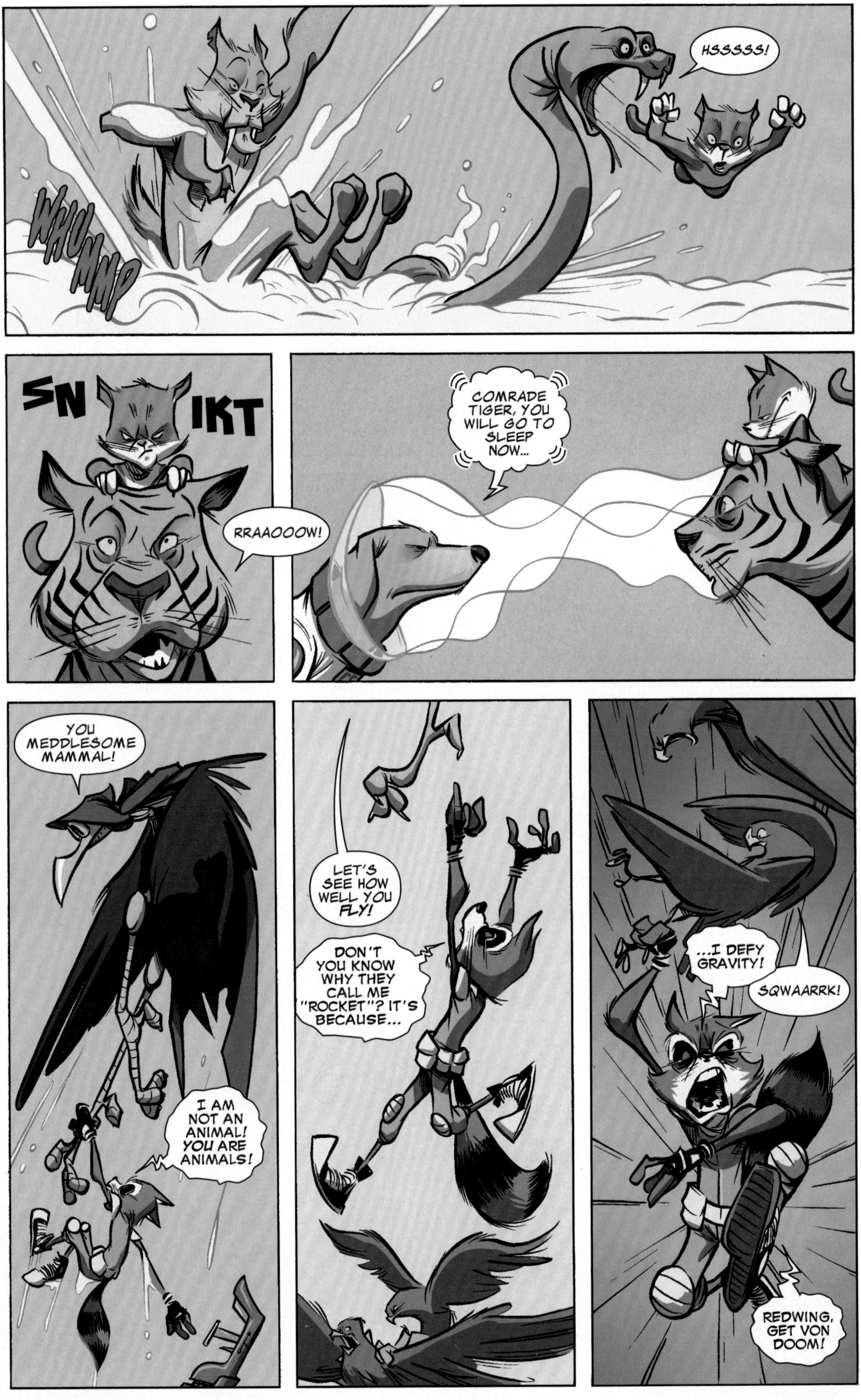
WHUMMP
HSSSSSS!
SN IKT
RRAAOOOW!
COMRADE TIGER, YOU WILL GO TO SLEEP NOW...
YOU MEDDLESOME MAMMAL!
I AM NOT AN ANIMAL! YOU ARE ANIMALS!
LET'S SEE HOW WELL YOU FLY!
DON'T YOU KNOW WHY THEY CALL ME "ROCKET"? IT'S BECAUSE...
...I DEFY GRAVITY!
SQWAARRK!
REDWING, GET VON DOOM!

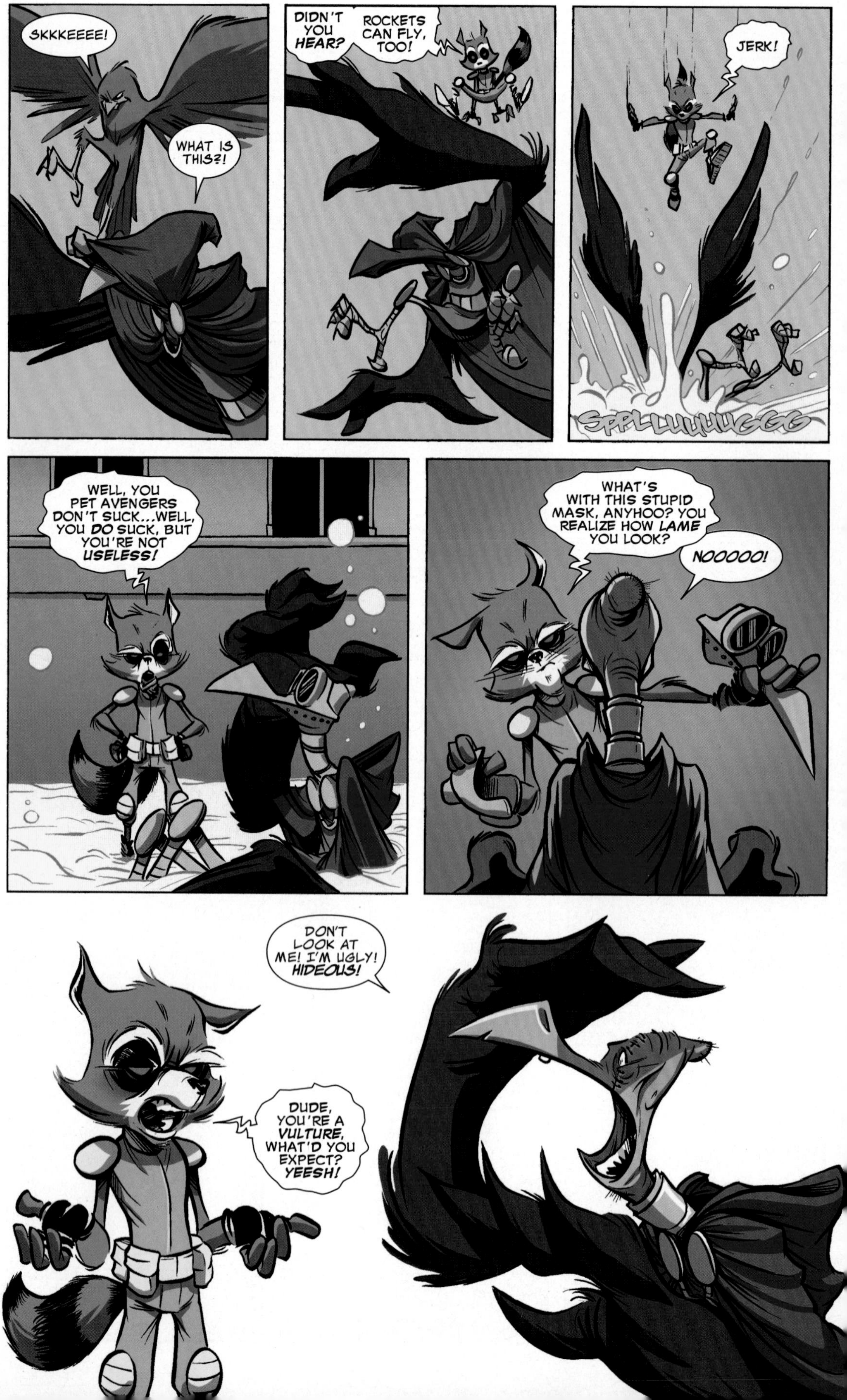
SKKKEEEE!
WHAT IS THIS?!
DIDN'T YOU HEAR?
ROCKETS CAN FLY, TOO!
JERK!
SPPLLUUUUGGG
WELL, YOU PET AVENGERS DON'T SUCK...WELL, YOU DO SUCK, BUT YOU'RE NOT USELESS!
WHAT'S WITH THIS STUPID MASK, ANYHOO? YOU REALIZE HOW LAME YOU LOOK?
NOOOOO!
DON'T LOOK AT ME! I'M UGLY! HIDEOUS!
DUDE, YOU'RE A VULTURE, WHAT'D YOU EXPECT? YEESH!

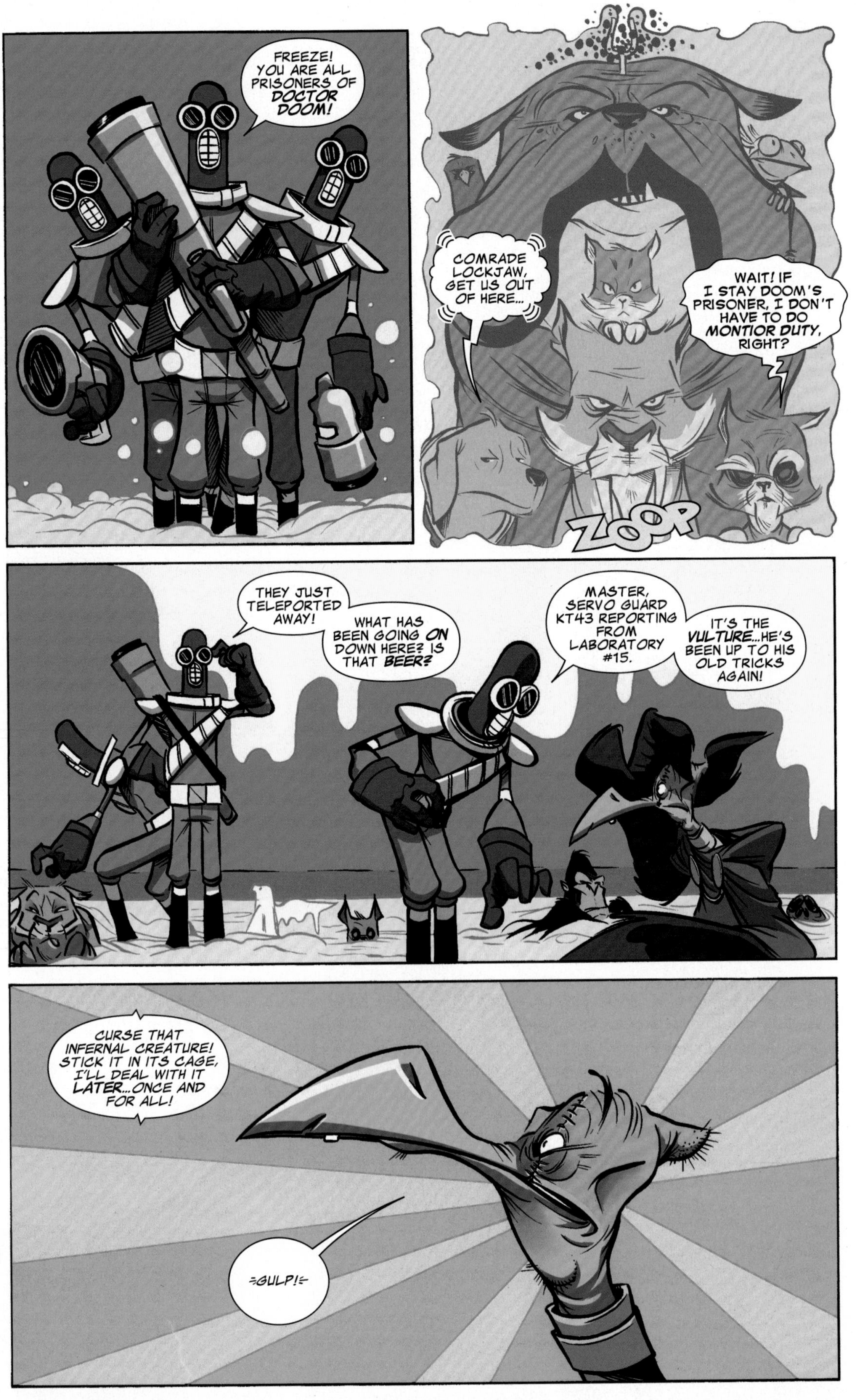
FREEZE! YOU ARE ALL PRISONERS OF DOCTOR DOOM!
COMRADE LOCKJAW, GET US OUT OF HERE...
WAIT! IF I STAY DOOM'S PRISONER, I DON'T HAVE TO DO MONTIOR DUTY, RIGHT?
ZOOP
THEY JUST TELEPORTED AWAY!
WHAT HAS BEEN GOING ON DOWN HERE? IS THAT BEER?
MASTER, SERVO GUARD KT43 REPORTING FROM LABORATORY #15.
IT'S THE VULTURE...HE'S BEEN UP TO HIS OLD TRICKS AGAIN!
CURSE THAT INFERNAL CREATURE! STICK IT IN ITS CAGE, I'LL DEAL WITH IT LATER...ONCE AND FOR ALL!
=GULP!=

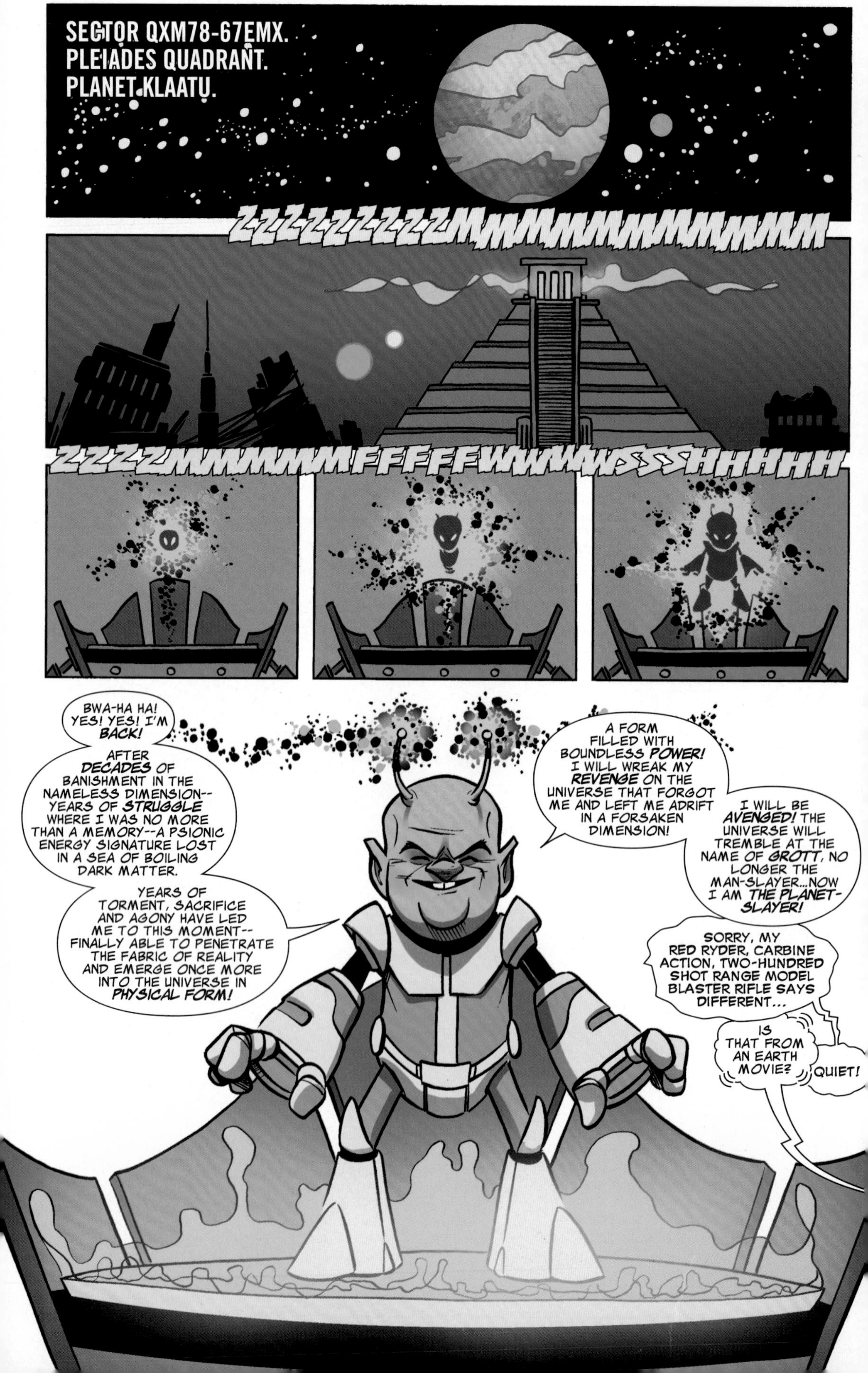
SECTOR QXM78-67EMX. PLEIADES QUADRANT. PLANET KLAATU.
Z-Z-Z-Z-Z-Z-Z-Z-Z-ZMMMMMMMMMMMMMMMM
ZZZZMMMMMMFFFFFWWWWSSSHHHHH
BWA-HA HA! YES! YES! I'M BACK!
AFTER DECADES OF BANISHMENT IN THE NAMELESS DIMENSION-- YEARS OF STRUGGLE WHERE I WAS NO MORE THAN A MEMORY--A PSIONIC ENERGY SIGNATURE LOST IN A SEA OF BOILING DARK MATTER.
YEARS OF TORMENT, SACRIFICE AND AGONY HAVE LED ME TO THIS MOMENT-- FINALLY ABLE TO PENETRATE THE FABRIC OF REALITY AND EMERGE ONCE MORE INTO THE UNIVERSE IN PHYSICAL FORM!
A FORM FILLED WITH BOUNDLESS POWER! I WILL WREAK MY REVENGE ON THE UNIVERSE THAT FORGOT ME AND LEFT ME ADRIFT IN A FORSAKEN DIMENSION!
I WILL BE AVENGED! THE UNIVERSE WILL TREMBLE AT THE NAME OF GROTT, NO LONGER THE MAN-SLAYER...NOW I AM THE PLANET-SLAYER!
SORRY, MY RED RYDER, CARBINE ACTION, TWO-HUNDRED SHOT RANGE MODEL BLASTER RIFLE SAYS DIFFERENT...
IS THAT FROM AN EARTH MOVIE?
QUIET!

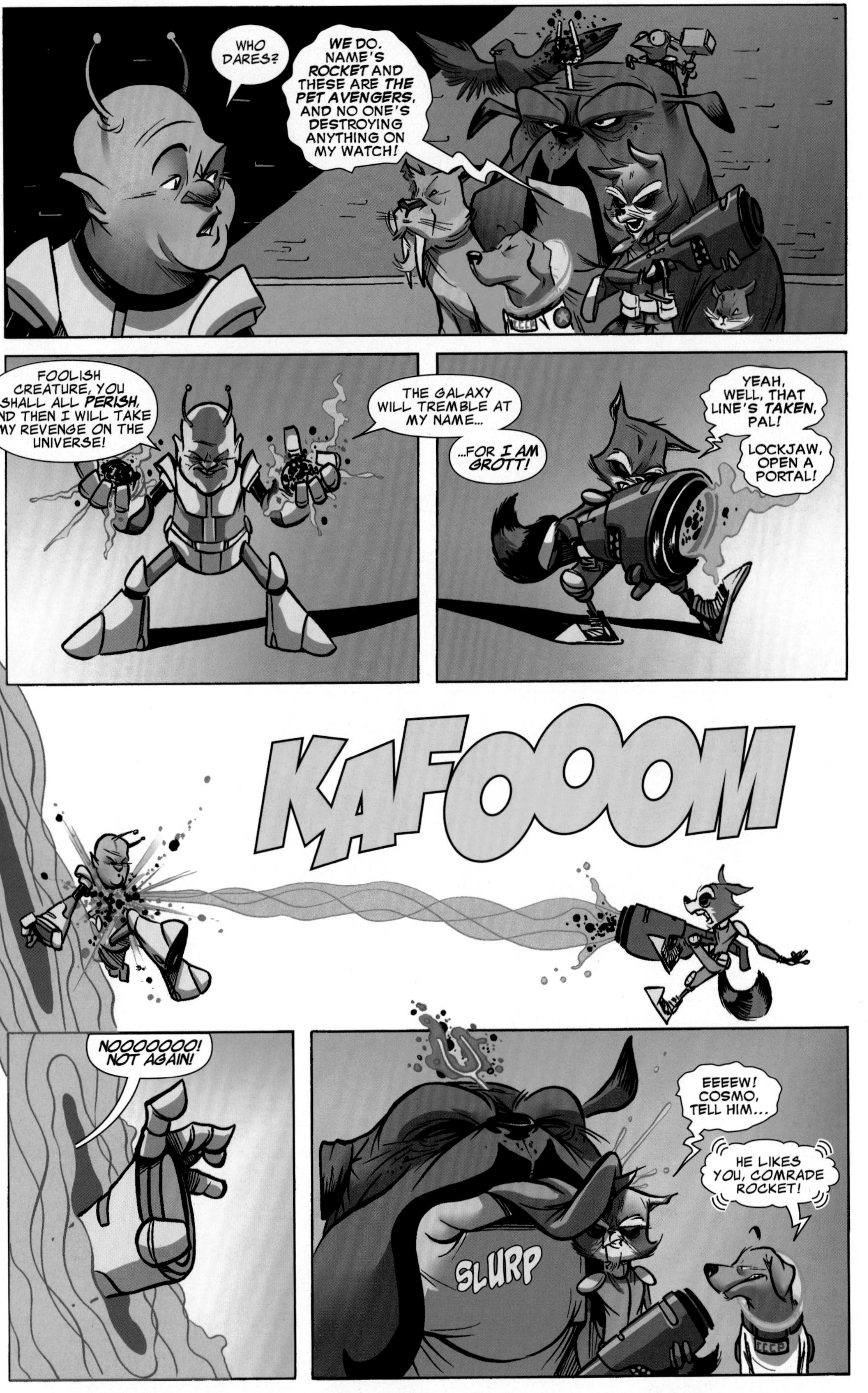
WHO DARES?
WE DO. NAME'S ROCKET AND THESE ARE THE PET AVENGERS, AND NO ONE'S DESTROYING ANYTHING ON MY WATCH!
FOOLISH CREATURE, YOU SHALL ALL PERISH, AND THEN I WILL TAKE MY REVENGE ON THE UNIVERSE!
THE GALAXY WILL TREMBLE AT MY NAME...
...FOR I AM GROTT!
YEAH, WELL, THAT LINE'S TAKEN, PAL!
LOCKJAW, OPEN A PORTAL!
KAFOOOM
NOOOOOOO! NOT AGAIN!
EEEEW! COSMO, TELL HIM...
HE LIKES YOU, COMRADE ROCKET!
SLURP

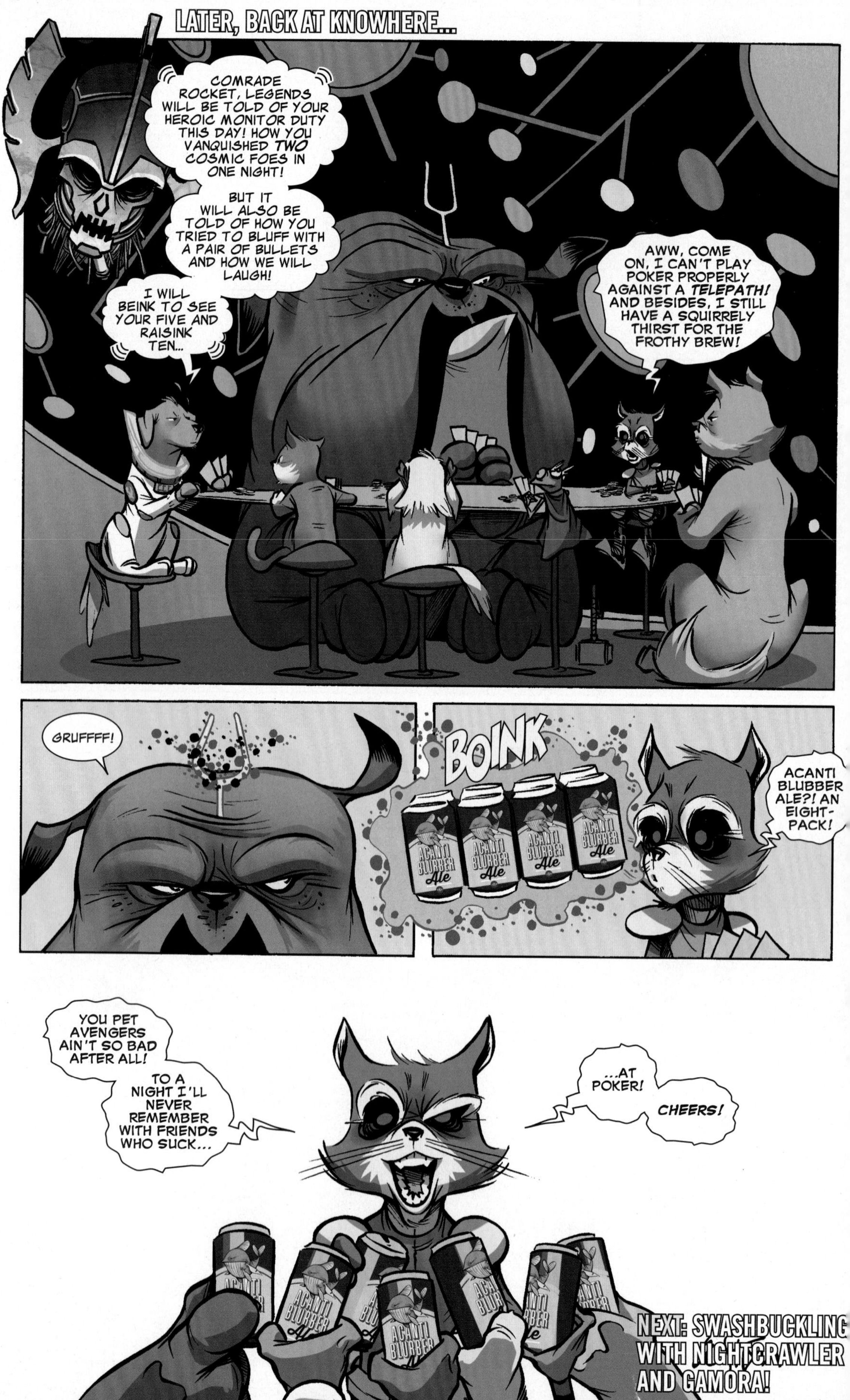
LATER, BACK AT KNOWHERE...
COMRADE ROCKET, LEGENDS WILL BE TOLD OF YOUR HEROIC MONITOR DUTY THIS DAY! HOW YOU VANQUISHED TWO COSMIC FOES IN ONE NIGHT!
BUT IT WILL ALSO BE TOLD OF HOW YOU TRIED TO BLUFF WITH A PAIR OF BULLETS AND HOW WE WILL LAUGH!
I WILL BEINK TO SEE YOUR FIVE AND RAISINK TEN...
AWW, COME ON, I CAN'T PLAY POKER PROPERLY AGAINST A TELEPATH! AND BESIDES, I STILL HAVE A SQUIRRELY THIRST FOR THE FROTHY BREW!
GRUFFFF!
BOINK
ACANTI BLUBBER Ale
ACANTI BLUBBER ALE?! AN EIGHT-PACK!
YOU PET AVENGERS AIN'T SO BAD AFTER ALL!
TO A NIGHT I'LL NEVER REMEMBER WITH FRIENDS WHO SUCK...
...AT POKER!
CHEERS!
NEXT: SWASHBUCKLING WITH NIGHTCRAWLER AND GAMORA!

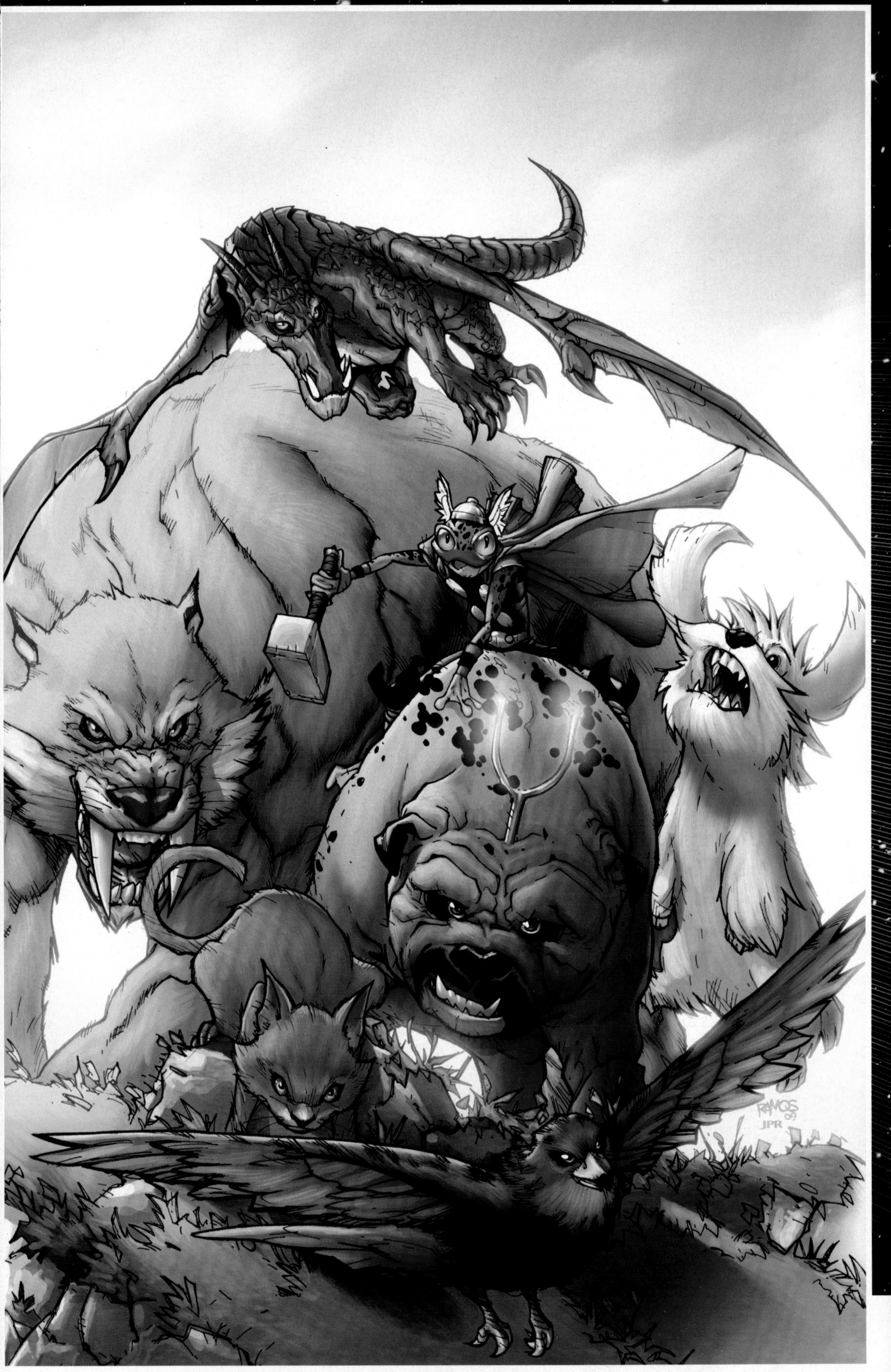
RAMOS 09
JPR

TAILS OF THE PET AVENGERS #1

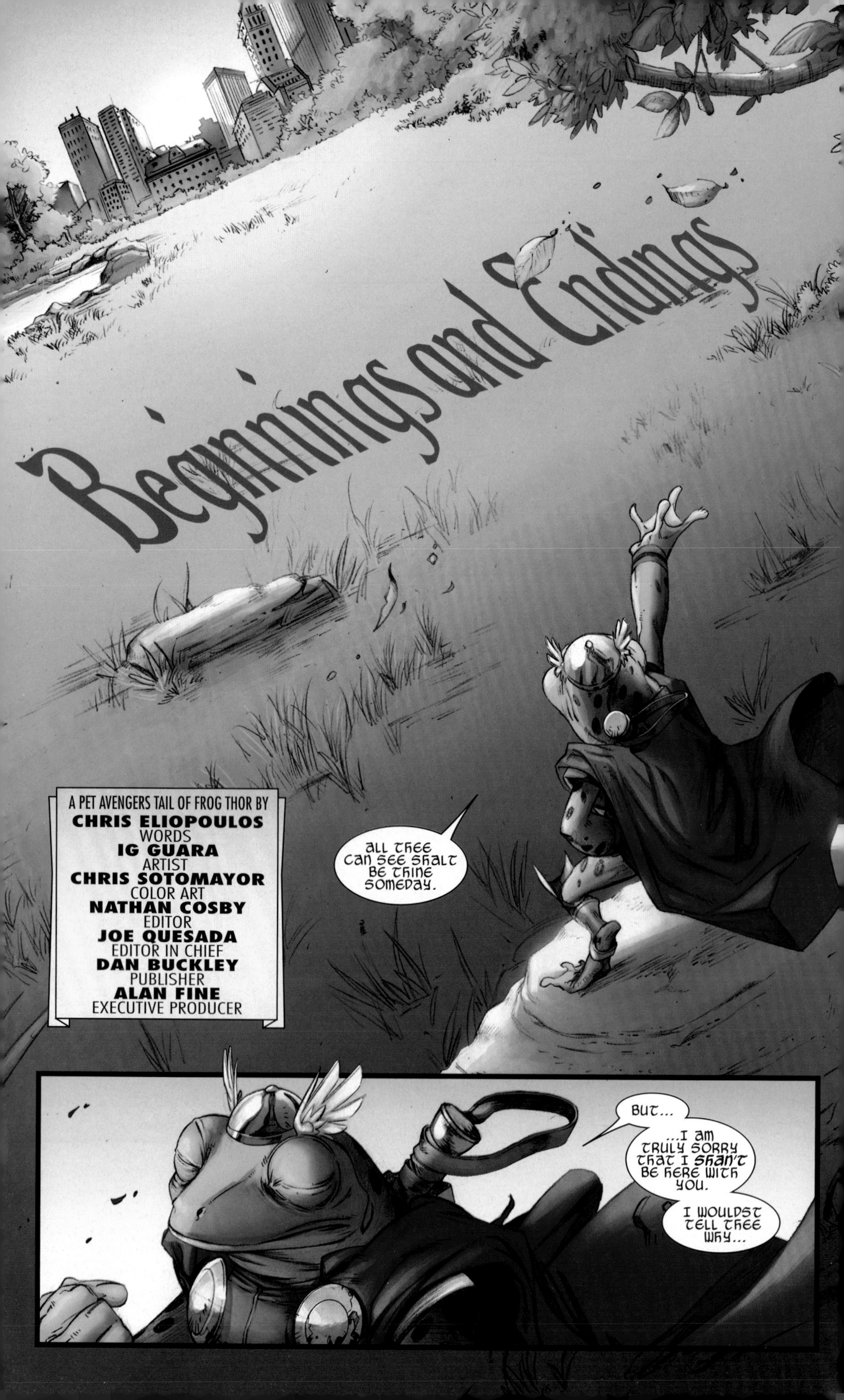

Beginnings and Endings
A PET AVENGERS TAIL OF FROG THOR BY
CHRIS ELIOPOULOS
WORDS
IG GUARA
ARTIST
CHRIS SOTOMAYOR
COLOR ART
NATHAN COSBY
EDITOR
JOE QUESADA
EDITOR IN CHIEF
DAN BUCKLEY
PUBLISHER
ALAN FINE
EXECUTIVE PRODUCER
ALL THEE CAN SEE SHALT BE THINE SOMEDAY.
BUT...
...I AM TRULY SORRY THAT I SHAN'T BE HERE WITH YOU.
I WOULDST TELL THEE WHY...

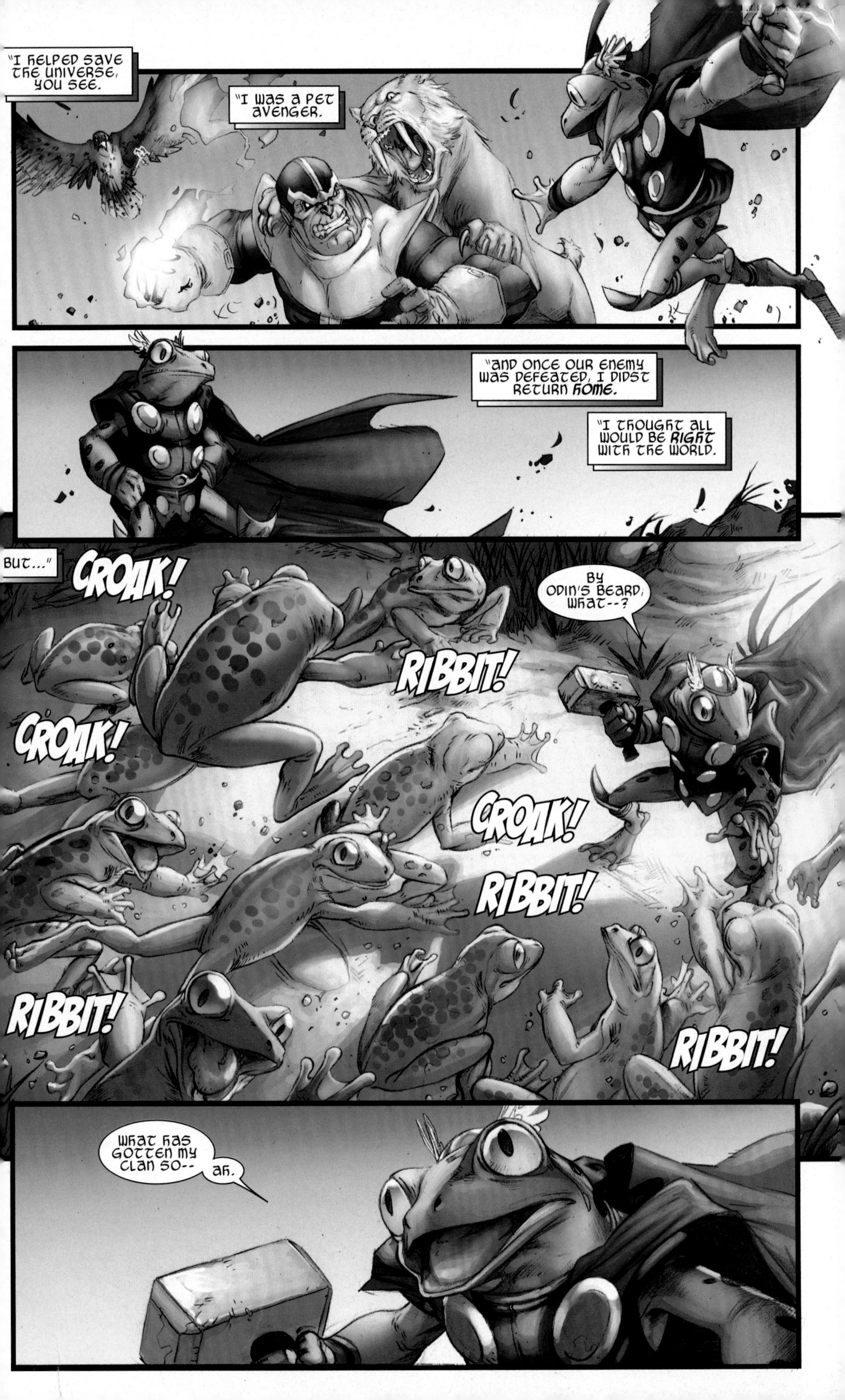
"I HELPED SAVE THE UNIVERSE, YOU SEE.
"I WAS A PET AVENGER.
"AND ONCE OUR ENEMY WAS DEFEATED, I DIDST RETURN HOME.
"I THOUGHT ALL WOULD BE RIGHT WITH THE WORLD.
BUT..."
CROAK!
BY ODIN'S BEARD, WHAT--?
RIBBIT!
CROAK!
CROAK!
RIBBIT!
RIBBIT!
RIBBIT!
WHAT HAS GOTTEN MY CLAN SO--
AH.

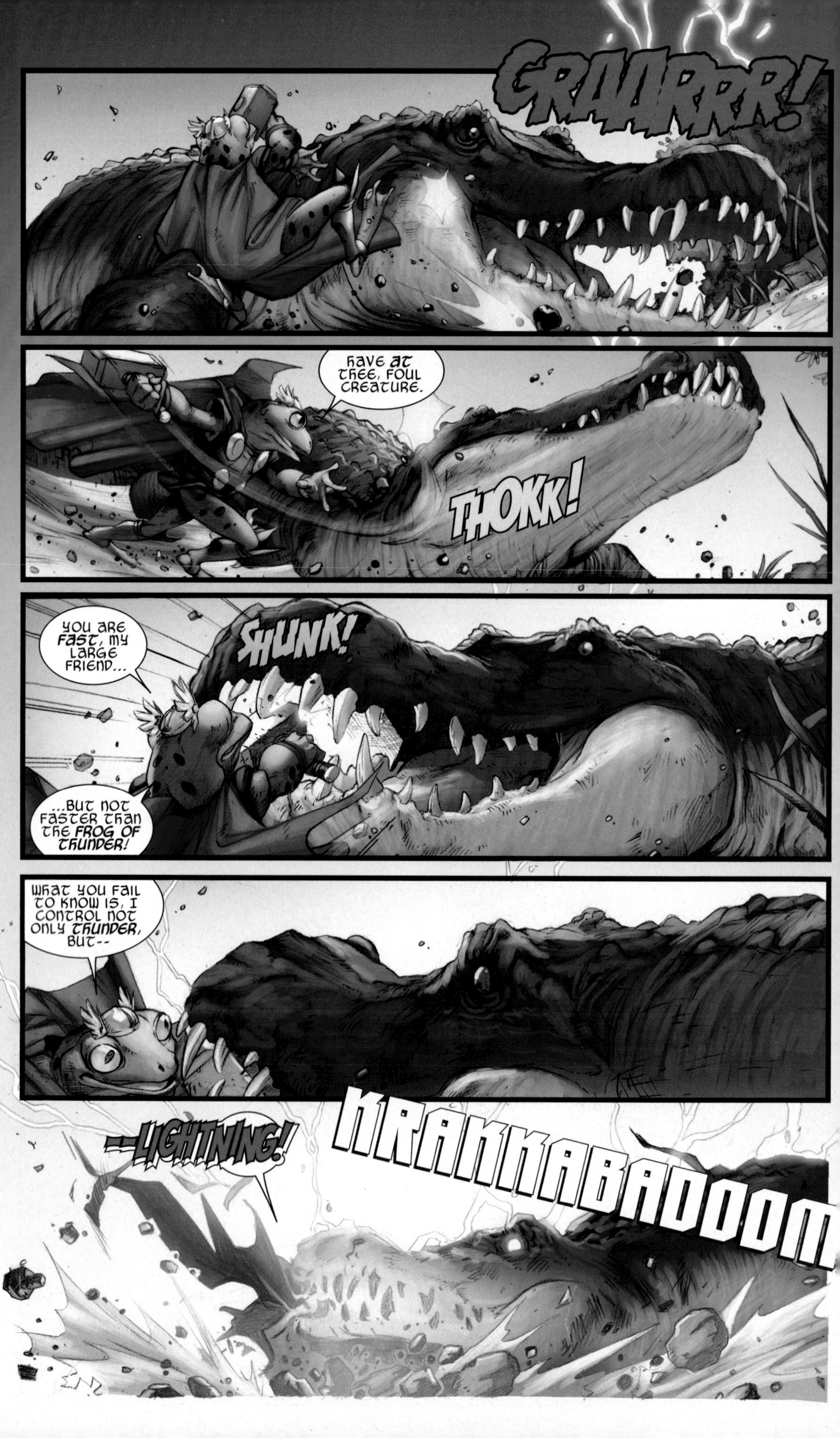
GRAARRR!
HAVE AT THEE, FOUL CREATURE.
THOKK!
YOU ARE FAST, MY LARGE FRIEND...
SHUNK!
...BUT NOT FASTER THAN THE FROG OF THUNDER!
WHAT YOU FAIL TO KNOW IS, I CONTROL NOT ONLY THUNDER, BUT--
--LIGHTNING!
KRAKKABADOOOM

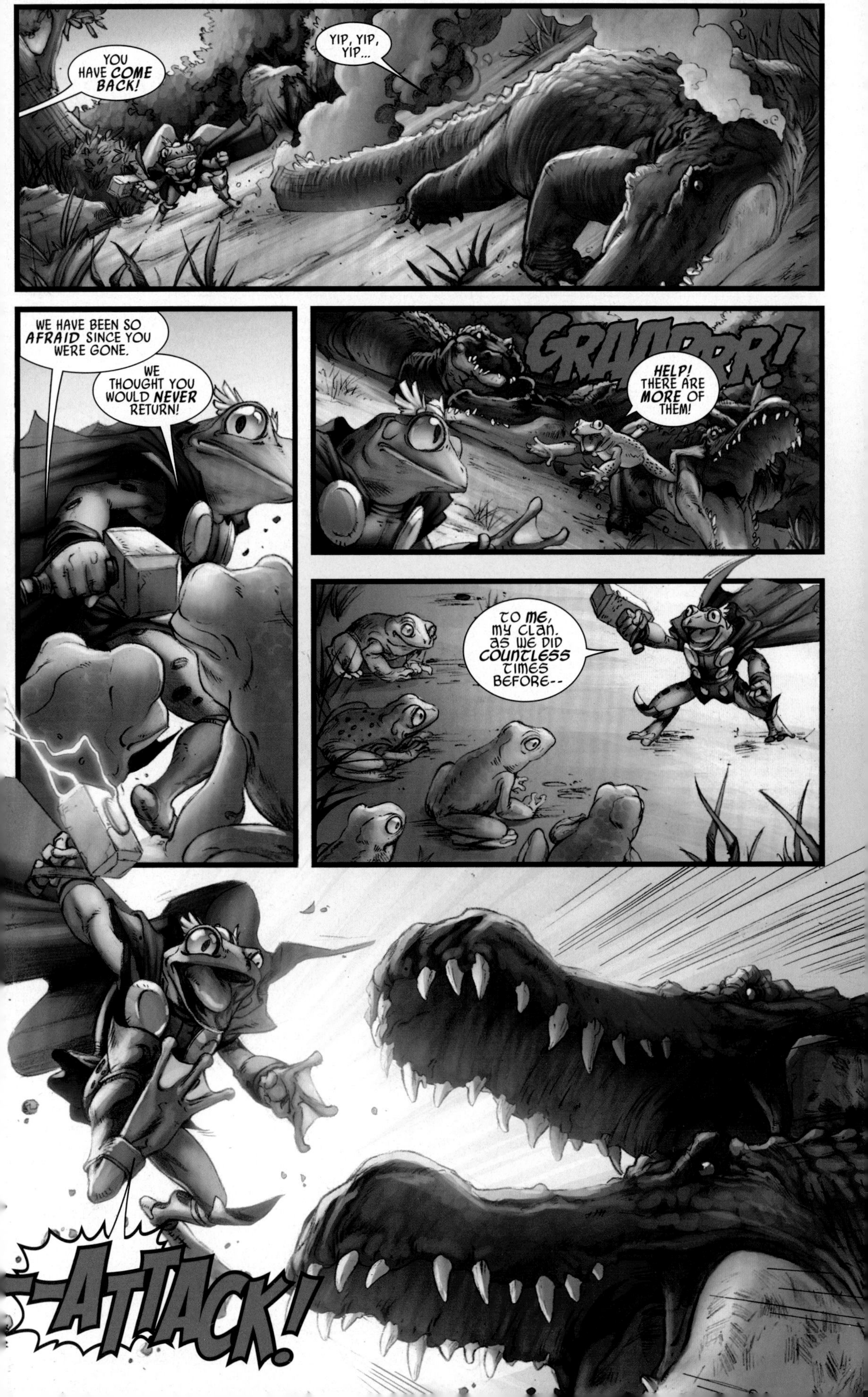
YOU HAVE COME BACK!
YIP, YIP, YIP...
WE HAVE BEEN SO AFRAID SINCE YOU WERE GONE.
WE THOUGHT YOU WOULD NEVER RETURN!
GRAAARR!
HELP! THERE ARE MORE OF THEM!
TO ME, MY CLAN. AS WE DID COUNTLESS TIMES BEFORE--
--ATTACK!

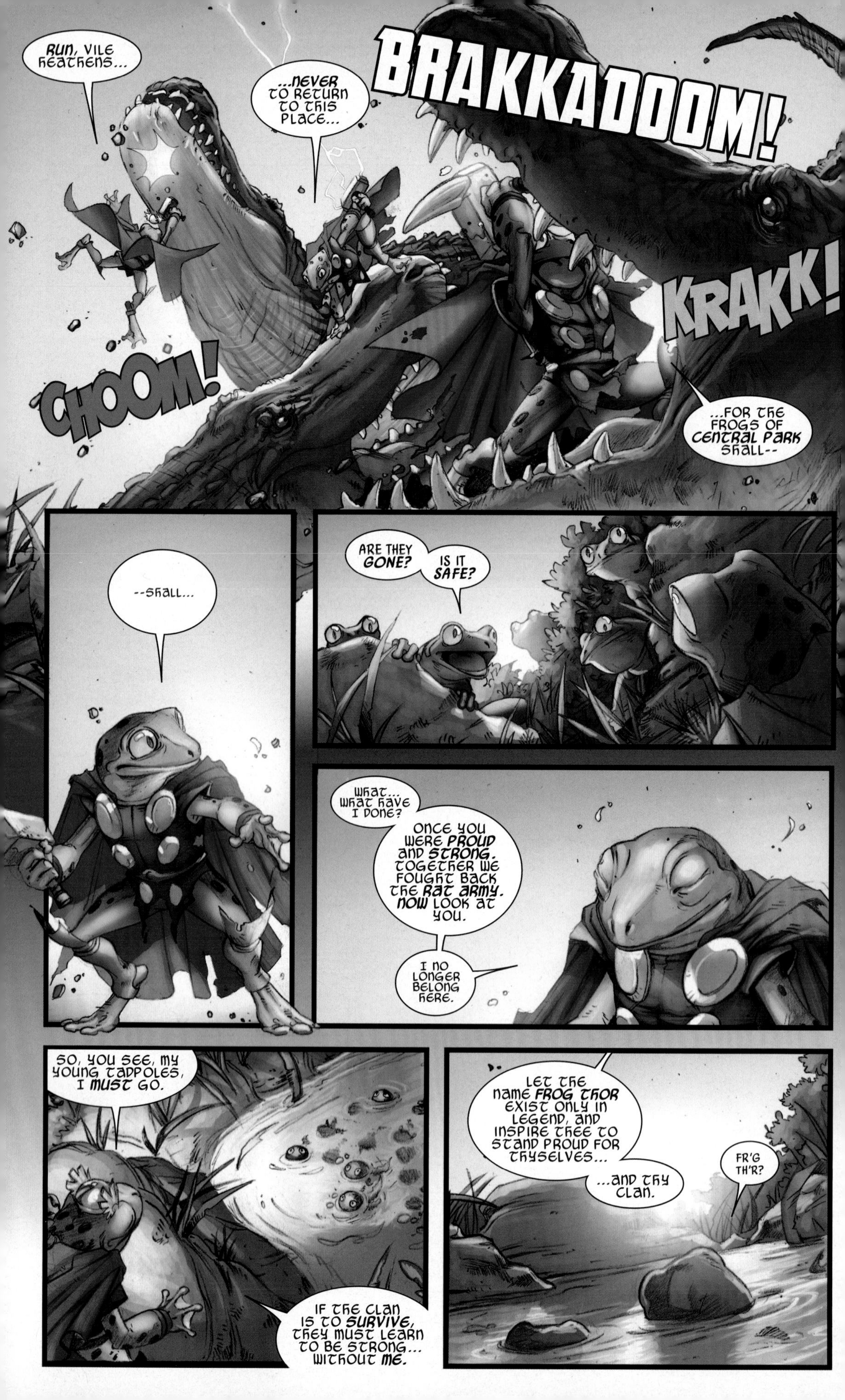
RUN, VILE HEATHENS...
...NEVER TO RETURN TO THIS PLACE...
BRAKKADOOM!
KRAKK!
CHOOM!
...FOR THE FROGS OF CENTRAL PARK SHALL--
--SHALL...
ARE THEY GONE?
IS IT SAFE?
WHAT... WHAT HAVE I DONE?
ONCE YOU WERE PROUD AND STRONG. TOGETHER WE FOUGHT BACK THE RAT ARMY. NOW LOOK AT YOU.
I NO LONGER BELONG HERE.
SO, YOU SEE, MY YOUNG TADPOLES, I MUST GO.
IF THE CLAN IS TO SURVIVE, THEY MUST LEARN TO BE STRONG... WITHOUT ME.
LET THE NAME FROG THOR EXIST ONLY IN LEGEND, AND INSPIRE THEE TO STAND PROUD FOR THYSELVES...
...AND THY CLAN.
FR'G TH'R?

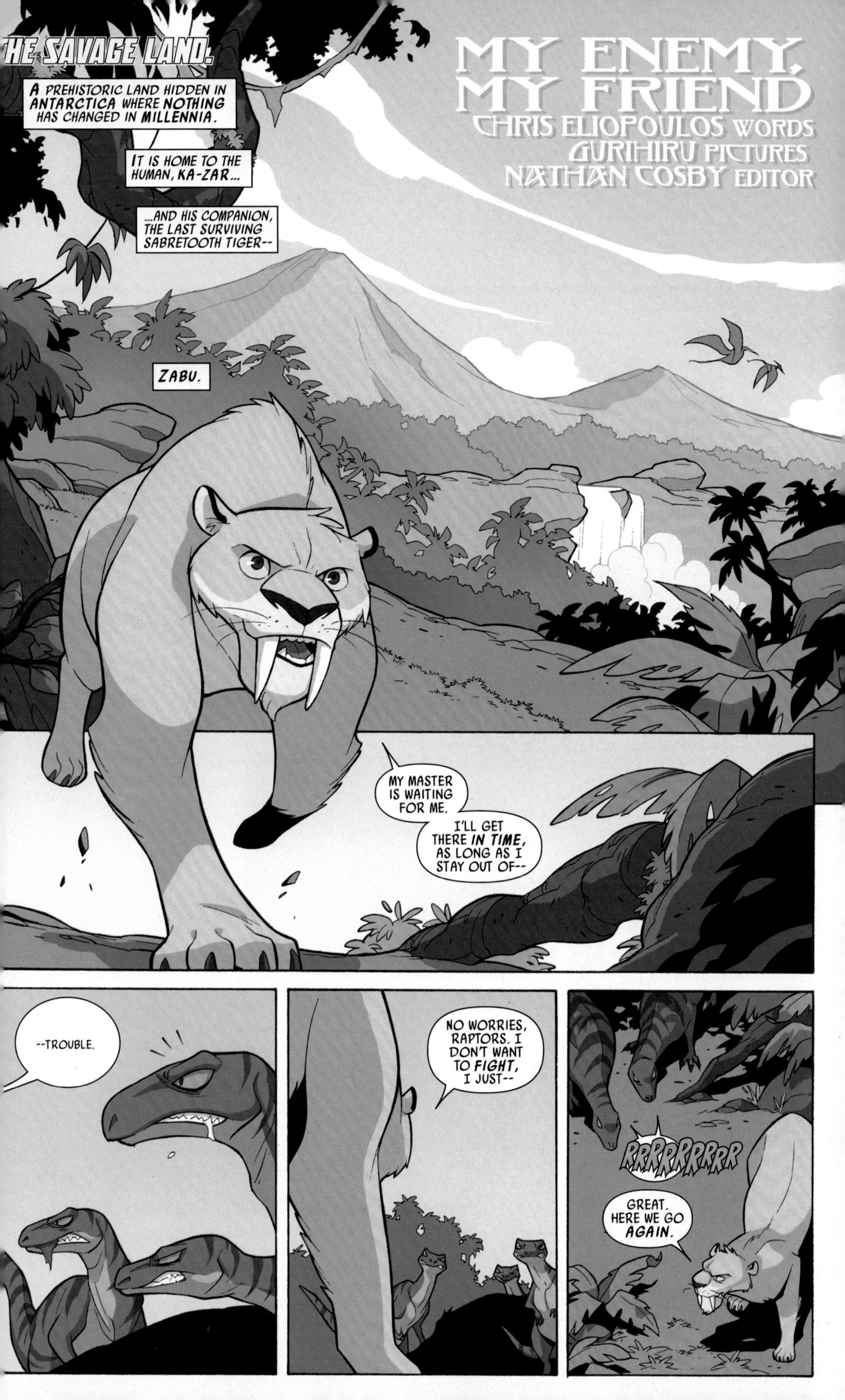
THE SAVAGE LAND.
A PREHISTORIC LAND HIDDEN IN ANTARCTICA WHERE NOTHING HAS CHANGED IN MILLENNIA.
IT IS HOME TO THE HUMAN, KA-ZAR...
...AND HIS COMPANION, THE LAST SURVIVING SABRETOOTH TIGER--
ZABU.
MY ENEMY, MY FRIEND
CHRIS ELIOPOULOS WORDS
GURIHIRU PICTURES
NATHAN COSBY EDITOR
MY MASTER IS WAITING FOR ME.
I'LL GET THERE IN TIME, AS LONG AS I STAY OUT OF--
--TROUBLE.
NO WORRIES, RAPTORS. I DON'T WANT TO FIGHT, I JUST--
RRRRRRRRR
GREAT. HERE WE GO AGAIN.

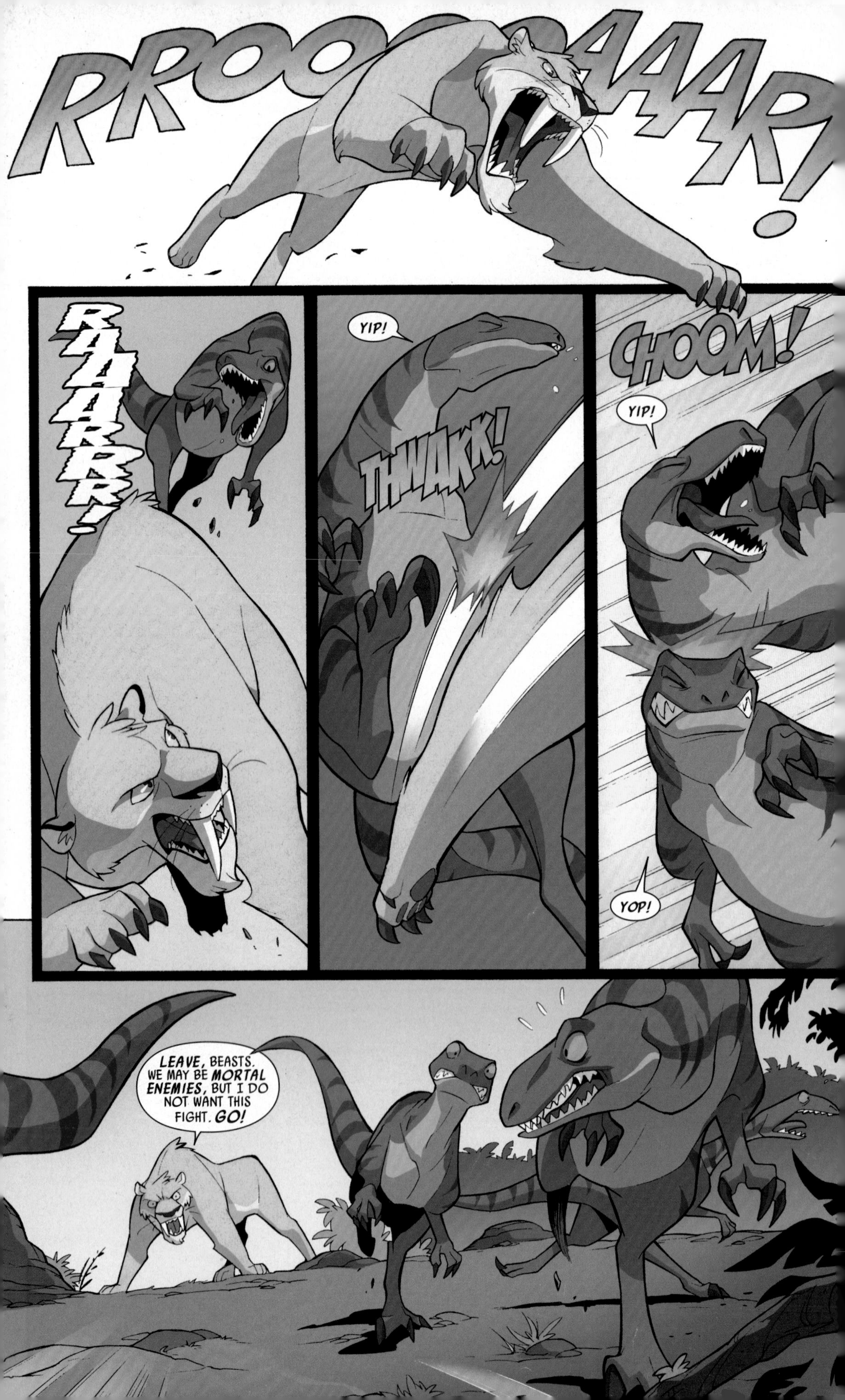
RROOOOAAAAR!
RAAARRR!
YIP!
THWAKK!
CHOOM!
YIP!
YOP!
LEAVE, BEASTS. WE MAY BE MORTAL ENEMIES, BUT I DO NOT WANT THIS FIGHT. GO!

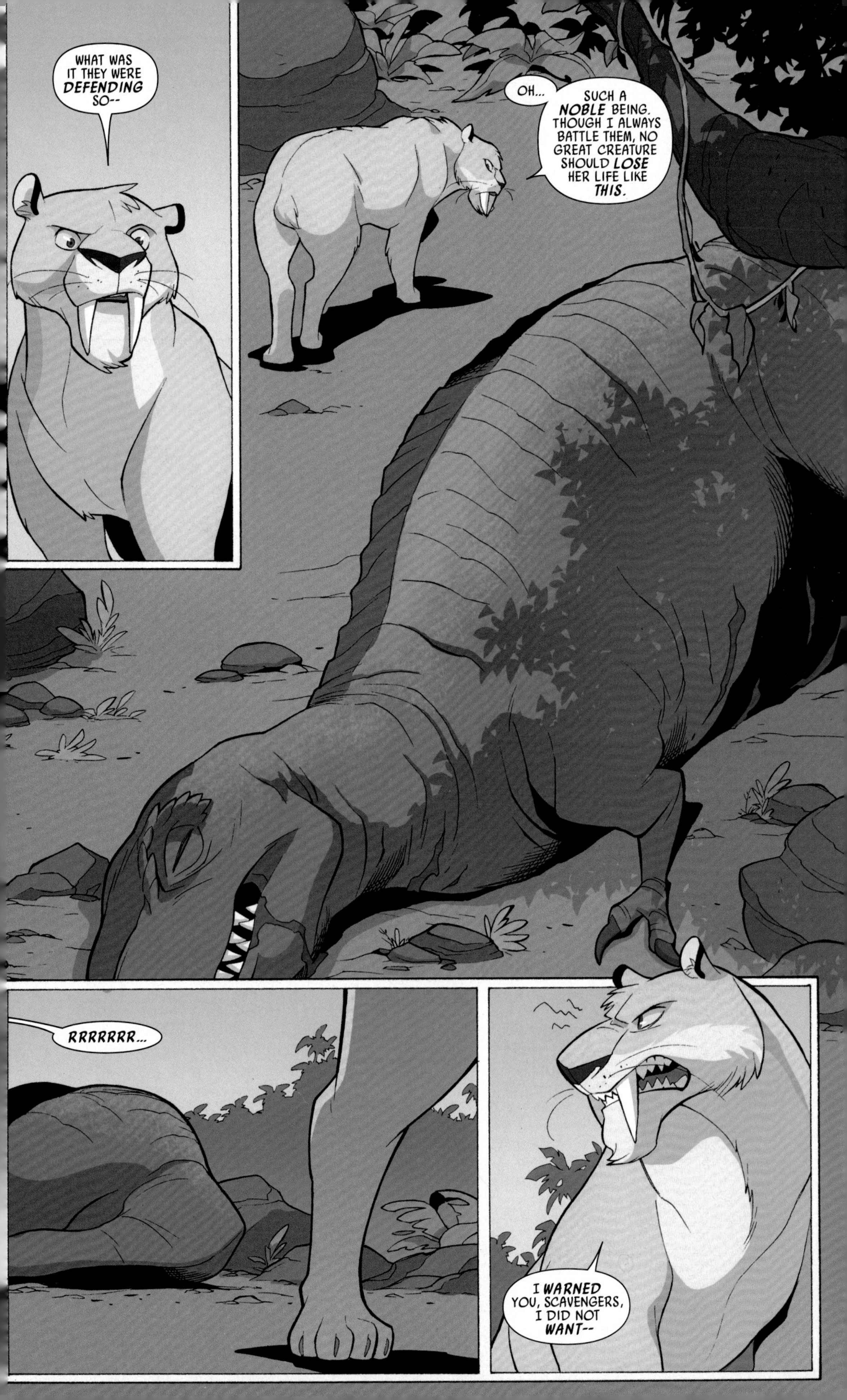
WHAT WAS IT THEY WERE DEFENDING SO--
OH...
SUCH A NOBLE BEING. THOUGH I ALWAYS BATTLE THEM, NO GREAT CREATURE SHOULD LOSE HER LIFE LIKE THIS.
RRRRRRR...
I WARNED YOU, SCAVENGERS, I DID NOT WANT--

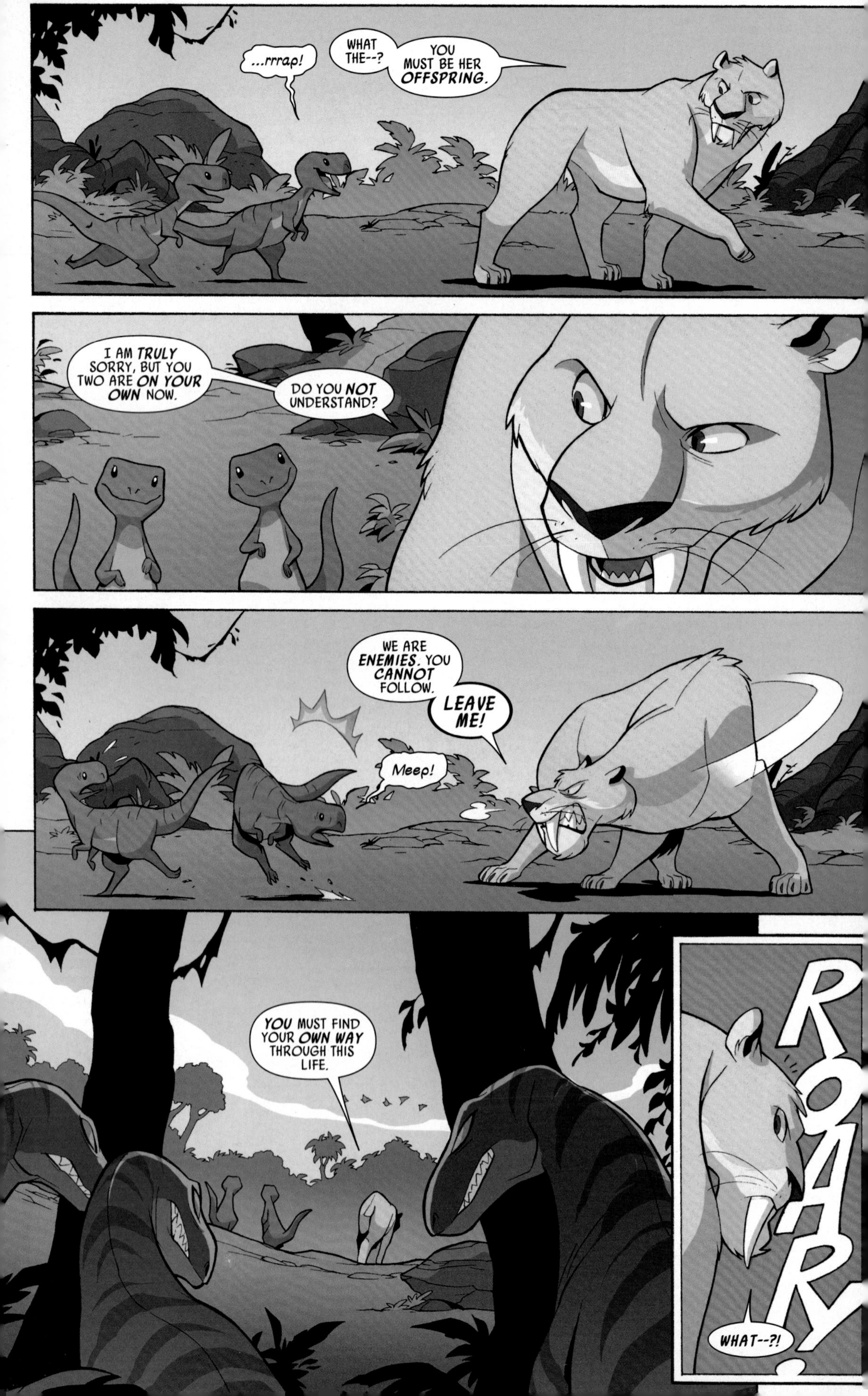
...rrrap!
WHAT THE--?
YOU MUST BE HER OFFSPRING.
I AM TRULY SORRY, BUT YOU TWO ARE ON YOUR OWN NOW.
DO YOU NOT UNDERSTAND?
WE ARE ENEMIES. YOU CANNOT FOLLOW.
LEAVE ME!
Meep!
YOU MUST FIND YOUR OWN WAY THROUGH THIS LIFE.
ROARY
WHAT--?!

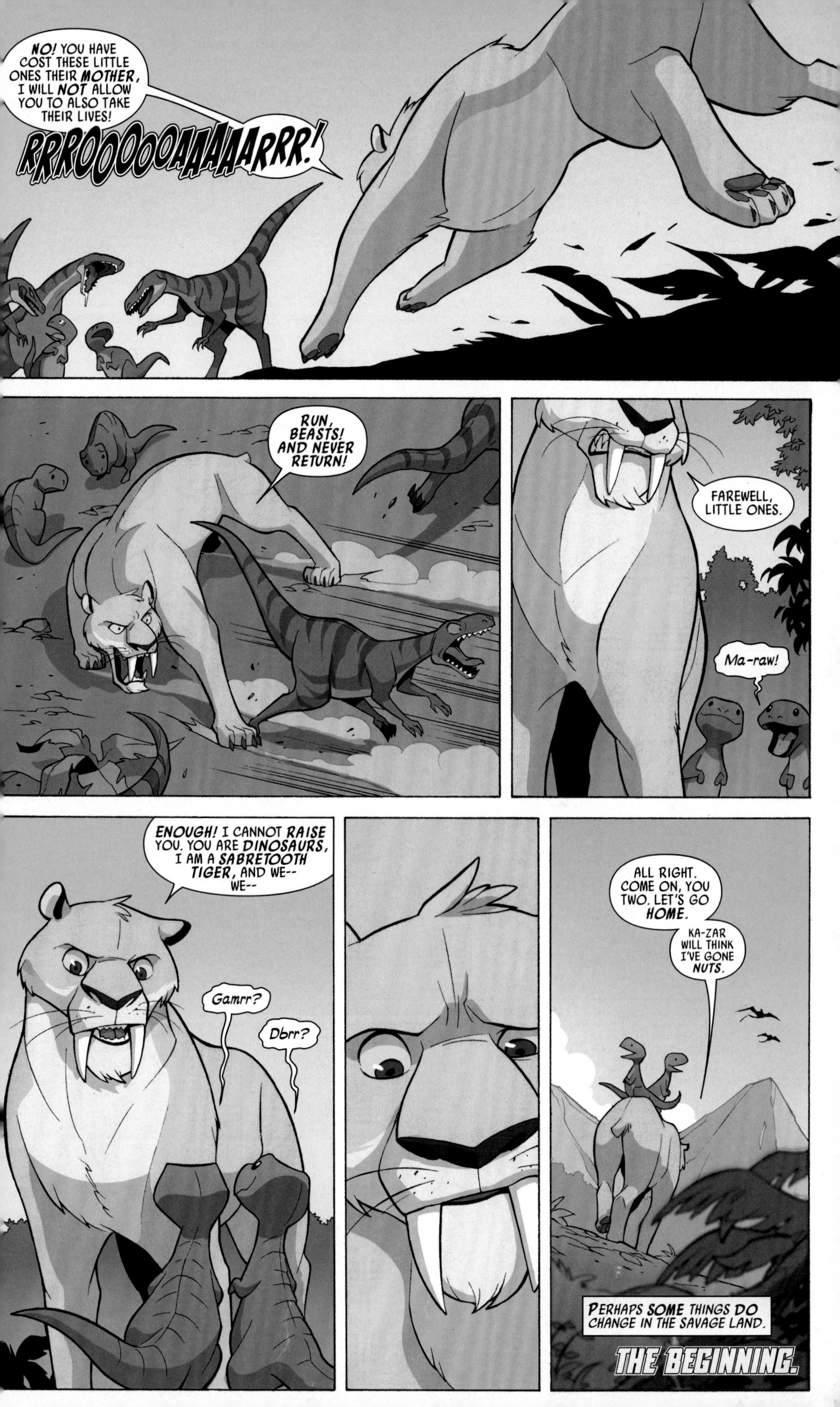

NO! YOU HAVE COST THESE LITTLE ONES THEIR MOTHER, I WILL NOT ALLOW YOU TO ALSO TAKE THEIR LIVES!
RRROOOOOOAAAAARRR!
RUN, BEASTS! AND NEVER RETURN!
FAREWELL, LITTLE ONES.
Ma-raw!
ENOUGH! I CANNOT RAISE YOU. YOU ARE DINOSAURS, I AM A SABRETOOTH TIGER, AND WE-- WE--
Gamrr?
Dbrr?
ALL RIGHT. COME ON, YOU TWO. LET'S GO HOME.
KA-ZAR WILL THINK I'VE GONE NUTS.
PERHAPS SOME THINGS DO CHANGE IN THE SAVAGE LAND.
THE BEGINNING.

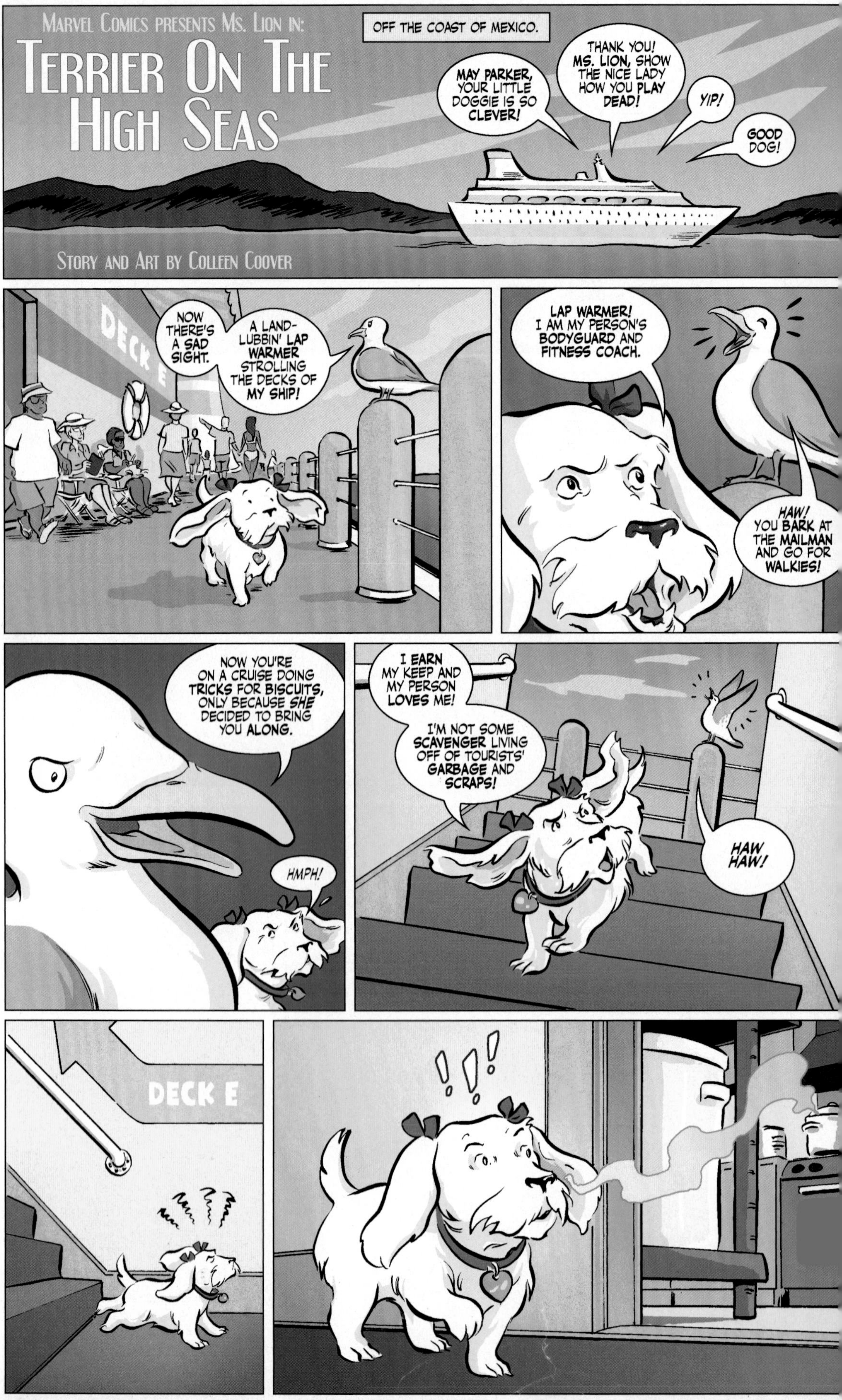
MARVEL COMICS PRESENTS MS. LION IN:
TERRIER ON THE HIGH SEAS
OFF THE COAST OF MEXICO.
MAY PARKER, YOUR LITTLE DOGGIE IS SO CLEVER!
THANK YOU! MS. LION, SHOW THE NICE LADY HOW YOU PLAY DEAD!
YIP!
GOOD DOG!
STORY AND ART BY COLLEEN COOVER
DECK E
NOW THERE'S A SAD SIGHT.
A LAND-LUBBIN' LAP WARMER STROLLING THE DECKS OF MY SHIP!
LAP WARMER! I AM MY PERSON'S BODYGUARD AND FITNESS COACH.
HAW! YOU BARK AT THE MAILMAN AND GO FOR WALKIES!
NOW YOU'RE ON A CRUISE DOING TRICKS FOR BISCUITS, ONLY BECAUSE SHE DECIDED TO BRING YOU ALONG.
HMPH!
I EARN MY KEEP AND MY PERSON LOVES ME!
I'M NOT SOME SCAVENGER LIVING OFF OF TOURISTS' GARBAGE AND SCRAPS!
HAW HAW!
DECK E
!!!

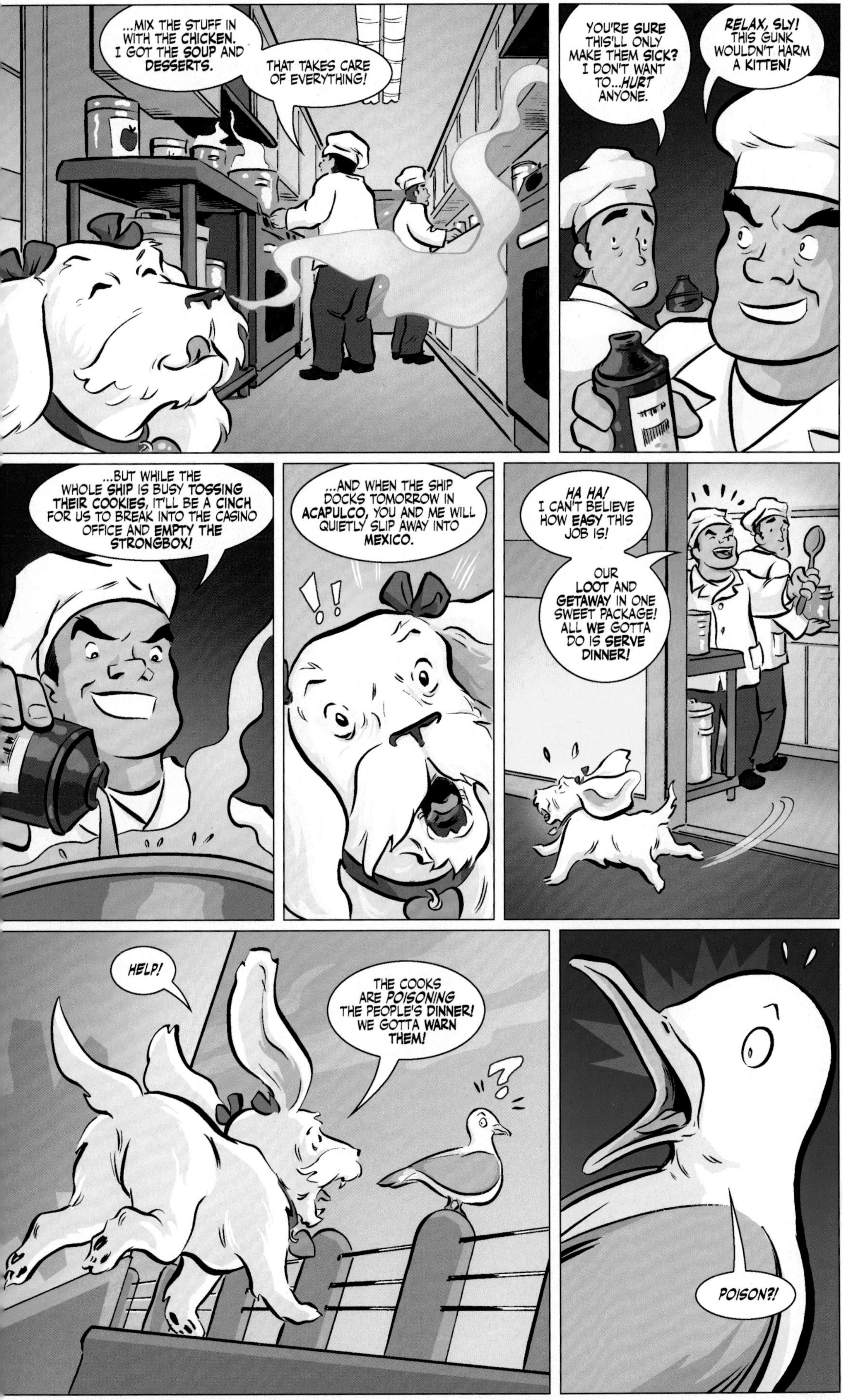
...MIX THE STUFF IN WITH THE CHICKEN. I GOT THE SOUP AND DESSERTS.
THAT TAKES CARE OF EVERYTHING!
YOU'RE SURE THIS'LL ONLY MAKE THEM SICK? I DON'T WANT TO...HURT ANYONE.
RELAX, SLY! THIS GUNK WOULDN'T HARM A KITTEN!
...BUT WHILE THE WHOLE SHIP IS BUSY TOSSING THEIR COOKIES, IT'LL BE A CINCH FOR US TO BREAK INTO THE CASINO OFFICE AND EMPTY THE STRONGBOX!
...AND WHEN THE SHIP DOCKS TOMORROW IN ACAPULCO, YOU AND ME WILL QUIETLY SLIP AWAY INTO MEXICO.
HA HA! I CAN'T BELIEVE HOW EASY THIS JOB IS!
OUR LOOT AND GETAWAY IN ONE SWEET PACKAGE! ALL WE GOTTA DO IS SERVE DINNER!
HELP!
THE COOKS ARE POISONING THE PEOPLE'S DINNER! WE GOTTA WARN THEM!
POISON?!

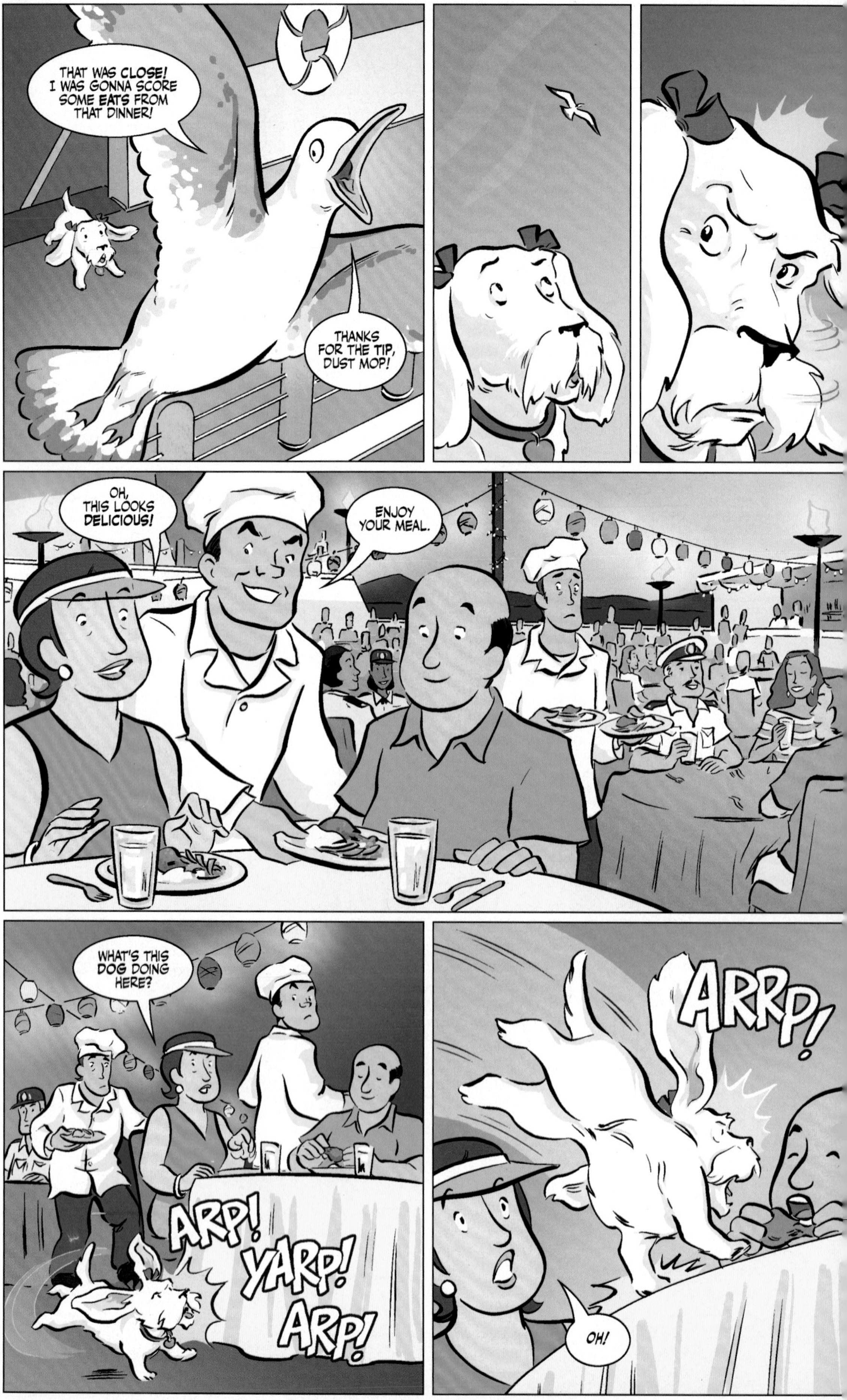
THAT WAS CLOSE! I WAS GONNA SCORE SOME EATS FROM THAT DINNER!
THANKS FOR THE TIP, DUST MOP!
OH, THIS LOOKS DELICIOUS!
ENJOY YOUR MEAL.
WHAT'S THIS DOG DOING HERE?
ARP! YARP! ARP!
ARRP!
OH!

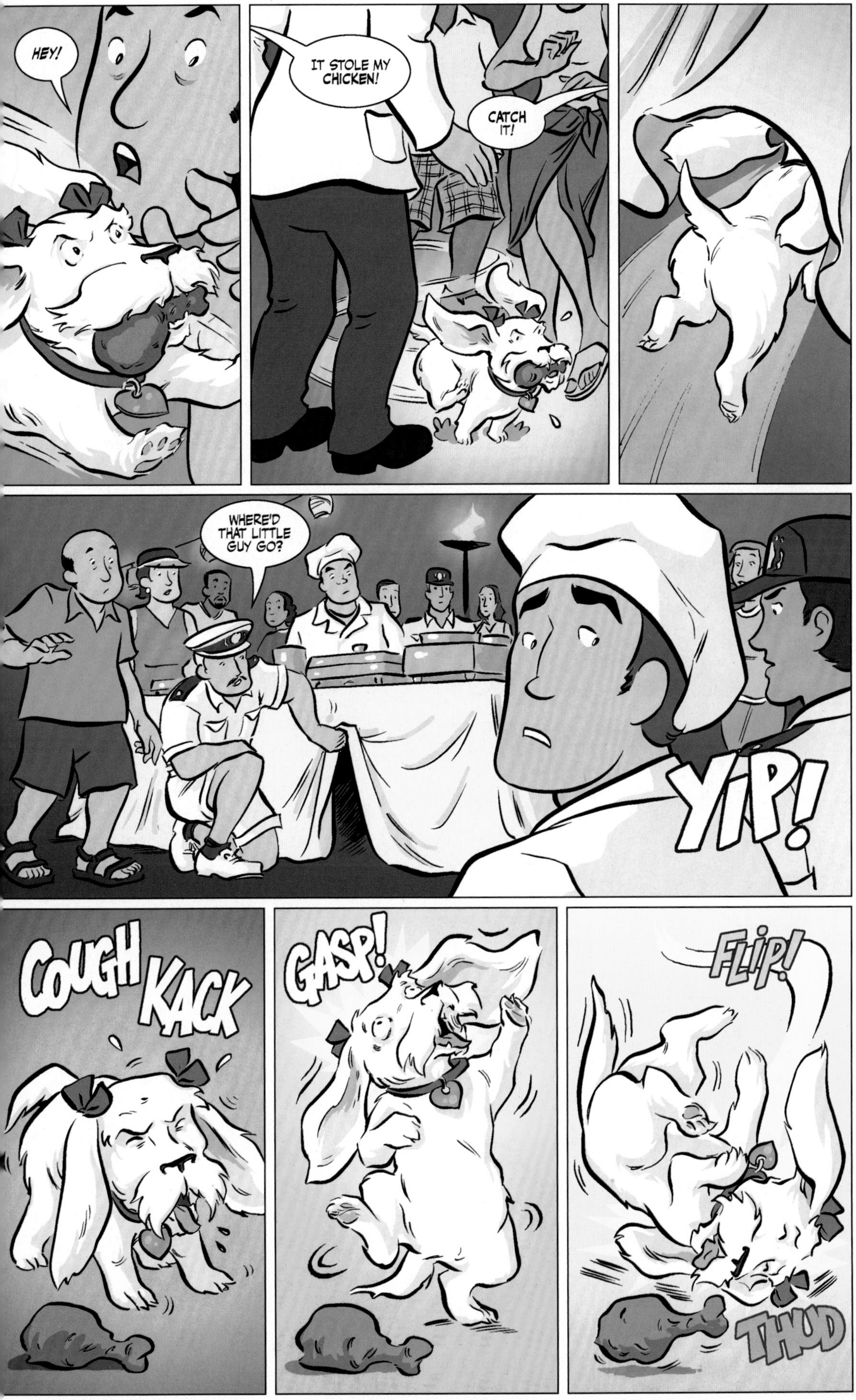
HEY!
IT STOLE MY CHICKEN!
CATCH IT!
WHERE'D THAT LITTLE GUY GO?
YIP!
COUGH
KACK
GASP!
FLIP!
THUD

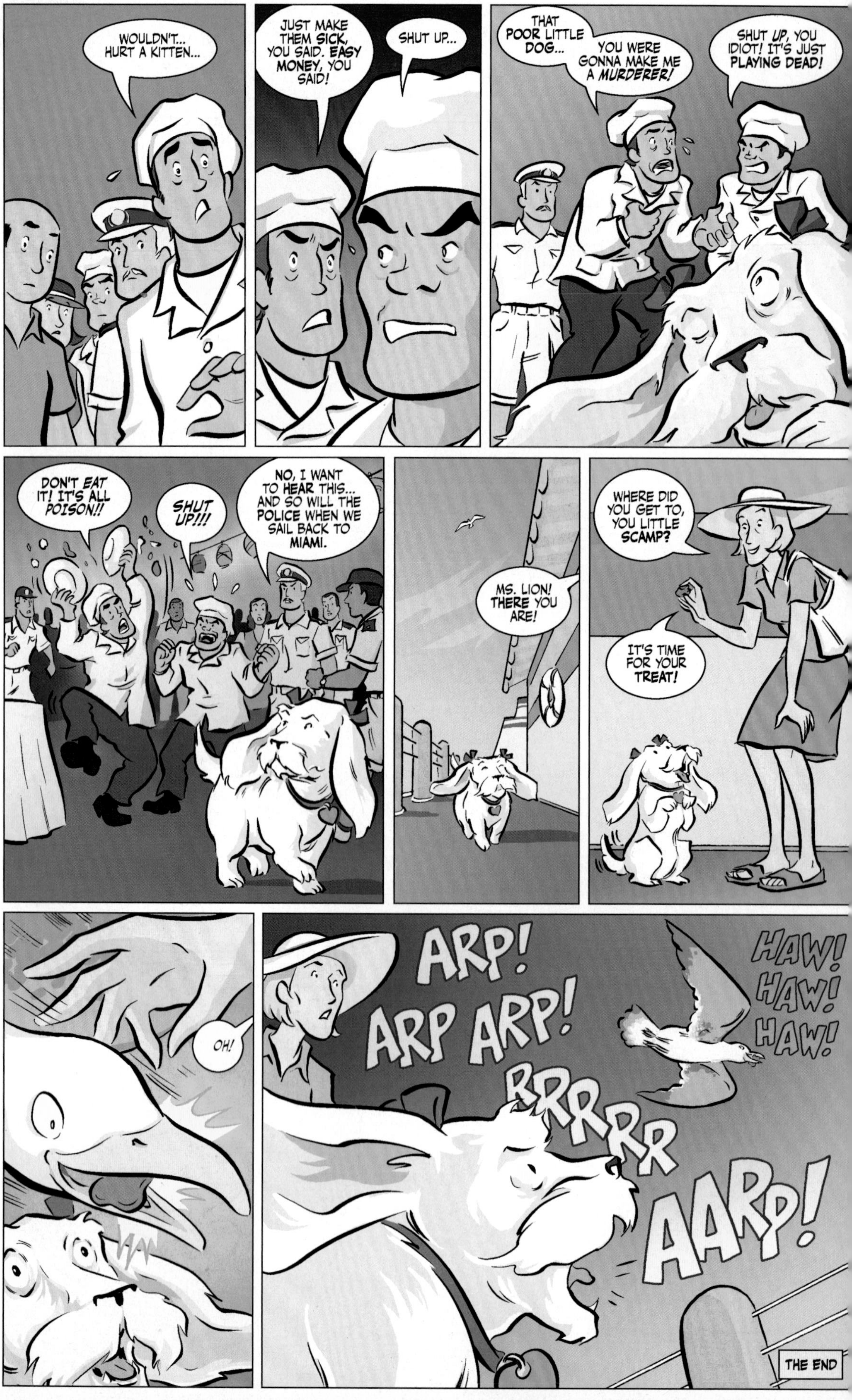
WOULDN'T... HURT A KITTEN...
JUST MAKE THEM SICK, YOU SAID. EASY MONEY, YOU SAID!
SHUT UP...
THAT POOR LITTLE DOG...
YOU WERE GONNA MAKE ME A MURDERER!
SHUT UP, YOU IDIOT! IT'S JUST PLAYING DEAD!
DON'T EAT IT! IT'S ALL POISON!!
SHUT UP!!!
NO, I WANT TO HEAR THIS... AND SO WILL THE POLICE WHEN WE SAIL BACK TO MIAMI.
MS. LION! THERE YOU ARE!
WHERE DID YOU GET TO, YOU LITTLE SCAMP?
IT'S TIME FOR YOUR TREAT!
OH!
ARP! ARP ARP!
RRRRRR
AARP!
HAW! HAW! HAW!
THE END

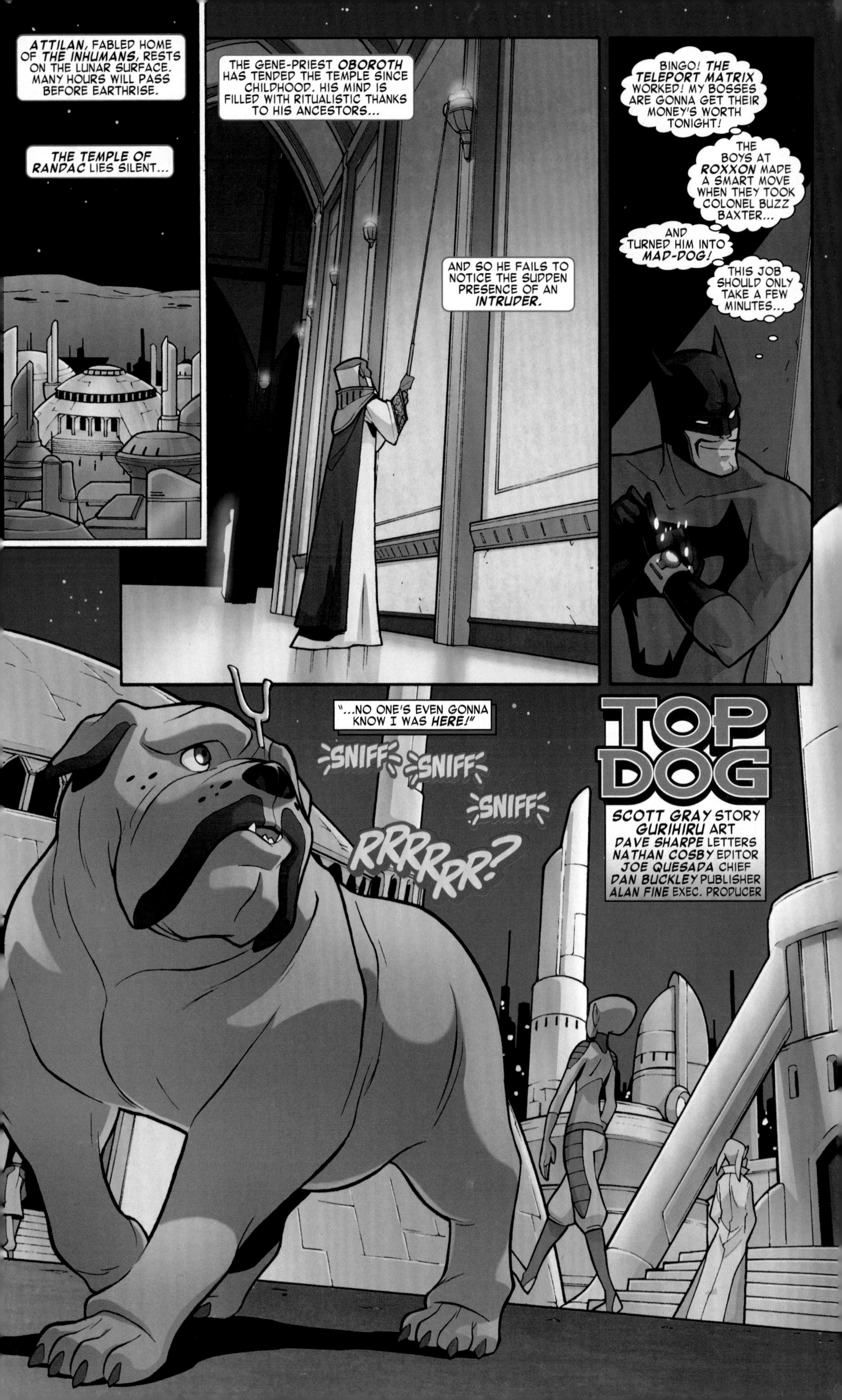

ATTILAN, FABLED HOME OF THE INHUMANS, RESTS ON THE LUNAR SURFACE. MANY HOURS WILL PASS BEFORE EARTHRISE.
THE TEMPLE OF RANDAC LIES SILENT...
THE GENE-PRIEST OBOROTH HAS TENDED THE TEMPLE SINCE CHILDHOOD. HIS MIND IS FILLED WITH RITUALISTIC THANKS TO HIS ANCESTORS...
AND SO HE FAILS TO NOTICE THE SUDDEN PRESENCE OF AN INTRUDER.
BINGO! THE TELEPORT MATRIX WORKED! MY BOSSES ARE GONNA GET THEIR MONEY'S WORTH TONIGHT!
THE BOYS AT ROXXON MADE A SMART MOVE WHEN THEY TOOK COLONEL BUZZ BAXTER...
AND TURNED HIM INTO MAD-DOG!
THIS JOB SHOULD ONLY TAKE A FEW MINUTES...
"...NO ONE'S EVEN GONNA KNOW I WAS HERE!"
SNIFF SNIFF
SNIFF
RRRRRR?
TOP DOG
SCOTT GRAY STORY
GURIHIRU ART
DAVE SHARPE LETTERS
NATHAN COSBY EDITOR
JOE QUESADA CHIEF
DAN BUCKLEY PUBLISHER
ALAN FINE EXEC. PRODUCER

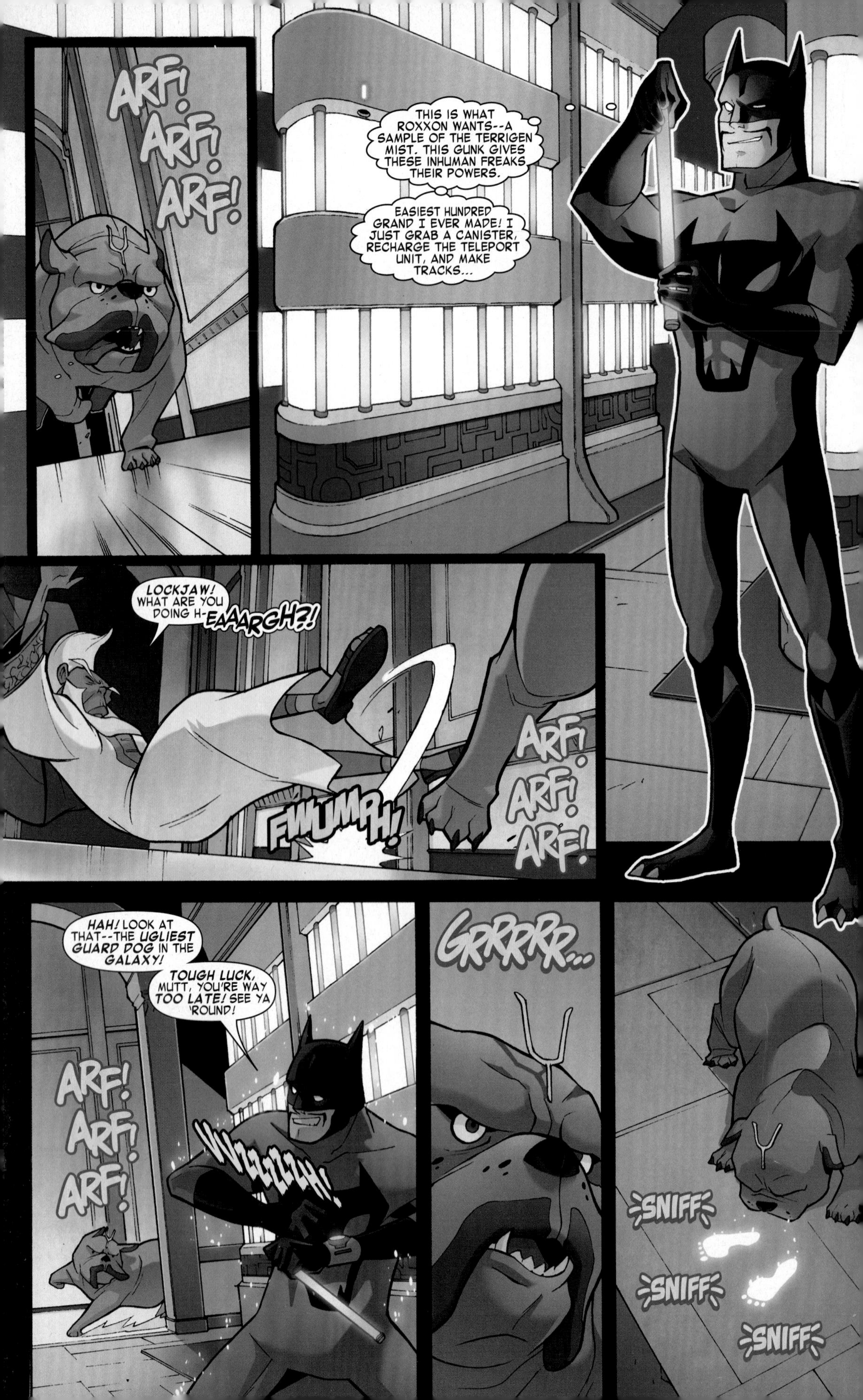
ARF! ARF! ARF!
THIS IS WHAT ROXXON WANTS--A SAMPLE OF THE TERRIGEN MIST. THIS GUNK GIVES THESE INHUMAN FREAKS THEIR POWERS.
EASIEST HUNDRED GRAND I EVER MADE! I JUST GRAB A CANISTER, RECHARGE THE TELEPORT UNIT, AND MAKE TRACKS...
LOCKJAW! WHAT ARE YOU DOING H-EAAARGH?!
FWUMPH!
ARF! ARF! ARF!
HAH! LOOK AT THAT--THE UGLIEST GUARD DOG IN THE GALAXY!
TOUGH LUCK, MUTT, YOU'RE WAY TOO LATE! SEE YA 'ROUND!
ARF! ARF! ARF!
VVZZZZZH!
GRRRRR...
SNIFF
SNIFF
SNIFF

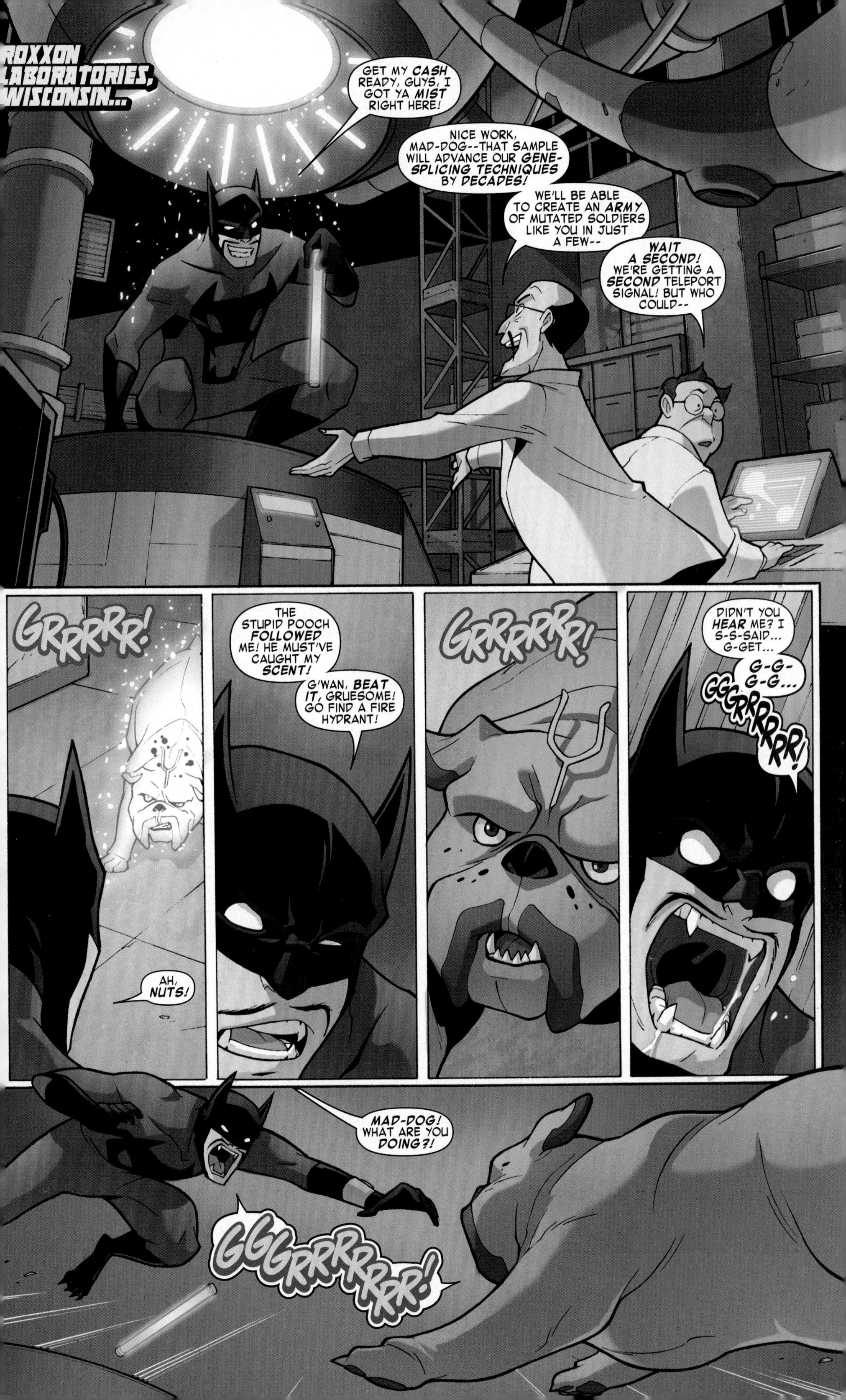
ROXXON LABORATORIES, WISCONSIN...
GET MY CASH READY, GUYS, I GOT YA MIST RIGHT HERE!
NICE WORK, MAD-DOG--THAT SAMPLE WILL ADVANCE OUR GENE-SPLICING TECHNIQUES BY DECADES!
WE'LL BE ABLE TO CREATE AN ARMY OF MUTATED SOLDIERS LIKE YOU IN JUST A FEW--
WAIT A SECOND! WE'RE GETTING A SECOND TELEPORT SIGNAL! BUT WHO COULD--
GRRRRR!
AH, NUTS!
THE STUPID POOCH FOLLOWED ME! HE MUST'VE CAUGHT MY SCENT!
G'WAN, BEAT IT, GRUESOME! GO FIND A FIRE HYDRANT!
GRRRRRR!
DIDN'T YOU HEAR ME? I S-S-SAID... G-GET...
G-G-G-G...
GGGRRRRRR!
MAD-DOG! WHAT ARE YOU DOING?!
GGGRRRRRRR!

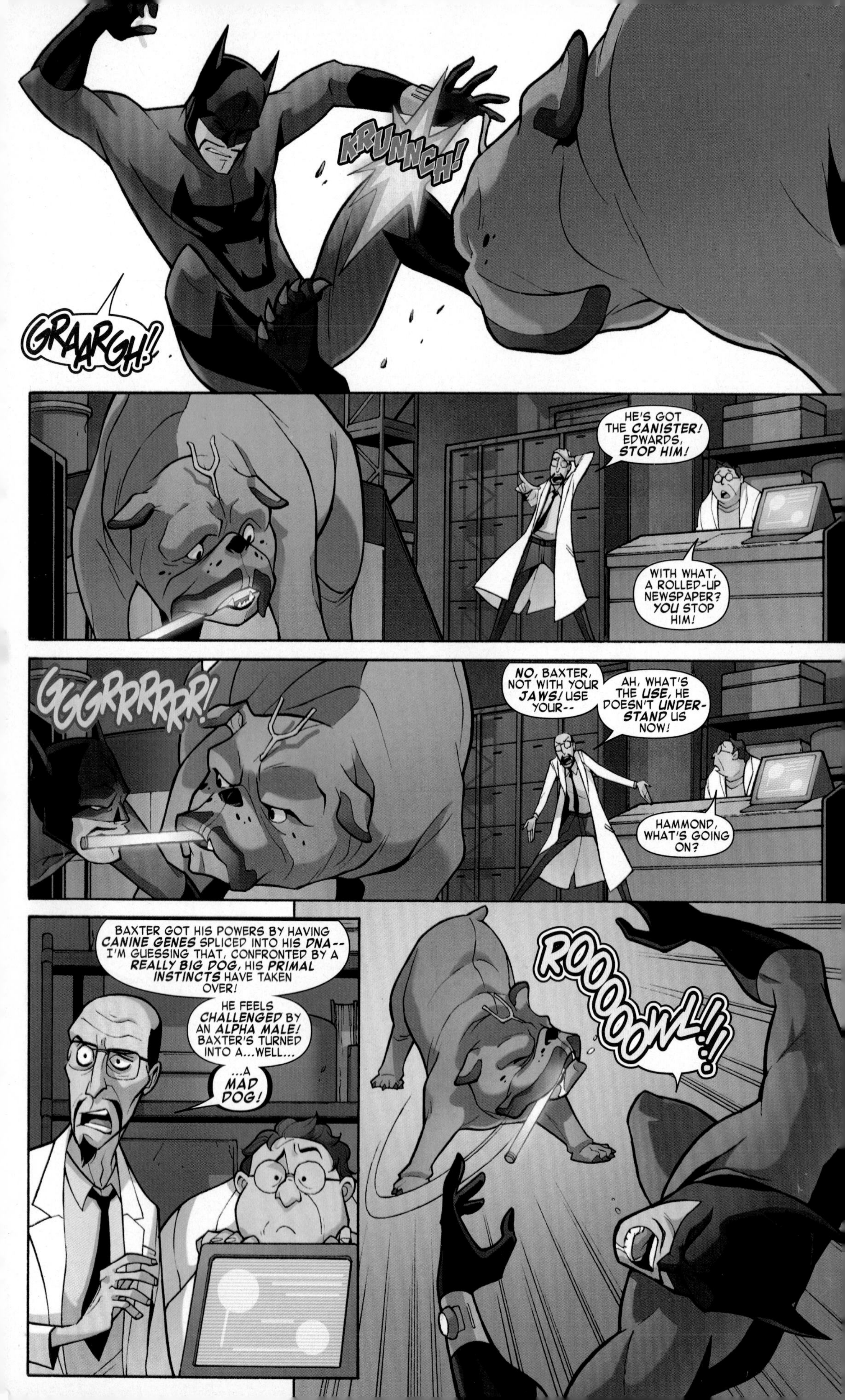
KRUNNCH!
GRAARGH!
HE'S GOT THE CANISTER! EDWARDS, STOP HIM!
WITH WHAT, A ROLLED-UP NEWSPAPER? YOU STOP HIM!
GGGRRRRRR!
NO, BAXTER, NOT WITH YOUR JAWS! USE YOUR--
AH, WHAT'S THE USE, HE DOESN'T UNDERSTAND US NOW!
HAMMOND, WHAT'S GOING ON?
BAXTER GOT HIS POWERS BY HAVING CANINE GENES SPLICED INTO HIS DNA-- I'M GUESSING THAT, CONFRONTED BY A REALLY BIG DOG, HIS PRIMAL INSTINCTS HAVE TAKEN OVER!
HE FEELS CHALLENGED BY AN ALPHA MALE! BAXTER'S TURNED INTO A...WELL...
...A MAD DOG!
ROOOOOWL!!

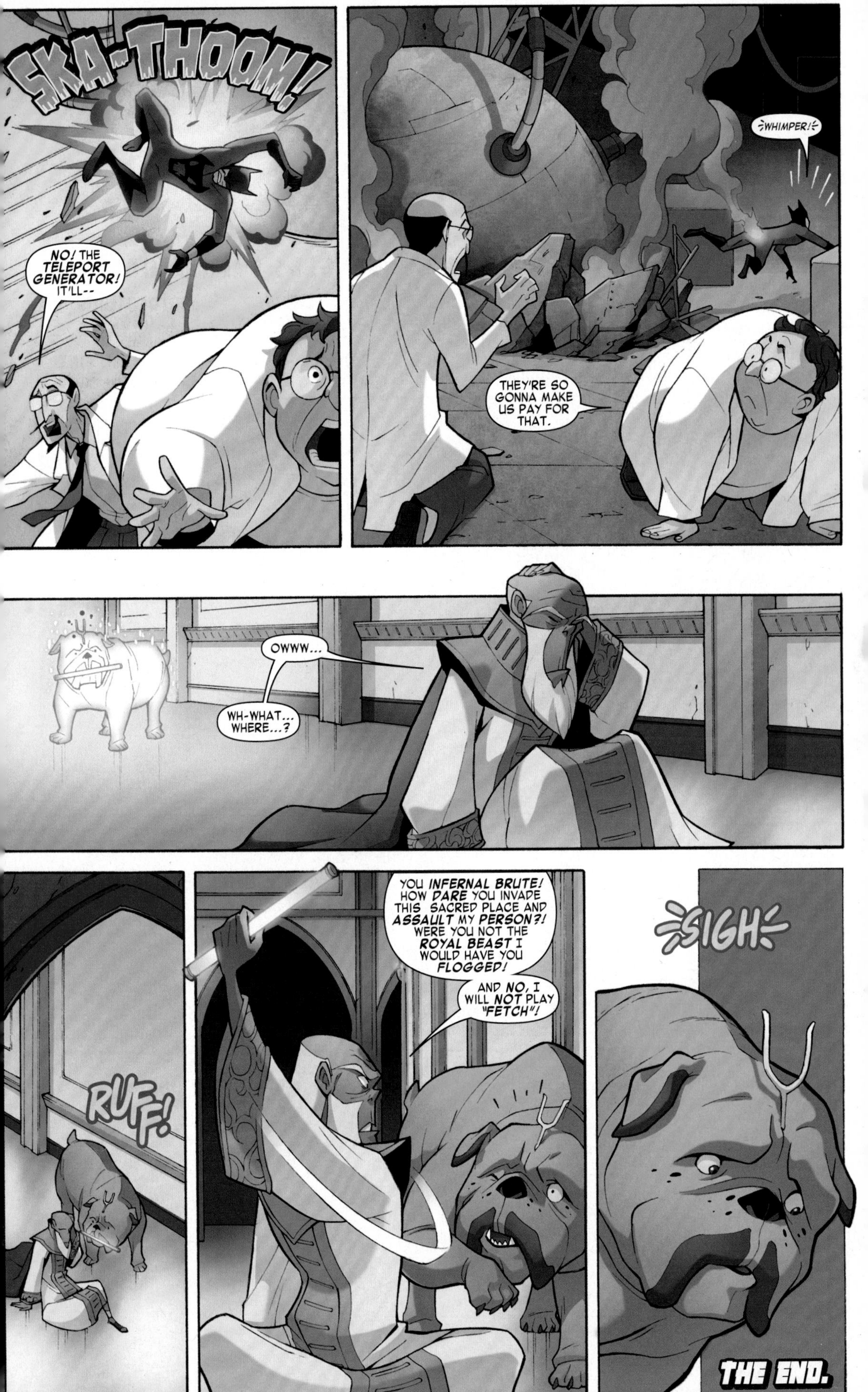

SKA-THOOM!
NO! THE TELEPORT GENERATOR! IT'LL--
WHIMPER!
THEY'RE SO GONNA MAKE US PAY FOR THAT.
OWWW...
WH-WHAT... WHERE...?
RUFF!
YOU INFERNAL BRUTE! HOW DARE YOU INVADE THIS SACRED PLACE AND ASSAULT MY PERSON?! WERE YOU NOT THE ROYAL BEAST I WOULD HAVE YOU FLOGGED!
AND NO, I WILL NOT PLAY "FETCH"!
SIGH
THE END.

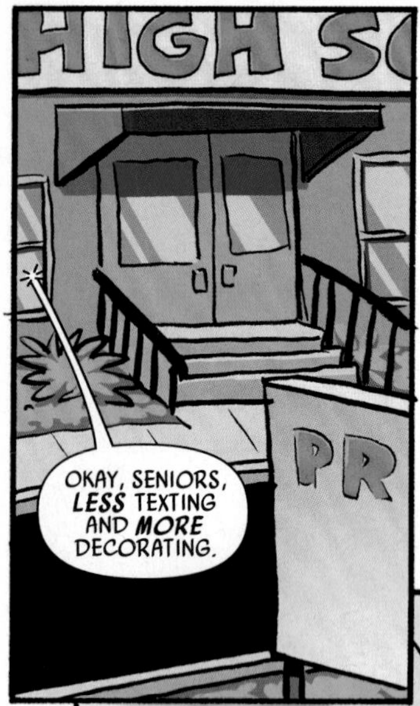
HIGH SC
PR
OKAY, SENIORS, LESS TEXTING AND MORE DECORATING.

Prom Queen

A TAIL OF THE **PET AVENGERS** STARRING **LOCKHEED**

BUDDY SCALERA WITH **CHRIS ELIOPOULOS** WRITERS
CHRIS ELIOPOULOS ARTIST
SOTOCOLOR'S C. GARCIA ARTIST
NATHAN COSBY EDITOR
JOE QUESADA EDITOR IN CHIEF
DAN BUCKLEY PUBLISHER
ALAN FINE EXECUTIVE PRODUCER

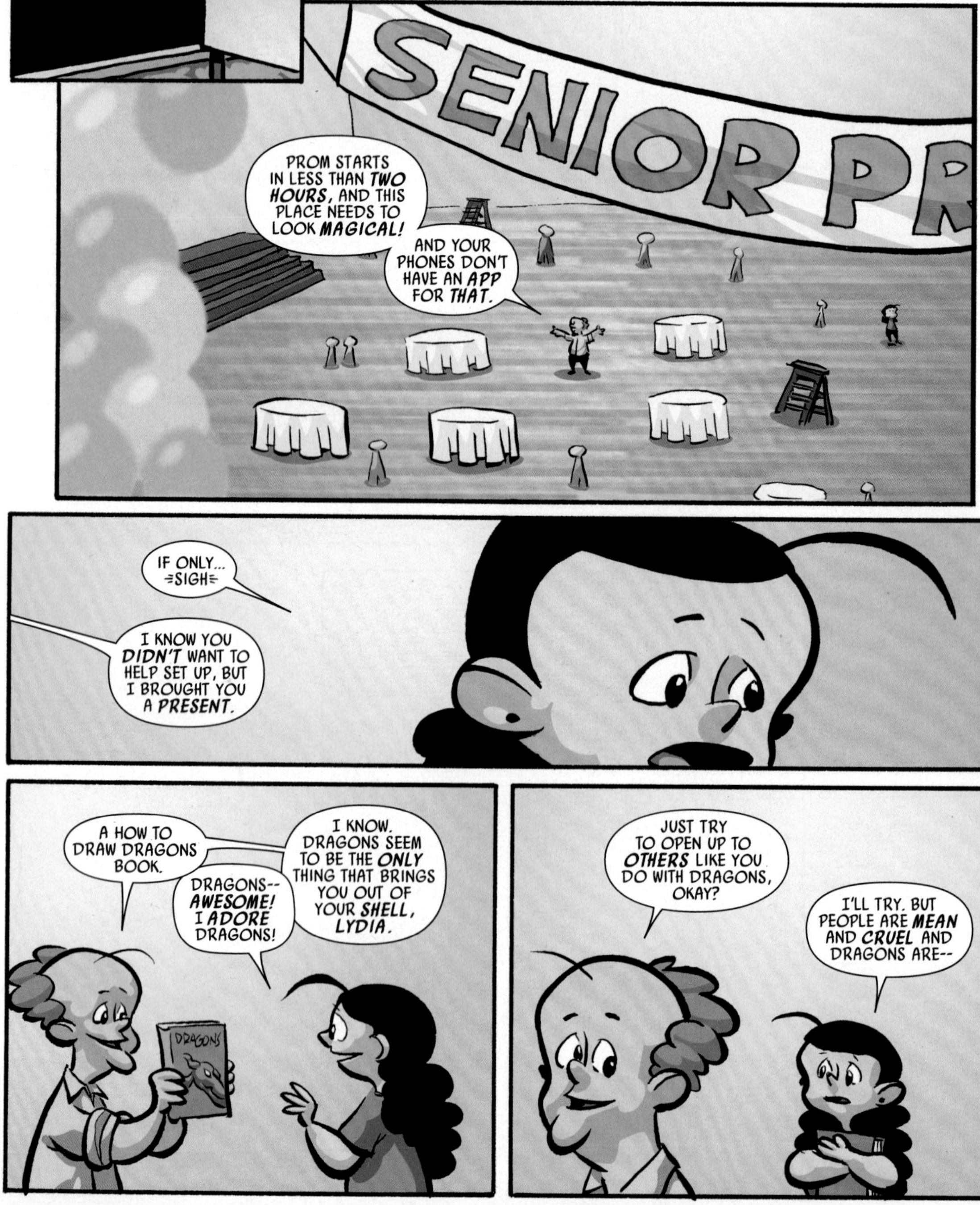
SENIOR PR
PROM STARTS IN LESS THAN TWO HOURS, AND THIS PLACE NEEDS TO LOOK MAGICAL!
AND YOUR PHONES DON'T HAVE AN APP FOR THAT.
IF ONLY... =SIGH=
I KNOW YOU DIDN'T WANT TO HELP SET UP, BUT I BROUGHT YOU A PRESENT.
A HOW TO DRAW DRAGONS BOOK.
DRAGONS-- AWESOME! I ADORE DRAGONS!
I KNOW. DRAGONS SEEM TO BE THE ONLY THING THAT BRINGS YOU OUT OF YOUR SHELL, LYDIA.
JUST TRY TO OPEN UP TO OTHERS LIKE YOU DO WITH DRAGONS, OKAY?
I'LL TRY. BUT PEOPLE ARE MEAN AND CRUEL AND DRAGONS ARE--

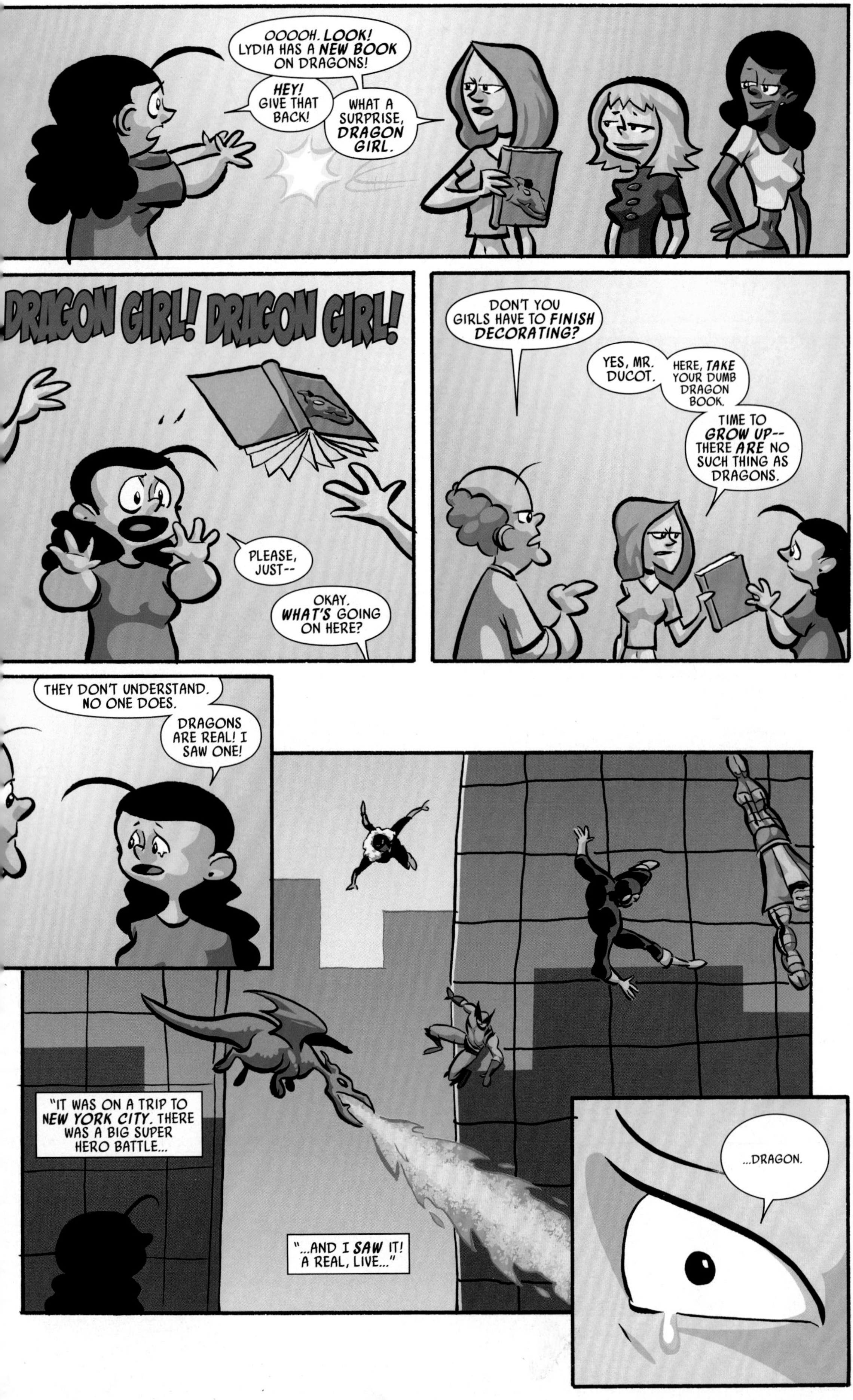
OOOOH. LOOK! LYDIA HAS A NEW BOOK ON DRAGONS!
HEY! GIVE THAT BACK!
WHAT A SURPRISE, DRAGON GIRL.
DRAGON GIRL! DRAGON GIRL!
PLEASE, JUST--
OKAY. WHAT'S GOING ON HERE?
DON'T YOU GIRLS HAVE TO FINISH DECORATING?
YES, MR. DUCOT.
HERE, TAKE YOUR DUMB DRAGON BOOK.
TIME TO GROW UP-- THERE ARE NO SUCH THING AS DRAGONS.
THEY DON'T UNDERSTAND. NO ONE DOES.
DRAGONS ARE REAL! I SAW ONE!
"IT WAS ON A TRIP TO NEW YORK CITY. THERE WAS A BIG SUPER HERO BATTLE...
"...AND I SAW IT! A REAL, LIVE..."
...DRAGON.

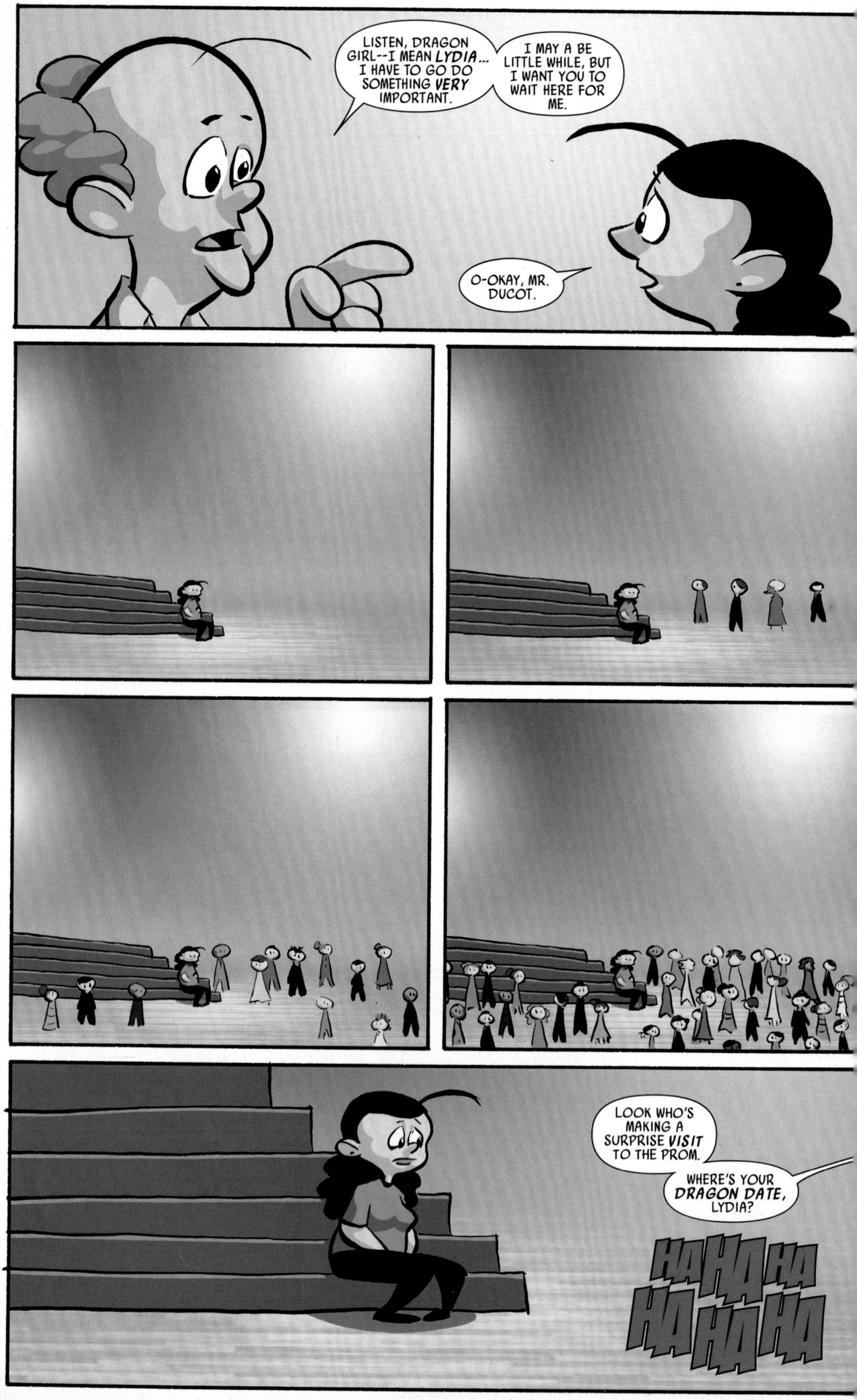
LISTEN, DRAGON GIRL--I MEAN LYDIA... I HAVE TO GO DO SOMETHING VERY IMPORTANT.
I MAY A BE LITTLE WHILE, BUT I WANT YOU TO WAIT HERE FOR ME.
O-OKAY, MR. DUCOT.
LOOK WHO'S MAKING A SURPRISE VISIT TO THE PROM.
WHERE'S YOUR DRAGON DATE, LYDIA?
HA HA HA HA HA HA HA

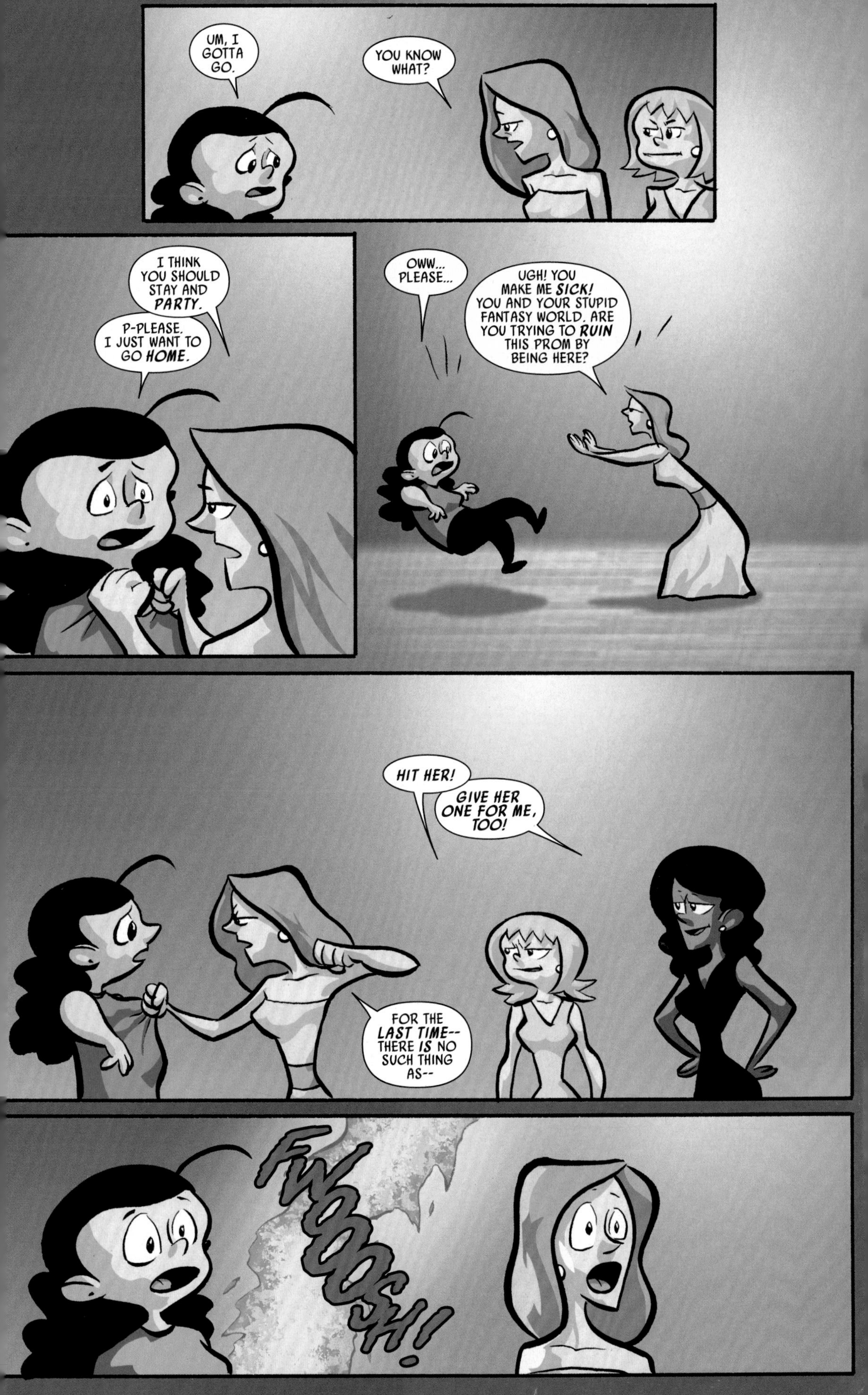
UM, I GOTTA GO.
YOU KNOW WHAT?
I THINK YOU SHOULD STAY AND PARTY.
P-PLEASE. I JUST WANT TO GO HOME.
OWW... PLEASE...
UGH! YOU MAKE ME SICK! YOU AND YOUR STUPID FANTASY WORLD. ARE YOU TRYING TO RUIN THIS PROM BY BEING HERE?
HIT HER!
GIVE HER ONE FOR ME, TOO!
FOR THE LAST TIME-- THERE IS NO SUCH THING AS--
FWOOOSH!

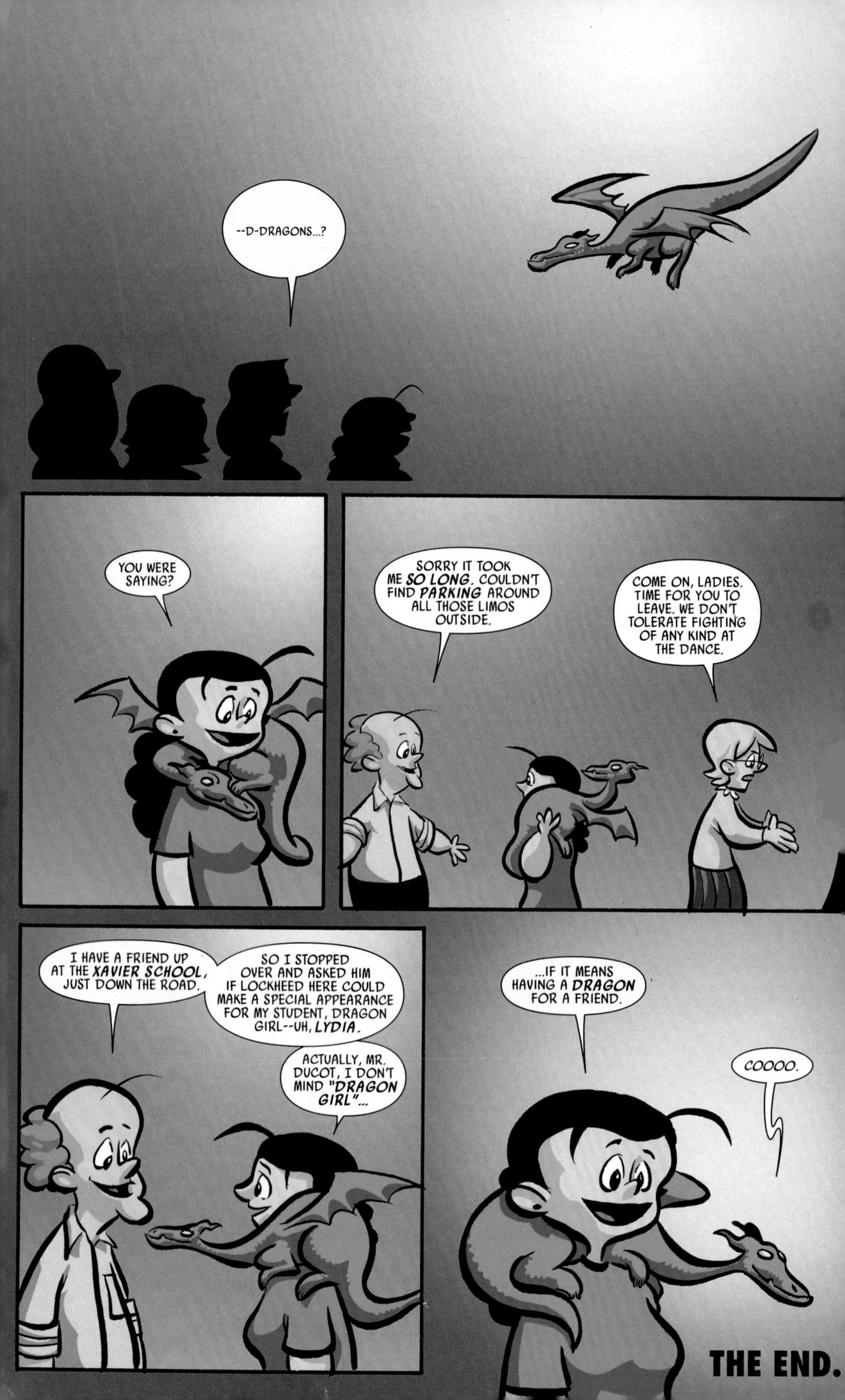
--D-DRAGONS...?
YOU WERE SAYING?
SORRY IT TOOK ME SO LONG. COULDN'T FIND PARKING AROUND ALL THOSE LIMOS OUTSIDE.
COME ON, LADIES. TIME FOR YOU TO LEAVE. WE DON'T TOLERATE FIGHTING OF ANY KIND AT THE DANCE.
I HAVE A FRIEND UP AT THE XAVIER SCHOOL, JUST DOWN THE ROAD.
SO I STOPPED OVER AND ASKED HIM IF LOCKHEED HERE COULD MAKE A SPECIAL APPEARANCE FOR MY STUDENT, DRAGON GIRL--UH, LYDIA.
ACTUALLY, MR. DUCOT, I DON'T MIND "DRAGON GIRL"...
...IF IT MEANS HAVING A DRAGON FOR A FRIEND.
COOOO.
THE END.

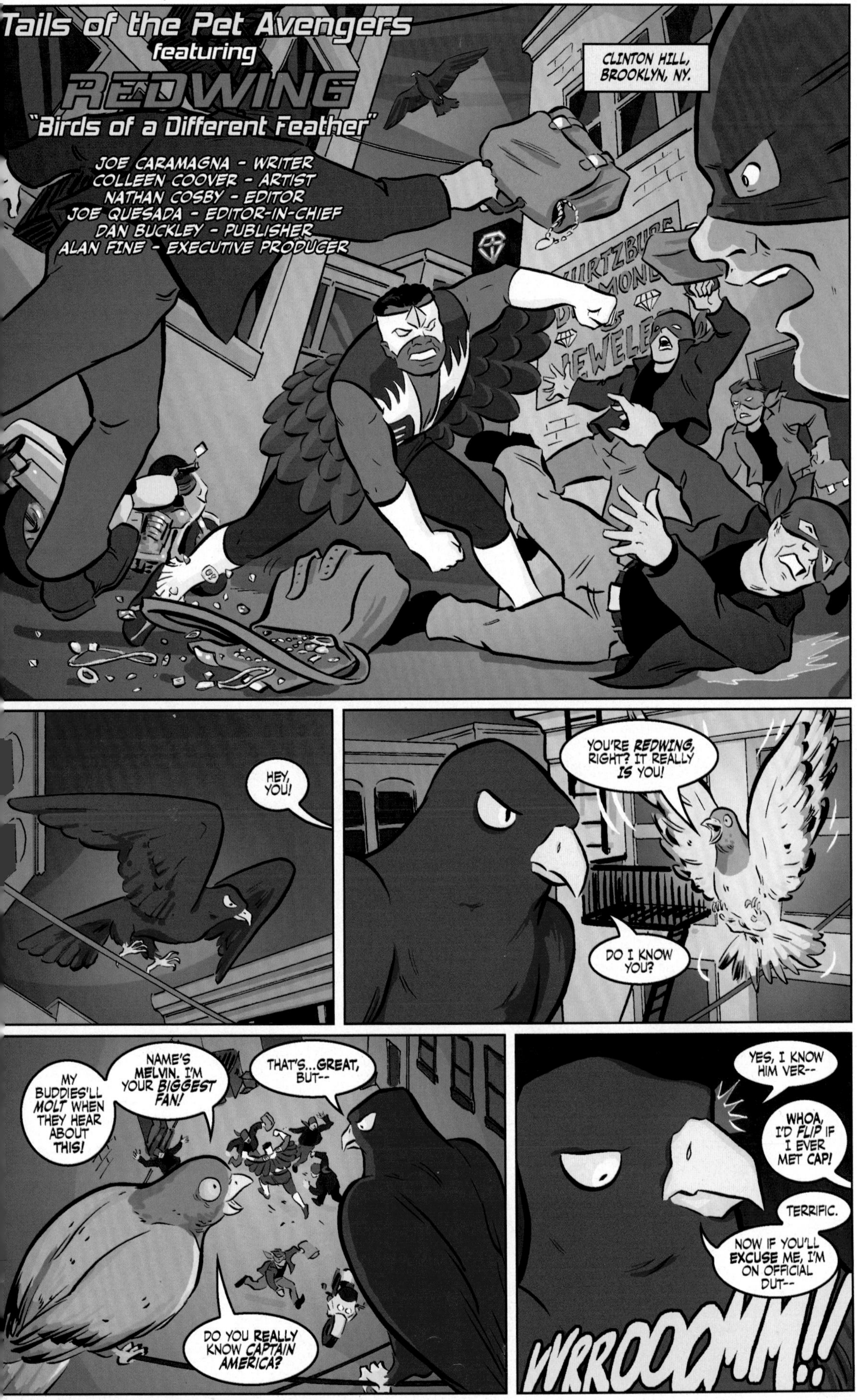
Tails of the Pet Avengers
featuring
REDWING
"Birds of a Different Feather"
JOE CARAMAGNA - WRITER
COLLEEN COOVER - ARTIST
NATHAN COSBY - EDITOR
JOE QUESADA - EDITOR-IN-CHIEF
DAN BUCKLEY - PUBLISHER
ALAN FINE - EXECUTIVE PRODUCER
CLINTON HILL, BROOKLYN, NY.
HEY, YOU!
YOU'RE REDWING, RIGHT? IT REALLY IS YOU!
DO I KNOW YOU?
MY BUDDIES'LL MOLT WHEN THEY HEAR ABOUT THIS!
NAME'S MELVIN. I'M YOUR BIGGEST FAN!
THAT'S...GREAT, BUT--
DO YOU REALLY KNOW CAPTAIN AMERICA?
YES, I KNOW HIM VER--
WHOA, I'D FLIP IF I EVER MET CAP!
TERRIFIC.
NOW IF YOU'LL EXCUSE ME, I'M ON OFFICIAL DUT--
VVRROOOMM!!

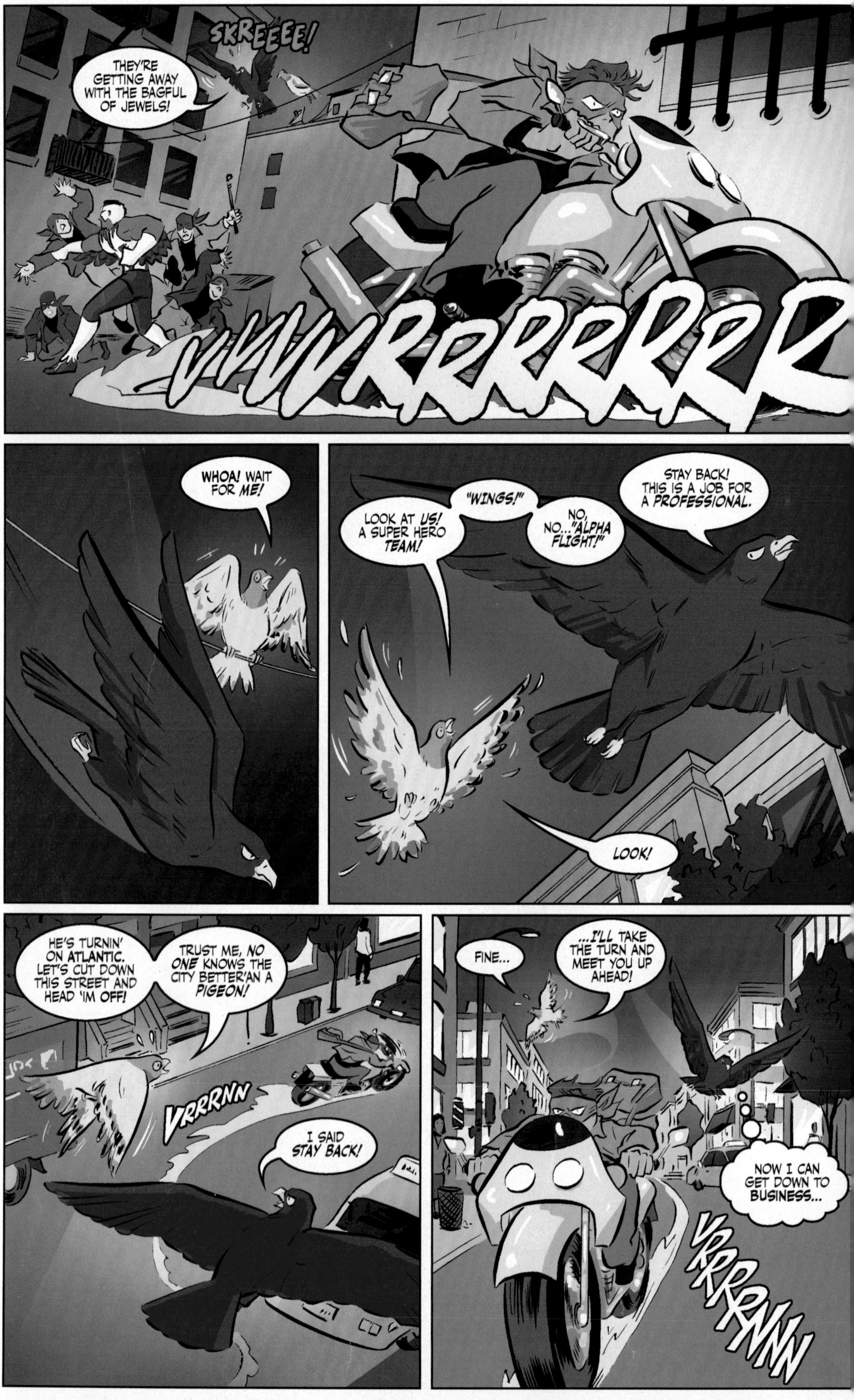
SKREEEEE!
THEY'RE GETTING AWAY WITH THE BAGFUL OF JEWELS!
VVVVVRRRRRRRRR
WHOA! WAIT FOR ME!
LOOK AT US! A SUPER HERO TEAM!
"WINGS!"
NO, NO..."ALPHA FLIGHT!"
STAY BACK! THIS IS A JOB FOR A PROFESSIONAL.
LOOK!
HE'S TURNIN' ON ATLANTIC. LET'S CUT DOWN THIS STREET AND HEAD 'IM OFF!
TRUST ME, NO ONE KNOWS THE CITY BETTER'AN A PIGEON!
VRRRNN
I SAID STAY BACK!
FINE...
...I'LL TAKE THE TURN AND MEET YOU UP AHEAD!
NOW I CAN GET DOWN TO BUSINESS...
VRRRNNN

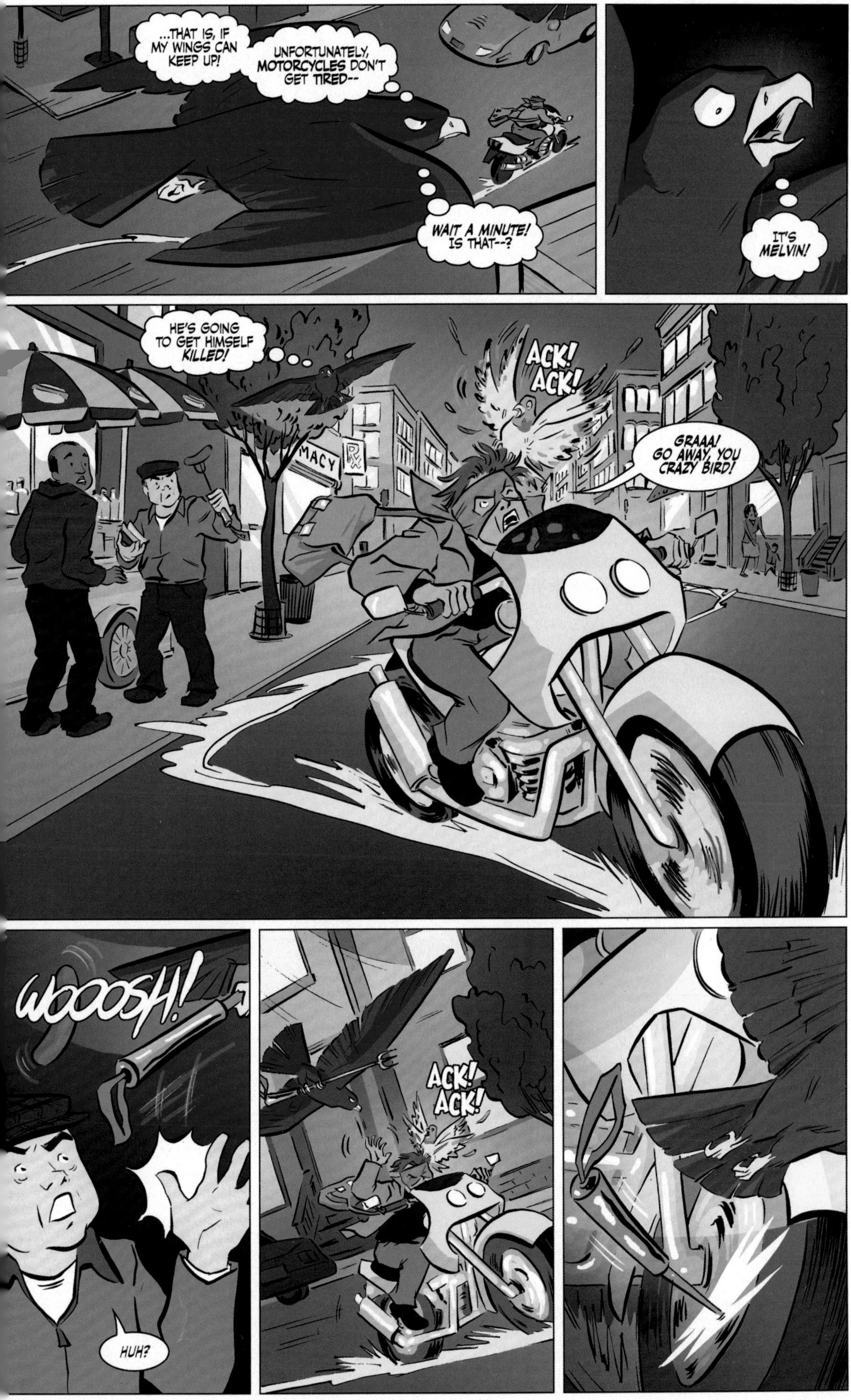
...THAT IS, IF MY WINGS CAN KEEP UP!
UNFORTUNATELY, MOTORCYCLES DON'T GET TIRED--
WAIT A MINUTE! IS THAT--?
IT'S MELVIN!
HE'S GOING TO GET HIMSELF KILLED!
ACK! ACK!
GRAAA! GO AWAY, YOU CRAZY BIRD!
MACY
Rx
WOOOSH!
HUH?
ACK! ACK!

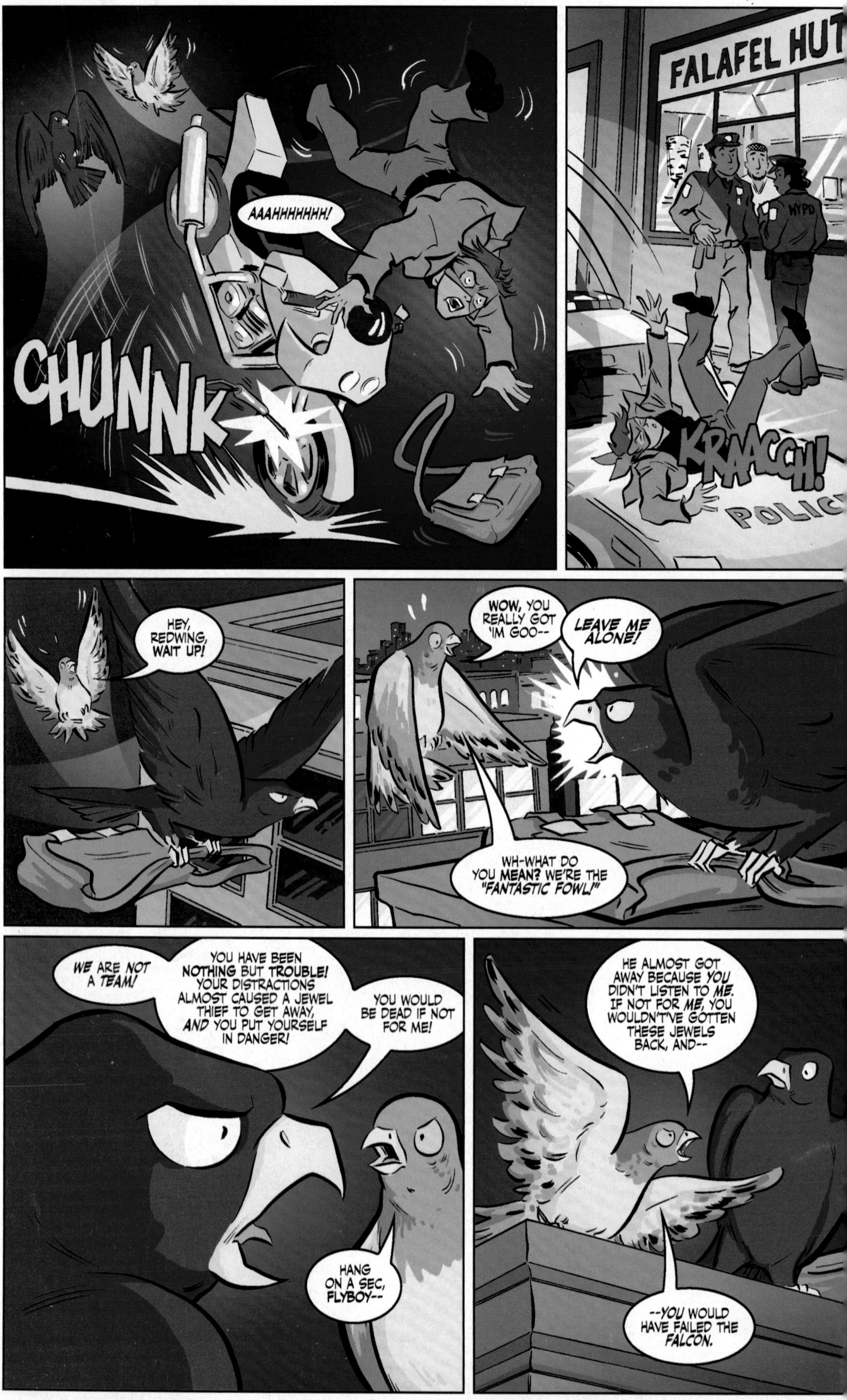
AAAHHHHHHH!
CHUNNK
FALAFEL HUT
NYPD
KRAACCH!
POLIC
HEY, REDWING, WAIT UP!
WOW, YOU REALLY GOT 'IM GOO--
LEAVE ME ALONE!
WH-WHAT DO YOU MEAN? WE'RE THE "FANTASTIC FOWL!"
WE ARE NOT A TEAM!
YOU HAVE BEEN NOTHING BUT TROUBLE! YOUR DISTRACTIONS ALMOST CAUSED A JEWEL THIEF TO GET AWAY, AND YOU PUT YOURSELF IN DANGER!
YOU WOULD BE DEAD IF NOT FOR ME!
HANG ON A SEC, FLYBOY--
HE ALMOST GOT AWAY BECAUSE YOU DIDN'T LISTEN TO ME. IF NOT FOR ME, YOU WOULDN'T'VE GOTTEN THESE JEWELS BACK, AND--
--YOU WOULD HAVE FAILED THE FALCON.

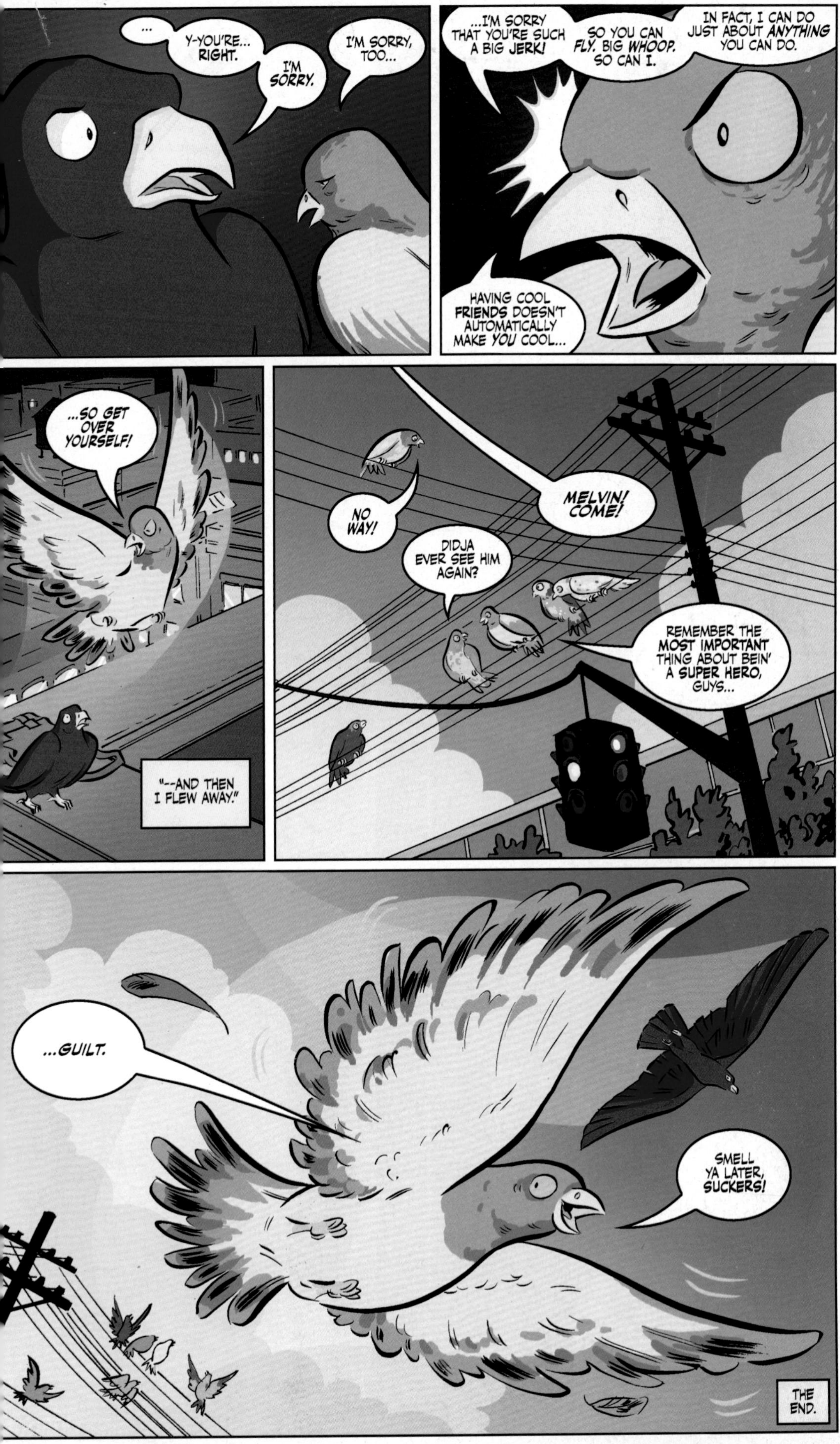
...
Y-YOU'RE... RIGHT.
I'M SORRY.
I'M SORRY, TOO...
...I'M SORRY THAT YOU'RE SUCH A BIG JERK!
SO YOU CAN FLY. BIG WHOOP. SO CAN I.
IN FACT, I CAN DO JUST ABOUT ANYTHING YOU CAN DO.
HAVING COOL FRIENDS DOESN'T AUTOMATICALLY MAKE YOU COOL...
...SO GET OVER YOURSELF!
"--AND THEN I FLEW AWAY."
NO WAY!
MELVIN! COME!
DIDJA EVER SEE HIM AGAIN?
REMEMBER THE MOST IMPORTANT THING ABOUT BEIN' A SUPER HERO, GUYS...
...GUILT.
SMELL YA LATER, SUCKERS!
THE END.

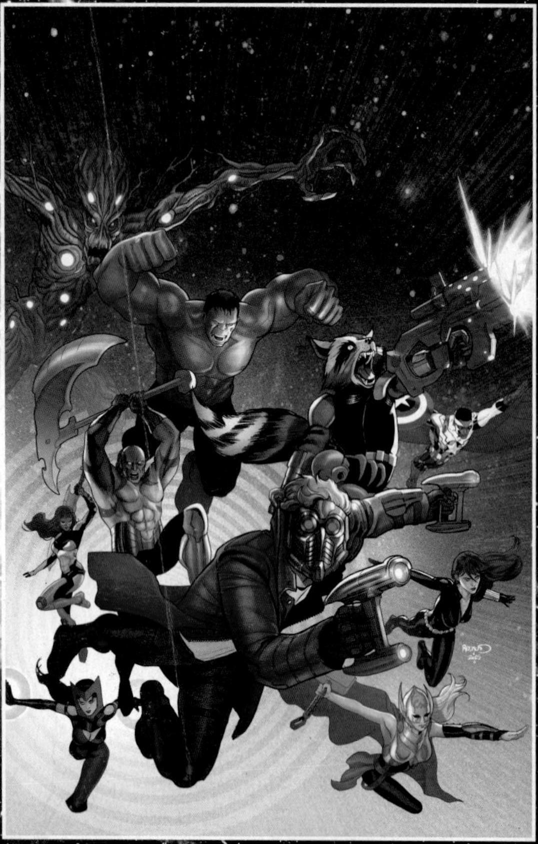

GUARDIANS TEAM-UP #2 VARIANT
BY PAUL RENAUD

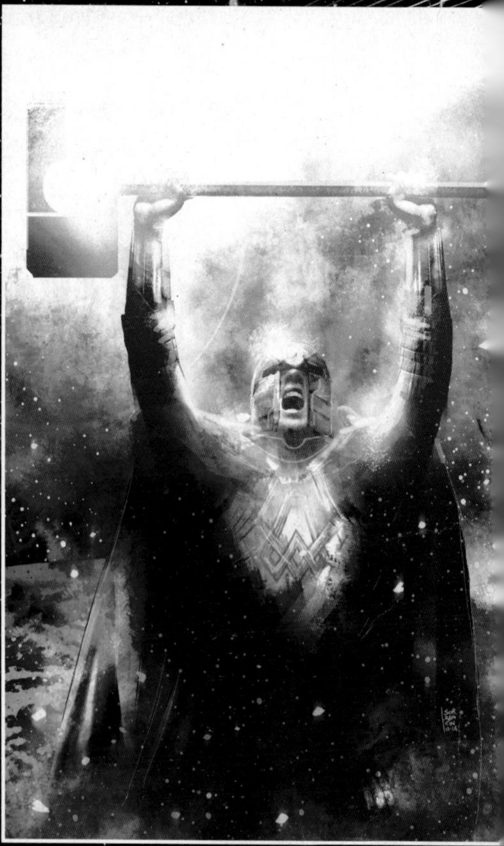

GUARDIANS TEAM-UP #3 COSMICALLY ENHANCED VARIANT BY ANDREA SORRENTIN

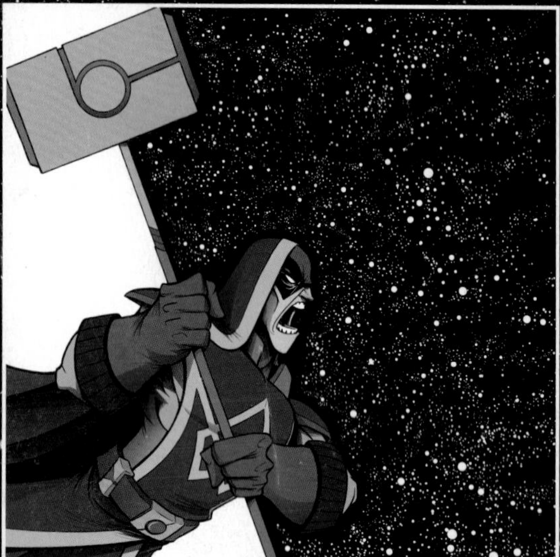

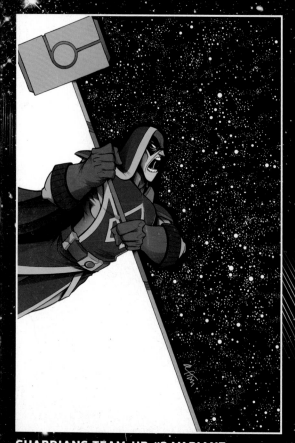

GUARDIANS TEAM-UP #3 VARIANT
BY GUSTAVO DUARTE

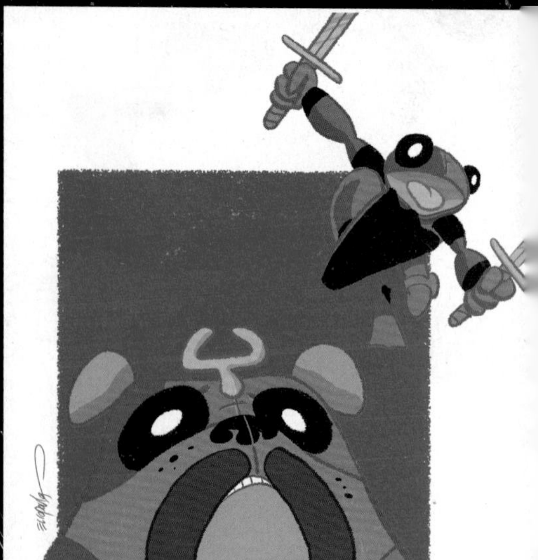

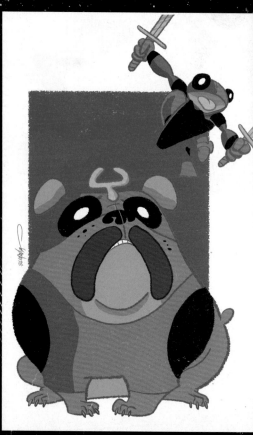

TAILS OF THE PET AVENGERS #1 DEADPOOL VARIANT BY CHRIS ELIOPOULOS